W9-BAX-204

DIFFER WE MUST

ALSO BY STEVE INSKEEP

Imperfect Union:
How Jessie and John Frémont Mapped the West, Invented Celebrity, and Helped Cause the Civil War

Jacksonland:
President Andrew Jackson, Cherokee Chief John Ross, and a Great American Land Grab

Instant City:
Life and Death in Karachi

Differ We Must

HOW LINCOLN SUCCEEDED IN A DIVIDED AMERICA

STEVE INSKEEP

PENGUIN PRESS NEW YORK 2023

PENGUIN PRESS
An imprint of Penguin Random House LLC
penguinrandomhouse.com

Illustration credits appear on page 317.

LIBRARY OF CONGRESS CATALOGING-IN-PUBLICATION DATA
Names: Inskeep, Steve, author.
Title: Differ we must : how Lincoln succeeded in a divided America / Steve Inskeep.
Other titles: How Lincoln succeeded in a divided America
Description: New York : Penguin Press, 2023. | Includes bibliographical references and index.
Identifiers: LCCN 2023005131 | ISBN 9780593297865 (hardcover) | ISBN 9780593297872 (ebook)
Subjects: LCSH: Lincoln, Abraham, 1809-1865—Friends and associates. |
Lincoln, Abraham, 1809–1865—Political and social views. | Presidents—United States—Biography. |
Political leadership—United States—History—19th century. |
United States—Politics and government—1849–1877.
Classification: LCC E457.2 .I47 2023 | DDC 973.7092 [B]—dc23/eng/20230420
LC record available at https://lccn.loc.gov/2023005131

Printed in the United States of America
1st Printing

Book design by Daniel Lagin

To Carolee, my first reader and critic;
and to Ava, Ana, and Molly,
who saw this book finished during
the final year we lived under one roof

Contents

SEPARATION

UNION

LINCOLN, 1863.

Introduction

ABRAHAM LINCOLN WAS A POLITICIAN. PEOPLE LIKE TO IDENtify him in ways that sound more noble—lawyer, statesman, husband, father. Contemporaries considered him a Christlike figure who suffered and died that his nation might live. Tolstoy called him "a saint of humanity" who realized "the greatest human achievement is love." But this revered American's vocation is not revered at all, seen as the province of money, power, cynicism, and lies.

Some writers suggest he was *only* a politician, who revived a stalled career by seizing on the slavery issue and who wasn't even advanced in his views. Lincoln himself modestly said he was only an "accidental instrument" of a "great cause"—but this book holds something different. Lincoln preserved the country and took part in a social revolution *because* he engaged in politics. He did the work others found dirty or beneath them. He always considered slavery wrong, but felt immediate abolition was beyond the federal government's constitutional power and against the wishes of too many voters. So he tried to contain slavery. He helped to build a democratic coalition supporting that position and held to it even when threatened with disunion and civil war. He moved forward when circumstances changed. "I shall adopt new views so fast as they appear to be true views," he said shortly before issuing the Emancipation Proclamation."

Just as athletes are best seen in motion on the field, Lincoln is best seen in action with other people. This biography views him in sixteen such encounters before and during his presidency, each one a face-to-face meeting with a person who differed with him—in background, experience, or opinion. In each meeting one or both people wanted something. These interactions show a master politician's practical and moral choices, along with his sometimes mysterious character.

Together the meetings make a book of arguments, as Lincoln matches wits with allies and adversaries alike. Their differences lead to this book's main insight: Lincoln learned, adapted, and sought advantage while interacting with people who disagreed with him. Senator Stephen A. Douglas said Lincoln misunderstood the nation's founders, and General George McClellan considered Lincoln "an idiot." Jessie Benton Frémont felt Lincoln was misled by advisers; George H. Pendleton that Lincoln was trampling the Constitution. Frederick Douglass excoriated Lincoln, saying he had a "passion for making himself seem silly and ridiculous," that his statements were "characteristically foggy, remarkably illogical and untimely," that he had shown "canting hypocrisy," and that he represented "American prejudice and Negro hatred." Even when Douglass celebrated the Emancipation Proclamation he said Lincoln had taken this "obvious" course only after "slothful deliberation." Lincoln had read some of this criticism before Douglass appeared in his crowded anteroom—but he met Douglass anyway, and you may judge who gained from it.

This book's title comes from an 1855 letter Lincoln sent to his best friend Joshua Speed, who came from a slaveholding family: "If for this you and I must differ, differ we must." He chided Speed for admitting the "abstract wrong" of slavery but failing to act accordingly: "Slave-holders *talk* that way" but "never *vote* that way." Yet he didn't abandon Speed, signing off as "your friend forever." He rarely wrote people off, because he knew they had the power of the vote. It's not that Lincoln greatly changed his critics' beliefs—some went to war against him—nor that they greatly changed his. Rather, he learned how to make his beliefs actionable. He started his career in the minority party and set out to make a majority. He perceived a social problem so vast it seemed impossible to address, and he slowly found ways to address it. Had he failed to engage with people who differed, he would not have become the Lincoln we know; and history would little note nor long remember him.

The encounters in this book showcase his political techniques. He's known for his speeches, of course—the Gettysburg Address, the Second Inaugural—but he used more personal methods, beginning with his skill in conversation. He was a storyteller. He told offbeat tales of growing up in Indiana. He repeated jokes he'd heard, mimicked dialects, and guffawed at his own punch lines. He used sarcasm. When Senator Douglas accused a rival of inconsistency, Lincoln said it was unfair: "Has Douglas the *exclusive right*, in this country, of being *on all sides of all questions*? Is nobody allowed that high privilege but himself?" He made fun of self-important clerics and his own ungainly face. Nothing was off-limits; he told a poop joke in the White House, recounting the day in his boyhood when he tried to relieve himself into a friend's upturned hat. (The friend foiled him by switching their hats.) Such self-deprecating banter helped him relate to people—and helped him hide. A storyteller could use his story as a mask, controlling the conversation and choosing what to say or withhold.

An ally considered Honest Abe evasive: "Beneath a smooth surface of candor," he "told enough only, of his plans and purposes, to induce the belief that he had communicated all; yet he reserved enough, in fact, to have communicated nothing." When he did give opinions, he sometimes urged people not to repeat them. "Let this be strictly confidential," he ended one letter, "not that there is anything wrong in it; but that I have some highly valued friends who would not like me any better for writing it." He was curating slightly different versions of himself for different people. Though history remembers him for what he said, he left many things unsaid. His campaigns addressed only issues he considered decisive, staying silent on all else. During his presidential campaign in 1860 an important politician questioned him on tariff policy, and he answered by forwarding a thirteen-year-old memorandum on the subject, not saying a single word that was new. Pressured to act against slavery in 1862, he wrote a famous public letter that gave his thinking without revealing his plans. In the last speech of his life, on April 11, 1865, he said he wouldn't answer a question in the news because it was "good for nothing at all—a merely pernicious abstraction."

Together, his reticence and his eloquence reflected something deeper than rhetorical style. It showed that he prioritized. He knew his limitations and those of the democratic system. He didn't try to win all arguments, nor to crush all opponents, nor to solve all problems. He concentrated his power on fights he had to win to keep from losing everything, which was harder to do than to say. Some of the most painful parts of this story are times when Lincoln left an injustice unaddressed, at least for the moment, to focus on goals he considered paramount. He often used the word *forbear*, as in "What I forbear, I forbear because I do *not* believe it would help to save the Union." This called on another of his character traits: exceptional patience.

In all that he said and did, he considered his audience, making calculations based on a straightforward understanding of human nature. He told his friend and law partner William Herndon that people acted entirely out of self-interest—that even their most loving, patriotic, or altruistic deeds were meant to bring them some benefit or pleasure. As president he said all people "look to their self-interest. . . . Unless among those deficient of intellect, everybody you trade with makes something." So he talked with them about it. In letters and speeches, he used the word *interest* far more often than *liberty*, *freedom*, or *moral*, and referred often to people's *motive*, by which he meant their self-interest. He embraced the spoils system, in which election winners distributed government jobs to political supporters. He appealed to the white electorate's self-interest against slavery: Workers in free states must resist it, or it would expand into their states and harm them. He spent little time urging charity or benevolence for enslaved people. Instead he said Black workers were denied their equal right to be paid for their labor—which white voters could relate to because they wanted fair pay for theirs. When white men questioned emancipation during the Civil War, Lincoln responded by invoking self-interest twice. He said Black men were fighting for the Union, which was in the national interest, and they had to be promised freedom, because they wouldn't fight unless there was something in it for them.

It still mattered to him *how* people pursued their interests. He said they could act out of "moral sense and self-interest," aligning their interests with a higher purpose, and this book is the story of his effort to do that. He navigated between rocks of political reality while trying not to lose sight of his moral compass.

While this is strictly a story of the past, it offers perspective on our disorderly present. Lincoln operated within the basic constitutional structure we know, with the Bill of Rights, separation of powers, and clashes between state and federal authority. It was a time of disorienting technological change. Railroads, the telegraph, and daily newspapers sped communications, bringing distant people together and forcing them to confront their differences with an intensity they'd never known. Rival camps offered contradictory, overlapping, and incoherent visions of the country. America was a beacon of freedom that was also an empire, a nation of immigrants that was suspicious of immigrants, a country of faith that was all about the money, and a land of equality that made people unequal in the eyes of the law.

After an opening chapter on Lincoln's early life and political education, this book is divided into three movements. "Coalition" follows his role in assembling disparate people to oppose slavery. "Separation" tracks the period of secession, when he encountered differences that could not be compromised. The longest section, "Union," follows his efforts to bring people of different views behind the Union cause in the Civil War. Together these chapters form a narrative of Lincoln's life as seen through his encounters.

DIFFER WE MUST

Young Lincoln in legend.

Chapter 1

PROTAGONIST: ABRAHAM LINCOLN

1809–1846

LINCOLN WAS BORN IN KENTUCKY AND WAS SEVEN WHEN HE suffered the first of several great disruptions. His father lost his farm in a dispute over the title, put his family on a wagon, and started for a new life in Indiana. A glance at a map doesn't convey how hard their journey was in 1816; they moved fewer than one hundred miles from their old home, but it took about five days, ending with a ferry across the Ohio and a trek through roadless woods. The travel time was longer than a modern journey from Kentucky to Afghanistan—and their destination was wilderness, the newest state of the Union, only recently cleared of most of the Indians after whom it was named.

Thomas Lincoln claimed land for a new farm, handed his son an axe, and told him to help clear the trees. He was not quite eight when he began this ceaseless labor and not even ten when his mother, Nancy Hanks Lincoln, died of a mysterious sickness. The year after that, Thomas returned to Kentucky to find a new wife, leaving Abraham and his sister Sarah behind. When Thomas reappeared many days later he brought a whole new family, having married a widowed mother of three. Abraham never detailed how he felt about these experiences, but an observation he made as an adult was revealing: "In this sad world of ours, sorrow comes to all; and to the young, it comes with bitterest agony, because it takes them unawares."

How did he escape obscurity on that farm? It's common to credit his reading. Though his schooling totaled less than a year, he learned to write by scratching letters on wood, and if he had to walk for miles to borrow a book he'd do it. His self-education is among the most inspiring stories about him, passed on in children's books to this day. But this story is incomplete. His reading was neither wide nor deep, limited to books within reach, and he once described his youth in two words: "Education defective." He needed a different form of learning, for which resources were more available: his study of his fellow human beings.

His stepmother, Sarah Bush Lincoln, said when grown-ups visited their cabin the boy listened, "never speaking or asking questions till they were gone and then he must understand everything—even to the smallest thing." He questioned his parents and repeated the answers "again and again" to remember. Thanks to his clear handwriting, he took dictation for settlers who were illiterate and said his "perceptions were sharpened" as he "learned to see other people's thoughts and feelings and ideas by writing their friendly confidential letters." By his twenties an acquaintance found his mind was "a great storehouse" of facts, "acquired by reading but principally by observation, and intercourse with men, women, and children, in their social and business relations; learning and weighing the motives that prompt each act in life." Not every book he found was worth finishing, but for a future democratic leader almost anybody was worth knowing.

The good listener became a good talker. Once after attending church he said he could repeat the sermon, and when friends challenged him he climbed on a log and did it. On other occasions, a friend said, "the boys would gather & cluster around him" to hear him tell jokes and stories. While there's no reliable record of his stand-up routine, it likely resembled things he said later, even while president, that brought out his inner twelve-year-old. He told of a lizard that crawled inside the pant leg of a preacher, who continued his sermon while desperately removing his clothes. To a man of Dutch ancestry, Lincoln once asked, What's the difference between an Amsterdam Dutchman and any other damn Dutchman? He told of an Irishman who went to the post office to ask for his mail. The postmaster said: Your name? And the man replied indignantly, It says my name on the letter! When Lincoln walked into Gentryville, a village near his home, he spent hours with other people "running rigs"—meaning "to tease, banter, or ridicule," apparently the sort of back-and-forth insults that in another context would be called "the dozens."

When he was twenty-one his family moved to Illinois, where he attended a rally for political candidates in front of a store. Though he wasn't running and didn't even have the six months' residence required to vote, he gave his own speech—an early sign of his invincible confidence. By then he'd had experiences that allowed him to prove himself, such as crewing a cargo boat all the way to New Orleans, enduring treacherous currents and even driving off would-be robbers. He was physically strong—all those years swinging the axe—and developed an idea that he had special gifts thanks to his late mother. He believed she was born out of wedlock, that illegitimate children grew up hardier and smarter than others, and that she had passed on her traits to him. No evidence supported any part of this, but far into adulthood he voiced his belief to a friend. If it helped him it didn't matter if it was true. Being born out of wedlock was considered a mark of shame, yet he privately adopted this identity, and made it a strength. It placed him on the side of people society shunned.

HE STARTED A POLITICAL CAREER AS SOON AS HE WAS ABLE, IN THE first place where he lived on his own: New Salem, in central Illinois, a frontier-style settlement without a single brick house or paved street. A wooden gristmill stood on stilts over the Sangamon River, and a few log cabins sat on a nearby bluff. While it wasn't an obvious destination for an ambitious young man, he got a job there in 1831, clerking for the man who ran the mill and a nearby store. He slept in that store, sharing a cot with another clerk, who said that "when one turned over the other had to do likewise." He was six feet four, his pants came nowhere near his shoes, and he was broke. But he followed political news, reading newspapers when he could get them and eventually hoarding enough cash to subscribe to the *Louisville Daily Journal*, out of Kentucky.

The *Journal* offered news of a nation dividing between two factions. Andrew Jackson of Tennessee, a war hero, claimed the 1824 presidential election had been stolen from him and carried his grievance to a landslide win in 1828; the Jacksonian movement evolved into the Democratic Party. Anti-Jacksonians organized as the Whig Party, led by Henry Clay of Kentucky. The *Journal* was a Clay paper, and Lincoln admired his fellow Kentuckian, an advocate of a strong federal government that promoted internal improvements—roads, bridges, and canals. He followed Clay into the opposition even though it was the minority party in Illinois. This meant that if he was going to succeed in politics, he had to build relationships with people whose politics differed.

His new neighbors included a group of Jackson men known as the Clary's Grove Boys, lawless toughs from a nearby farm community. Their leader, Jack Armstrong, had a habit of hazing newcomers and was a bully; one story involved his gang stuffing a man in a barrel and rolling it downhill. But Lincoln managed him well when Armstrong challenged him to a wrestling match. People gathered outside the store in New Salem and bet on the outcome. Lincoln's skill with words helped him as much as his greater height: he refused Armstrong's plan to wrestle with no holds barred, insisting that Armstrong agree to rules he wasn't disciplined enough to follow. Witnesses gave many versions of this encounter—Lincoln won, Lincoln lost, Lincoln was fouled—and in most versions the match dissolved into chaos. But Lincoln showed he couldn't be pushed around.

From then on the Clary's Grove Boys respected him, which allowed him to befriend their whole community: they were less a gang than part of a clan, seven families who had intermarried as they migrated out of the Appalachians. Lincoln spent long hours at the Armstrong farm outside town, where Jack's wife, Hannah, fed him. While there's no evidence that Lincoln joined Armstrong's lawless activities—at least once the Clary's Grove Boys vandalized and robbed a store in New Salem—they supported each other's ambitions. The first time Lincoln ever voted, in August 1831, he cast a ballot for Jack Armstrong, the bully, for constable.

In 1832 the Clary's Grove Boys voted twice for Lincoln. The first came when the state raised troops to fight Black Hawk, a chief of the Sauk people who had brought his followers into Illinois. The militia company raised around New Salem elected its own officers, choosing Lincoln as captain while Armstrong became first sergeant. Soon after their brief service, a widening circle of Democrats voted for Lincoln out of personal friendship as he ran for the state legislature. Though he failed to win election in the countywide district, he received almost all the votes from both parties in the New Salem precinct.

Making a living wasn't easy in the village—Lincoln lost his clerk's job when the store closed, then started his own store that failed, leaving him in debt—but Democrats helped him again: He got a job as postmaster of New Salem. Though he said the part-time federal position was "too insignificant to make [my] politics an objection," it's hard to see how he would have been appointed by President Jackson without the support of local Jacksonians. The Democratic county surveyor also hired him as a part-time deputy, and he gained more than money as he carried a compass and chain across rough countryside. People discussed their land with Lincoln, a personal matter that touched on their wealth, their identity, and the reason they had come to Illinois; and this allowed him to continue studying people. In 1834 he surveyed the farm of a Democrat named Russell Godbey and won his trust while measuring the distance in chain lengths between certain white oak trees at the corners. When Lincoln ran for the legislature again that year, Godbey said, "I voted for him . . . against my political creed and principles." Leading Democratic politicos were also supporting Lincoln, hoping to defeat another Whig they liked less. Their plan backfired: four seats were up for election, and both Whigs won.

For his first legislative session he borrowed money from a friend to buy a new suit and began his climb into the Illinois elite. He was young and inexperienced, just twenty-five at the start, but it was a young country where life was short, the median age was eighteen, and many lawmakers were in their first terms. By his second term he counted as a veteran and was leading the Whig minority—supporting bridges and canals to open the state for development, and proposing to reform a law concerning "insolvent debtors," a subject he knew uncomfortably well. He was still paying the creditors of his failed New Salem store, and the sheriff once auctioned his belongings.

He read law, borrowing books from a fellow legislator to study under a tree, and obtained his law license. And having supported a bill that moved the state capital to the prosperous town of Springfield, he moved there himself. He spent time with wealthy Whigs, mostly the sons and daughters of slaveholding families who had migrated from Kentucky. One, Joshua Speed, became his roommate and best friend, while another, Mary Todd, married him. He courted her in the Springfield mansion where she was living—the home of her brother-in-law, Ninian Edwards, a Whig politico and son of a former governor, who threw parties for as many as one hundred well-connected guests at a time.

HE HAD TO DO HIS SOCIAL CLIMBING CAREFULLY, BECAUSE HE LIVED in a culture of equality; citizens would drag down any man who acted like their better. He always stressed his modest roots. "I was born and have ever remained in the most humble walks of life," he said in his first campaign announcement. Though he didn't like manual labor, having had all he wanted in his youth, he appealed for the votes of farmworkers by helping them harvest grain from a field. His expressions of humility continued right through the Gettysburg Address three decades later. ("The world will little note, nor long remember what we say here.") Always he hid his self-confidence behind a cloak of modesty.

President Jackson, who remained in office until 1837, kept equality at the center of politics by labeling Whigs aristocrats. A Jacksonian newspaper said his movement favored "natural equality, and breaking down the contrivances of the old world [that] maintain and perpetuate distinctions in society." Jackson was a wealthy slave owner but had risen from poverty, and his party attracted the common white farmer and workingman. He destroyed the national bank, saying it supported the aristocracy. He threw veteran government servants out of office, saying their jobs weren't hard and other people deserved a chance to do them. Illinois Democrats took a similar approach, and Lincoln sometimes faced the charge of aristocracy even though he had a negative net worth.

Lincoln himself played the politics of equality, where fact mattered less than appearance. In 1840 he campaigned for the Whig presidential candidate William Henry Harrison, an aristocrat who posed as if he wasn't. The college-educated son of a Virginia governor, General Harrison battled some of the last Indians of Indiana while living with his family in a brick mansion. But when he ran for president, a Democratic newspaper mocked him as a tired old man who should retire to a cabin, and Harrison's managers seized on the imagery to recast him as a simple frontiersman. They said Whigs were the "Log-Cabin Party." Lincoln promoted Harrison by coediting a campaign newspaper that, in eighteen issues, referred to log cabins more than twenty times, cheering the "Log Cabin Candidate." His paper remade incumbent Martin Van Buren, son of a rural tavern keeper, into a clueless aristocrat—detailing his payment of $3,875.35 for silk curtains in the presidential mansion.

Harrison won in a landslide, and his inaugural parade included a log cabin on wheels—but the culture of equality turned back against Lincoln. When he married Mary Todd in 1842 it cost him, because a man who tried to rise in the world was vulnerable to the charge that he was getting above himself. William Herndon, his friend and later law partner, thought Lincoln sought "a political marriage" to align himself with "the cultured—the refined—the wealthy—the aristocratic—and the powerful family of the state," meaning Ninian Edwards's family. Herndon thought "Lincoln lost" by his connection with Mary, "and he knew it. The young and active Whigs—self-made men—men who had power, were strong. . . . They loved Lincoln because he was one of them. But what was going on between Mary Todd and Lincoln did not advance Lincoln." Even his best man wondered what Lincoln was doing, which forced him to reply, "I am, as I have always been, one of the boys and expect to be so always. I am yet poor."

His wife married him for his potential, not his present circumstances, and they lived at first in a room in Springfield's Globe Tavern. When they had their first child, Robert Todd Lincoln, the space grew crowded. But in 1843, when he first tried to run for Congress, Whigs held a meeting and decided to support another candidate. "I have been put down here as the candidate of pride, wealth, and aristocratic family distinction," he said. He'd been a "strange, friendless, uneducated penniless boy, working on a flat boat"; his marriage undermined that image.

He tried never to be painted as an aristocrat again. Whenever he confessed his poor education or talked of growing up in Indiana, he was telling a story about what kind of person he was. Sometimes he used his humility like a spear. In a speech, he said an opponent was a "greater man than all the rest of us," meaning he was self-important and overrated. In another speech he mocked a Democrat's exaggerated war record by invoking his own: "Did you know that *I* am a military hero?" He recounted his brief service in the Black Hawk War, when he saw no combat but had "bloody struggles with the mosquitoes."

His image was so simple it was easy to miss how much work it took to maintain it. Though his finances improved, he didn't buy a house in Springfield until 1844, and it was a small one for his growing family. He added to it in later years but never traded up to another; Mary, who'd grown up in mansions, would have to wait for her chance to live in one. Unlike other politicos he didn't take advantage of his connections to buy land or run a side business. And it was no accident that when he ran for president in 1860 his backers portrayed him as a rural rail-splitter—packaging him even more brilliantly than the Log Cabin Candidate. Never mind that by then he was a lawyer for railroads, and prosperous enough to send Robert to Harvard.

His image told ordinary voters he was one of them and shared their interests, which mattered in his later career when he talked about slavery. When he said of a Black woman, "She is my equal" in "her natural right to eat the bread she earns with her own hands," he spoke as a man who'd earned *his* bread with his hands.

THE MOST PROFOUND CONTRADICTION IN THE CULTURE OF EQUALity was its coexistence with slavery. Before Lincoln's time, the ideals of the Revolution had inspired Northern states to abolish slavery, and some states allowed Black men to vote. In the South, Henry Clay promoted gradual emancipation in Kentucky in 1799, and Virginia's legislature debated it as late as 1832, but these efforts failed; the enslaved of Southern states were more numerous, leading white men to a different calculation of their interests. Southern leaders cast slavery as the foundation of society, and even of *free* society: assigning subservient jobs to Black people assured equality among white men.

Illinois was nominally a free state but made accommodations for settlers from the South. The state constitution allowed indentured servants, typically young people held to labor until they reached a certain age; one was a girl in Ninian Edwards's home. A man might also bring his slaves from out of state and claim they were just passing through. Lincoln occasionally handled court cases for slave owners, and had many encounters with people held as property.

One came in 1841, when he visited the family home of his friend Joshua Speed in the slave state of Kentucky. He spent weeks at the estate called Farmington, where his hosts introduced him to luxury he'd rarely seen. Leading him between the columns on the front porch, the family directed him down the hallway to his room—his own room!—where he could sleep off the rigors of travel by stretching out on one of the house's nine feather beds. Speed's family noticed his discomfort at dinner; he wasn't sure of his manners in such an elegant setting. They were still chuckling about this two decades later when he was elected president, although they left unspoken a notable feature of the meals: the black hands that almost certainly served them, having carried food from the kitchen where enslaved people prepared it on the cast-iron stove. Joshua's late father had left his family an inheritance of fifty-seven people who worked the farm.

When it was time to return to Illinois, Abraham and Joshua went to Louisville and caught a steamboat heading west. It was a low-water journey in summer; the boat spent days avoiding sandbars in the Ohio, and Lincoln passed time on deck with a group of enslaved men. He later wrote a description. "They were chained six and six together. A small iron clevis," a kind of handcuff, "was around the left wrist of each, and this fastened to the main chain by a shorter one at a convenient distance from, the others; so that the negroes were strung together precisely like so many fish upon a trot-line." One had a fiddle, which he played "almost continually." His companions "danced, sung, cracked jokes, and played various games with cards from day to day."

Lincoln didn't record the fiddler's name, only that he was being shipped out of Kentucky. Six thousand people were sold out of that state each year; demand for Black labor was declining as the state economy changed, and property owners disposed of the surplus as they would any items in a market economy, sending them to newly developed land farther south. "They were being separated forever from the scenes of their childhood, their friends, their fathers and mothers, and brothers and sisters, and many of them, from their wives and children, and going into perpetual slavery." In the fiddler's case, the "offense for which he had been sold was an over-fondness for his wife." Had his master taken his wife? Lincoln didn't say, but eventually wrote two letters about this journey, making it his sole encounter with enslaved people of which he left a detailed account. It's not obvious why he felt it was so important. It didn't introduce him to slavery, because he'd been born in a slave state; nor did it turn him against slavery, because he already opposed it. It wasn't even a rare experience for him; "I see something like it every time I touch the Ohio, or any other slave-border," he wrote to Speed. What differed was Lincoln's traveling companion. He felt a conflict between the fiddler, trapped in the slave system, and his best friend who was invested in it. Lincoln's moral sense was always on the side of the fiddler, but his interests lay uncomfortably near the people who enslaved him.

Though the conflict stayed on his mind—he wrote one of his letters about the men in chains a full fourteen years afterward—it was not yet part of his politics. In his early career he wrote that slavery was based on "injustice and bad policy," but acknowledged that the Constitution left it for states to decide. This gave him little say in it. He left few clues about the origin of his antislavery beliefs, which led to many later efforts to deduce it; but the absence of an origin story was itself a clue. It took no special revelation for a nineteenth-century American to understand that slavery was wrong. Many did; even some slaveholders professed this while continuing to practice it. The harder question was how to *act* against an institution so securely fenced in by interest, custom, prejudice, and law.

His early years had given him an identity and enough success to reinforce his belief in himself. Now he needed a larger arena for his ambition, which he found after his first failed bid for Congress. He negotiated an agreement with other ambitious Whigs: They would run for the central Illinois congressional seat one at a time, hoping to share it in rotation with a new congressman every two years. Lincoln waited for his turn in 1846. He expected to campaign on protective tariffs and internal improvements, the platform of Henry Clay—leading issues of an era that was about to end.

COALITION

Lincoln in the 1850s.

Giddings, 1795–1864.

Chapter 2

PROVOCATEUR: JOSHUA GIDDINGS

January 8, 1849

FOR MOST OF THE 1840S LINCOLN SAID LITTLE ABOUT SLAVERY. This was normal for an ambitious man in the two-party system. Both parties sought votes North and South, so silence served their interests, and when that was impossible they used coded or ambiguous terms. Slave-state leaders spoke of their "domestic institution" without naming it. Free-state leaders framed it as unfortunate but not their business. Henry Clay opposed slavery in principle but didn't free the workers on his own Kentucky farm. A few abolitionists spoke clearly—free Black citizens, white activists, a Boston editor named William Lloyd Garrison—but were called extremists. Southern leaders said their talk incited slave rebellions, and slave states seized abolitionist tracts when they appeared in bookstores or the mail.

Lincoln himself considered abolitionists counterproductive. He was distressed when Clay ran for president in 1844 only to be derailed by an antislavery third party. Clay would have won had he received the electoral votes of New York, but the Liberty Party candidate drained just enough of his support there to leave him five thousand votes short. Clay, who favored at least gradual emancipation, lost to James K. Polk, a Tennessee plantation owner who went on to weave a defense of "domestic institutions" into his inaugural address. A year later Lincoln met a Liberty Party voter, and this defeat was still on his mind: "If the whig abolitionists of New York had voted with us last fall, Mr. Clay would now be president," he told the man. Instead, "all that either had at stake in the contest, was lost."

Polk's election made it harder to downplay slavery. He favored the annexation of Texas, a breakaway Mexican province that entered the Union as a slave state. In 1846 he provoked a war with Mexico, and when he sent troops to conquer its territories of New Mexico and California, critics feared he wanted that land, too, for slavery. The war and slavery became dominant issues—but Lincoln resisted engaging with them. Under his agreement with local Whigs it was his turn to run for the central Illinois congressional seat that year, and he took no chances, campaigning in a way that seemed detached from the crisis. One of the few newspaper accounts of his stump speeches didn't mention slavery, saying his "principal subject" was protective tariffs, and that he made only "some general observations on the Mexican war" at the end. The campaign's only memorable moment came when his equally off-topic opponent accused him of lacking faith in God. Lincoln, who'd never been a member of a church, published a lawyerly reply that he had "never denied the truth of the Scriptures," without saying if he believed them. He won as expected—it was one of the few Whig districts in his Democratic state—and a supportive newspaper predicted that in Congress he would find "many men who possess twice the good looks, and not half the good sense."

He brought his family to Washington in 1847 and settled in a boardinghouse. It was in a line of houses called Duff Green's Row, named after a Whig politico who owned this prime real estate; when boarders peered out the windows they saw the Capitol dome across the street. It was sheathed in green-tinted copper in those days, and a spectacular addition topped it: An inventor had just persuaded Congress to pay for a spruce shaft that rose seventy-five feet, holding a giant lantern visible for miles at night. It burned "solar gas," an early form of natural gas, which flowed through pipes from a tank in the basement—one of the emerging technologies that defined the era, like the new railroads that brought the Lincolns partway from Illinois and the telegraph wires that brought high-speed news of the war.

Lincoln crossed the park each morning to the high-ceilinged House chamber, where he sat among other legislators beneath a solar gas chandelier. It beamed so brightly on the desks that a visitor marveled, "We could read the smallest print and ordinary letter writing with perfect ease." In the glow of progress, he took an antislavery view but wasn't strident. He voted for the Wilmot Proviso, which called for slavery to be banned in any territory conquered from Mexico, but this never passed. He questioned the way Polk had provoked the war—calling Polk's explanations the "half-insane mumbling of a fever-dream"—but his speech didn't mention slavery. Polk didn't answer Lincoln's criticism; the war was providing its own justification. Early in 1848 a treaty confirmed Mexico's surrender of New Mexico and California, changing the very shape of the United States, and Lincoln was distracted. Mary quarreled with other guests in the boardinghouse and eventually returned westward with their two small children. He wrote her on April 16, "All the house—or rather, all with whom you were on decided good terms—send their love to you. The others say nothing." He seemed depressed. "I hate to stay in this old room by myself," he said. He told her he'd been planning a speech on the House floor, but lost interest while waiting to speak.

Even as he wrote this lethargic letter, events nearby were screaming for his attention. Slavery was practiced in the District of Columbia, and a group of Washingtonians was trying to escape. On April 15 they bought passage on a schooner called the *Pearl*, sailing away from the Seventh Street docks and planning to navigate to the free state of New Jersey. Seventy-seven Black people crowded the boat crewed by three white men, but unfavorable winds allowed a posse to catch up using a steamboat, another technological wonder of the age. An ominous crowd met the returning schooner at the docks a few days later. A newspaper said that without a police escort, the schooner's white captain "would have fallen victim to the mob which collected around him. He was put into a hack, and carried off to jail, for security." A slave dealer took fifty captured fugitives to sell them for their crime. White rioters smashed the doors of an antislavery newspaper, roaming streets illuminated by the beaming light from the Capitol.

Lawmakers gave speeches in the gaslight of the House, minimizing the violence and criticizing those who sought freedom. But one congressman, Joshua Giddings, chose a different course. He visited the boat's crew in jail and told them they were entitled to a lawyer. He was still there when someone gave rioters a key to the jail and they flooded inside. A jailer urged the congressman to flee for his safety, but Giddings, a solidly built man with a shock of gray hair, defiantly finished his business, stared down the mob, and walked out unharmed. Then he returned to his boardinghouse on Duff Green's Row, the same one Lincoln used, where the guests shared their meals at a common table.

Giddings was from Lincoln's party but represented different interests, which explained why he could approach slavery differently. While Lincoln's district was largely populated by Southern migrants whose trade flowed with the rivers to New Orleans, Giddings was a schoolteacher and lawyer from Ashtabula County, Ohio, settled by New Englanders. Ashtabula was a port on Lake Erie, and its trade ran eastward to the Erie Canal and New York. This left him free to express antislavery views that grew out of his faith. Elected to the House in 1838, he was unimpressed by his colleagues—"Our Northern friends are in fact afraid of these Southern bullies"—but made friends with John Quincy Adams, whose opinions aligned with his own. The former president, now a representative from Massachusetts, was waging a parliamentary war against a gag rule in the House that prevented discussion of antislavery petitions; he said "liberty of speech" was being "abandoned." Giddings joined the fight and in 1842 introduced a resolution relating to a controversy on slavery. The House voted to censure him. He resigned his seat, went home to Ohio, and was returned to Congress in a special election. By 1844 the House gag rule was overturned.

So when he visited the prisoners of the *Pearl* in 1848, his colleagues were unsurprised but didn't like him any better for it. Lawmakers condemned him when the House met on April 25. An Indiana representative said Giddings liked "troubled waters" and may have visited the jail "on purpose to get into a scrape." Giddings gave his own speech, which sounded conciliatory at first: He accepted that the Constitution left slavery to the states. But he turned this obligatory point against the South: *Free* states had the same "indisputable right to be free and exempt from the support of slavery which the slave states have to sustain it. . . . This Government has no constitutional power to involve us of the free States in the turpitude of slavery. We possess the positive, unqualified and indisputable right to remain exempt from its continuation, unstained with its guilt, and disconnected from its crimes." Learning that a slaveholding lawmaker was Presbyterian he said, "It cannot be so. No man can be a true Presbyterian who barters his fellow-men for gold." He spoke of people denied the ability to read the Bible and whose backs were torn by the lash. This wounded the feelings of the slaveholding Presbyterian, who rose to protest that he didn't use the lash.

Lincoln was present for this exchange, but didn't join the debate. Not until later that year did events give him a motive to speak. In June he attended the Whig national convention and was excited when delegates nominated General Zachary Taylor, a hero of the recent war who was so popular he seemed sure to win even though nobody knew his political views. This uncertainty had consequences: Neither Taylor nor his Democratic rival endorsed the Wilmot Proviso, so antislavery activists bolted both parties. They established the Free Soil Party and nominated former president Martin Van Buren in a challenge to the two-party system. Whigs faced the distressing possibility of losing a second consecutive election by dividing their vote—and those who broke with the party included Joshua Giddings.

Horace Greeley, the Whig editor of the *New York Tribune*, sent Giddings a private warning. "The Free Soil platform will hardly carry a state," he wrote. It might give Democrats the presidency, "throw the anti-slavery element of both parties out of Congress, and enable the expansionists to carry slavery to the Pacific." He agreed with Giddings's principles but said nobody could win a national election by asking white voters to take an interest in slavery: "Each man has a keen regard for his own rights," but as for the rights of Black people, voters would ask, "Who cares?" Giddings remained on his course.

To save the election Whigs would have to compete against the third party, and Lincoln volunteered to help. He campaigned for the Whig ticket by delivering multiple speeches across the antislavery state of Massachusetts, and told an audience on September 12 that his party was as antislavery as the Free Soilers: "This question of the *extension* of slavery to new territories" made it a proper subject for federal action. In Boston he shared a stage with William Henry Seward, a leading Whig from New York, who not only called to keep slavery out of the West but said "the time will soon arrive when further demonstrations will be made against the institution."

Taylor triumphed, but only because he had votes to spare; Free Soilers captured 10 percent of the popular vote, impressive for a third party. When Congress resumed after the November election, energized antislavery lawmakers followed up. They pressed Congress to abolish slavery in the District of Columbia. Giddings proposed a local referendum on slavery, in which both Black and white residents would be eligible to vote. The House batted away that idea, and rejected another lawmaker's call to ban the District slave trade. Then the antislavery men learned they had a new ally: Lincoln told them he was drafting his own bill.

Giddings wrote in his journal on January 8: "Mr. Lincoln called on me this evening, read his bill and asked my opinion which I freely gave."

LINCOLN SEEMED TO BE TRYING TO REPAIR THE BREACH IN HIS party. Other Whigs had stopped speaking to Giddings—his biographer said he suffered "absolute social ostracism" for failing to support his party's presidential candidate—but Lincoln was still talking. In Giddings's room at the boardinghouse he said he, too, wanted a referendum on slavery. In other ways Lincoln's approach differed: Giddings's call for Black people to vote guaranteed the House would kill his proposal, and Lincoln wanted a bill that could pass. Giddings approved his idea for getting one: crafting a conservative plan supported by the District's leading white citizens, which might induce the House to approve it. Lincoln intended to meet the next day with the mayor of Washington and incorporate his ideas.

Mayor William Winston Seaton seemed a good person for Lincoln to recruit—part of the permanent national establishment, an insider who influenced affairs for decades. An admirer called him "noble looking, singularly handsome, with most prepossessing manners, of great dignity." His office as mayor was not his most powerful post; he ran the *National*

Intelligencer, a venerable newspaper, and affected the city in ways that were visible centuries later. He was on the board of the Smithsonian Institution, created on his watch in 1846; President Polk favored one location for the museum and Seaton another, and the Smithsonian building known as the Castle was built where the mayor wanted. Weeks before Lincoln went to see him, he presided over a dinner for congressional leaders including the Speaker of the House, who said the capital should be the home of "the model schools, the model charities, the model libraries, the model prisons." A model emancipation plan could add to Seaton's legacy.

The mayor had freed his own enslaved workers, though he was less progressive than he seemed. In a portrait written after his death, his daughter said Seaton hoped for a "gradual solution" to slavery, a "patriarchal institution" that led to "the happiness of the race subjected to its protecting administration," but unfortunately corrupted and divided white people. Seaton himself said slavery was "the whole framework and foundation of society" across the South, and its "demolition" was not "the work of a day" but "one of an age." But he was the man available to work with, and at their meeting on January 9 Lincoln offered something the mayor might seriously consider. "Every free white male citizen" over twenty-one should be eligible to vote in a referendum in April 1849, and if voters approved, emancipation would come so gradually that few people would notice. Freedom would apply to Black children born from 1850 onward, while their parents would remain in bondage. The government would compensate any owners who chose to free people sooner, creating a framework that might lead to rapid change—but in theory a person born into slavery in 1849 might remain in slavery far into the twentieth century. This resembled gradual abolition laws that Northern states had adopted after the Revolution.

Seaton found the proposal so congenial that he doubted antislavery figures would favor it. He mentioned Giddings and said the Ohio provocateur would oppose this bill.

Lincoln knew Giddings favored the bill. ("I believed it as good a bill as we could get at this time," Giddings said.) But Seaton was more likely to support it if he thought Giddings didn't, so Lincoln kept the truth to himself. He "did not undeceive" the mayor, as he later put it.

Any emancipation would be an earthquake, and Lincoln left the meeting believing Seaton was on his side. He returned to the boardinghouse and reported to Giddings, who was delighted. On January 10 they crossed the park and climbed the white steps to the House, where Lincoln rose beneath the chandelier and described his proposal. He had shown it to "about fifteen of the leading citizens of the District of Columbia," and all approved. He didn't know if they would all *vote* for emancipation, but all agreed that there should *be* a vote.

Chaos erupted. Other lawmakers shouted, "Who are they? Give us their names!" Lincoln sat without replying, probably feeling he wasn't authorized to name Seaton or anyone else; but reporters took note. The next day a report on his action appeared in the *Illinois State Journal* in Springfield, having been sent across the country by telegraph—and it suggested the emotions he had unleashed: "Great confusion throughout the House. Nothing definite was done. Adjourned."

He seemed to be on the verge of making a difference. And then nothing happened. He never filed his bill, and the House never voted on it.

He later explained, "I was abandoned by my former backers and having little personal influence, I dropped the matter knowing it was useless." Apparently public reaction caused Mayor Seaton and other Washingtonians to back away from whatever they supported in private. Seaton was known to be anxious about the contagion of antislavery talk; debates in the House about freedom might reach the ears of enslaved people, with perilous consequences. Of more immediate concern was the reaction of white Southerners, to which Seaton as a Virginian would naturally be sensitive. In Northampton County, Virginia, the District slavery debate triggered a mass meeting. White men adopted resolutions that "Congress has no power" over abolition in the District, which must not happen without the "consent" of the neighboring slave states of Maryland and Virginia. Otherwise "we will *resist*, even if it be at the cost of our lives." The meeting further resolved that their threat should be sent for publication in the *National Intelligencer*. Seaton's paper didn't publish it but a Democratic paper in the city did.

Proslavery lawmakers turned Lincoln's proposal into misinformation and propaganda. South Carolina senator John C. Calhoun, the great tribune of slavery, mentioned it in his "Address of the Southern Delegates in Congress to their Constituents," which many lawmakers endorsed a few days later. Calhoun recounted antislavery debates in Congress—one outrageous bill after another!—topped by the proposal of a "member from Illinois," who supposedly had offered a resolution abolishing slavery not merely in Washington but in *all* federal territories, and even the "forts, magazines, arsenals, dock-yards, and other needful buildings" that the federal government maintained in slave states. It was likely the only time Lincoln ever came to the attention of slavery's most capable spokesman, who threw all his energy into erasing Lincoln's moderation, casting him as a Giddings-style radical who was easier to attack. Possibly the aged Calhoun didn't feel he was lying so much as carrying Lincoln's plan to its logical extreme: if Congress abolished slavery in the District it could abolish slavery on other land under federal control.

To Calhoun, antislavery figures were waging demented war against the natural order of society. They were also hypocrites, as he'd said in a speech years earlier: "The wealth of all civilized communities" had always been "unequally divided," with a small share "allotted to those by whose labor it was produced," and a large share "given to the non-producing classes." Ancient princes and priests enforced inequality with raw power and superstition; modern inequality was produced using "artful fiscal contrivances," the workings of Northern financiers. The South had "a more direct, simple and patriarchal mode" of dividing society: White people profited and Black people toiled. Wasn't this more honest than other systems?

Lincoln's failed effort showed his evolving political style. He tried to align his interest (a unified party) with his moral sense (opposition to slavery). In his strategy session with Giddings he sought common ground with a radical. Using some sleight of hand, they then tried for an alliance with conservatives. They didn't find the right formula: When Congress finally acted against slavery in the District one year later, it was an even more modest step, banning only the slave trade. But his effort thrust Lincoln into the national debate as an antislavery man.

Douglas, 1813–1861, as seen on a Civil War–era envelope.

Chapter 3

PARTISAN: JUDGE DOUGLAS

October 4, 1854

LINCOLN HAD NO ENCORE TO HIS MOMENT ON THE NATIONAL stage. He left Congress after his term ended in March 1849, returning to Springfield. He thought he'd get a federal job for helping to elect President Taylor, but it didn't work out: Taylor offered the governorship of Oregon Territory, and Mary vetoed a move to the Pacific. Her father had just died of cholera, and it was the start of a dark period. In early 1850 the Lincolns' younger child, Edward, died just short of his fourth birthday. "I suppose you had not learned that we lost our little boy," Lincoln reported to his stepbrother. "He was sick fifty-two days and died the morning of the first day of this month. We miss him very much." The agony was in the counting, the exact number of days. The death strained his marriage; Mary showed big emotions even in better times, feeling the world did her wrong. Then in 1851 Abraham's father died. He didn't attend the funeral, a sign of how distant they had become, but was forced to consider Thomas Lincoln's life and by extension his own. He obtained his father's family Bible and recorded the names, birth dates, and deaths of his relatives—work his illiterate father couldn't have done.

In an ordinary life these wouldn't count as wasted years. The Lincolns had two more children, Tad and Willie, and Lincoln improved his income; Illinois companies had more need for lawyers as the economy grew more sophisticated. But politics offered no possibilities, because only Democrats could advance in Illinois. The governor was always a Democrat. United States senators were always Democrats, chosen not by popular vote but by the state legislature that Democrats always controlled. Even Lincoln's old House seat, once thought safe for Whigs, was captured by a Democrat after Lincoln gave it up; and so Lincoln was no more than a spectator to the events that divided the country in those years.

He'd hardly departed Washington when a message reached the capital: California, its population swollen by the Gold Rush, was seeking admission to the Union as a free state. Congress had to answer this appeal, and the resulting conflict between free and slave interests threatened to split the Union until the aged Senator Henry Clay proposed the Compromise of 1850. Congress admitted California to statehood and banned the slave trade in Washington. The South was compensated with the Fugitive Slave Act, which strengthened a requirement for Northern states to return people escaped from slavery. But this brought destabilizing consequences. Though the number of renditions under the act was small—125 cases over more than a decade, not quite one per month nationwide—those proved more politically potent than the daily reality of four million people enslaved in the South. The prospect of seizures in their own communities radicalized white Northerners.

Lincoln followed all this from his law office, where each morning, according to his partner William Herndon, "the first thing he did was to pick up a newspaper, spread himself out on an old sofa, one leg on a chair, and read aloud," which "used to annoy me almost beyond the point of endurance." Lincoln said he read the news aloud so that "two senses," seeing and hearing, "catch the idea." And he kept on reading until 1854, when the papers told of a debate in Washington that threatened to disrupt the political system.

Lincoln knew the lawmaker at the center of that debate: Senator Stephen Douglas of Illinois. He was the coming man, just past forty yet deeply experienced and widely seen as a future president. He was a Democrat, a successor to Andrew Jackson and James K. Polk—an advocate of national expansion, limited government, and himself. He knew how to sell Northern audiences on the ideas of his Southern-dominated party. He had favored annexing Texas, not for slavery but for national greatness. He opposed high tariffs, which Southern plantation owners hated paying on the luxury goods they imported; Douglas said they hurt Northern workingmen. Loudly prejudiced against Black people who couldn't vote, he was perfectly unprejudiced against immigrants who could, and courted the Irish who were filling the growing neighborhoods of Chicago.

Every description began with his height, five feet four or less, but this failed to capture his charisma. He made everyone feel he was their "frank and personal friend," with a melodious voice, an imposing face, and deep-blue eyes. When he was twenty, just arrived in Illinois from Vermont, he turned those eyes on a judge and talked him into granting him a law license without studying first. He then talked the legislature into naming him a prosecutor. He won a legislative seat at twenty-three, then found he could gain advantage by criticizing unelected judges. In the 1840 election he coordinated an attack on the supposedly biased state supreme court, and Democrats won a mandate to appoint extra supreme court justices—one of whom was Douglas. Confirmed to the bench at twenty-seven, Judge Douglas was often a guest in the bipartisan parties at Ninian Edwards's mansion. A biographer said he would "sit on a red piano stool, laughing quite as merrily as the girls, giving back jest for jest."

Having joined the majority party, he enjoyed opportunities Lincoln never had. He hadn't been on the state supreme court long when the

Democratic legislature redrew congressional district boundaries, creating a new district that Douglas won. In 1847, though he was only thirty-four, the legislature promoted him to the US Senate. That same year he came into a fortune: He married the daughter of a wealthy Southerner, and her father offered Douglas an entire Mississippi cotton plantation as a wedding present, complete with its enslaved labor force. It was awkward for a free-state man to own human beings, so Douglas declined—but his wife soon inherited the plantation. Her father's will named Douglas its manager, and he left the property in his wife's name while using its profits to finance his career. Critics called him a slave owner, but he turned his blue eyes to the mirror and persuaded himself this was untrue. The charge didn't hurt him. A newspaper claimed "his remarkable energy and boldness" had given him a "world wide reputation" as "the very embodiment" of "true American progress."

He used that boldness in the Senate, where he took charge of guiding Clay's Compromise of 1850 to passage. It was daunting to attempt it with the country on the line, but he welcomed the responsibility. The bill's various provisions were so hated that he had to break it into several parts and pass them separately, each firmly supported and violently opposed by differing coalitions of lawmakers. It was the perfect project for him because it wasn't ideological. It was a dodge. It was an effort to straddle the most urgent question of his time, which was exactly what Douglas wanted to do. He wanted to save the Union—there was no reason to doubt his sincerity—and wanted to run for president, which demanded that he win support from both free and slave states. He sought the Democratic nomination in 1852 and though he fell short he was young enough to try again. It was natural that in 1854 he devised another straddle—proposing to do a favor to the South, but selling it in a way that, he hoped, would not fatally offend the North.

Under an 1820 law known as the Missouri Compromise, Congress had divided the West, the land of Thomas Jefferson's Louisiana Purchase, and banned slavery in its northern portion. The bulk of the southern part became the slave states of Missouri and Arkansas, but Southerners looked with apprehension as the time came to establish governments to the north. Too many free states would outnumber slave states at election time and also limit the market for slave property. They appealed to Douglas, the chairman of the Committee on Territories—a territory being an area that Congress organized for settlement so it could apply for eventual statehood. Douglas wanted to organize Nebraska Territory, which was north of the dividing line between free and slave areas, and he agreed on a bill that would repeal the line. The people of each new territory should decide on slavery themselves: What could be more democratic? He called it "popular sovereignty." His bill also split Nebraska in two, which implied that Kansas, the southern territory, would be a slave state, and Nebraska free.

He expected a Northern backlash, predicting during a carriage ride with a Kentucky senator that "I shall be assailed by demagogues and fanatics," probably "hung in effigy," and possibly forced to "end my political career." On the same ride he cast himself as a statesman and said the attacks would last only "for a season." But the debate over slavery had eroded Northern patience with what was called the slave power. His proposal shattered the parties; many Northern Democrats opposed it, while Southern Whigs defected to support it. Douglas forced it through Congress, but that was only the beginning of his trouble. Proslavery and antislavery settlers raced to the Kansas River valley, knowing majority rule would decide the territory's fate. The valley soon had proslavery and antislavery towns, along with proslavery and antislavery gunmen, whose conflicts generated stories in proslavery and antislavery newspapers. Many politicos abandoned the major parties to join a new antislavery party, the Republicans. Party label mattered less than a single issue: there were

Nebraska men who supported Douglas, and anti-Nebraska men who did not.

Desperate to defend their legislation, Nebraska men invoked the culture of equality: They said it violated equal rights to prevent a white man from settling in the West with his property. A North Carolina newspaper complained that "meetings opposed to the Nebraska bill" showed hostility to "the equal rights of the States. . . . The bill introduced by Judge Douglas proposes nothing more than to place all states . . . on the same footing." It was unsurprising to read this in a slave state, but a paper in Bath, Maine, published an article headlined EQUAL RIGHTS.

> *The right of settlement in the territories of the United States is a common right belonging to the citizens of all the states. If a citizen of Maine can plant himself in Nebraska, so can a citizen of Kentucky. . . . The Nebraska bill sets this question at rest, establishing equal rights to the citizens of all the states.*

Douglas himself, addressing a raucous crowd in New York, answered a heckler by saying his bill protected "equal rights." He then returned to Illinois and tried to give a speech in front of Chicago's North Market, where hecklers shouted him down. Undaunted, he traveled to parts of the state where settlers from the South might offer support. He didn't face reelection that year, but many of his allies did, and he was determined to sustain the party on which his career rested.

LINCOLN DECIDED TO CRACK THAT PARTY, UNDERSTANDING THAT Douglas had made himself vulnerable by separating himself from many Democratic voters. As a congressional leader of a later generation said, a leader without followers was just a man taking a walk—and Douglas was out on a walk. Lincoln, reading his newspapers, was a biased but perceptive observer: "The masses" in the North, "democratic as well as whig," were nearly "unanimous" against the bill. This gave him a weapon to use against the Democrats who had blocked his progress for five years.

He was seen in the summer of 1854 "nosing for weeks in the State Library," digging up Douglas's past statements. Then he traveled fifty miles out of Springfield for an obscure Whig county convention, and when he was "loudly called for" he denounced the "injustice of the repeal of the Missouri Compromise." It was one of many speeches he gave, though it wasn't clear what his interest was. He wasn't running for office, at least not eagerly. Other anti-Nebraska men pushed Lincoln to run for the state legislature because his name on the ballot would help other candidates in the same area; Lincoln reluctantly consented but didn't seem to want the job. Instead he gave speeches outside the legislative district. He tried to speak wherever Douglas did—following the national figure, the future president: the man who had what Lincoln wanted.

In Bloomington, where Douglas addressed a "Democratic Mass Meeting," the senator turned aside a proposal to let Lincoln reply at the same location. Lincoln instead visited Douglas at his hotel—"most cordially as old friends," according to a man in the room. Douglas gestured toward a bottle on a sideboard and offered a drink, but Lincoln declined, and their courteous exchange did nothing to moderate Lincoln's tone when he delivered a speech by candlelight at a separate location that evening. He alleged that Douglas had sold out his principles. Douglas had called the Missouri Compromise "sacred" before opportunism caused him to reject it. "Who was it that uttered this sentiment? What Black Republican?" Lincoln howled, drawing laughter and applause. "No other than Judge Douglas himself." Douglas had been trying out the label "Black Republicans" for the new antislavery party.

Douglas took note. Days later he spoke at the Springfield statehouse, in the white-walled chamber of the House of Representatives, which was often opened for such events. The governor introduced him, and "between ten and twelve hundred persons" filled the room, but even in this supportive atmosphere he was looking over his shoulder: "Before I proceed, it is understood by some gentlemen that Mr. Lincoln, of this city, is expected to answer me. If this is the understanding, I wish Mr. Lincoln would step forward and arrange some plan." Douglas wanted to respond to *him.*

Lincoln didn't step forward, and Douglas began. He said abolitionists were twisting the meaning of his legislation: "They burn in effigy, and get up mobs, and incite insurrection.... This is a simple matter, and easily settled. Shall the people of the Territories determine their local affairs for themselves?" He drew great applause, and people afterward filed out of the second-floor chamber into a lobby—where Lincoln stood by the stairs, singing out that he would respond to Douglas in the same place the following day.

The chamber filled again by two o'clock the next afternoon, October 4. Women as well as men attended; hundreds jammed the curving balcony and stood amid the legislators' wooden desks. Autumn light slanted through the oversized windows, and as the sun moved during the lengthy speech the light fell on Douglas, who had chosen to attend.

A fellow politician said Lincoln on stage was "awkward in his posture and leaning a little forward," and spoke "in a somewhat familiar, yet very earnest, way, with a clear, distinct, and far-reaching voice," though "sometimes rather shrill." The tenor voice was part of his power because it carried so well. He defended the Missouri Compromise, and then, according to a newspaper, challenged his opponent's notion of equality. "It is said that the slaveholder has the same right to take his negroes to Kansas that a freeman has to take his hogs or his horses. This would be true if negroes were property in the same sense that hogs and horses are. But is this case? It is notoriously not so. . . . [Even slave owners knew] the creatures had mind, feeling, souls, family affections, hopes, joys, sorrows—something that made them more."

He offered a different concept of equality.

> *What social or political right, had slavery to . . . claim entrance into States where it has never before existed? The theory of our government is Universal Freedom. "All men are created free and equal," says the Declaration of Independence. The word "Slavery" is not found in the Constitution.*

This was new ground for Lincoln, the first time on record that he invoked the Declaration's creed on behalf of the enslaved. Abolitionists had done this for generations, as Lincoln would have known; Frederick Douglass, the writer and orator who had escaped from slavery, had done it in a speech in 1852. Though Lincoln still didn't identify with abolitionists, he needed to reach for their idea—the way a man in a brawl must make a weapon out of anything that comes to hand. Having grasped it, he never let go, answering Douglas with the same concept that he used nine years later at Gettysburg.

Lincoln, a sympathetic audience member said, received "cheer after cheer," as "women waved their handkerchiefs." Then he sat, and a witness said "all was still, and deep attention" because Douglas, having come to listen, now had a chance to reply. He spoke in a voice that a biographer compared to "the effortless volume of a great organ tone." A onetime ally said Douglas was unmatched before a crowd, "bold in his assertions, maledictory in his attacks, impressive in language, not caring to persuade, but intent to force the assent of his hearers." Though no detailed record showed Douglas's speech, it was said that he attacked Lincoln's arguments one by one, painting him as a divisive abolitionist. Douglas advocated group rights, or what would later be called "national self-determination," and defined the nation as white Americans, who had the sovereign right to decide their fate. The white people of a state had this right, and so should the white people of a territory. It was in the interest of white voters to guard the power that went along with their group identity.

Later that month Douglas spoke in Peoria, and Lincoln responded from the same stage, challenging the senator's view of sovereignty. "Self government is right—absolutely and eternally right," he said, but whether self-government applied to slavery "depends on whether a negro *is* or *is not* a man.... If the negro *is* a man, is it not to that extent, a total destruction of self-government to say that he too shall not govern *himself*?" Lincoln invoked individual rather than group rights, then rejected the idea that the white people of a territory should decide on those rights.

> *This declared indifference, but as I must think, covert real zeal for the spread of slavery, I can not but hate. I hate it because of the monstrous injustice of slavery itself. I hate it because it deprives our republican example of its just influence in the world—enables the enemies of free institutions, with plausibility, to taunt us as hypocrites—causes the real friends of freedom to doubt our sincerity, and especially because it forces so many really good men amongst ourselves into an open war with the very fundamental principles of civil liberty—criticising the Declaration of Independence, and insisting that there is no right principle of action but self-interest.*

Nineteenth-century Americans thought of their republic as a lighthouse in the worldwide fog of despotism and empire, and Lincoln said slavery dimmed its lamp. He foreshadowed an argument Americans made a century later against legal segregation—that it allowed "the enemies of free institutions" to "taunt us as hypocrites" during the Cold War. In each case, the national interest demanded greater equality. The Peoria speech was the most sophisticated of Lincoln's life up to then, and he had Douglas to thank for making it necessary.

THE NOVEMBER ELECTION REVEALED DRAMATIC MOTION TOWARD Lincoln's side. He won the legislative seat he hadn't even wanted, and Douglas's Democrats lost their hold on the legislature. It was divided between Nebraska Democrats, anti-Nebraska Democrats, Whigs, independents, and members of the new Republican party. If anti-Nebraska lawmakers united they'd have a majority.

Now Lincoln's interest became apparent: The new legislature would choose a senator to serve alongside Douglas. For close to thirty years they'd chosen Democrats, but now, Lincoln told an ally, "It has come round that a whig may, by possibility, be elected to the U.S. Senate; and I want the chance of being the man." A few years earlier he had advised other lawyers, "Never take your whole fee in advance. . . . When fully paid beforehand, you are more than a common mortal if you can feel the same interest in the case. . . . And when you lack interest in the case the job will very likely lack skill and diligence in the performance. Settle the amount of fee and take a note in advance. Then you will feel that you are working for something." His approach to the 1854 campaign was similar: he had contested the election without asking for anything, and now wanted to collect.

He likely had foreseen his chance before the election, when he so reluctantly agreed to run for the legislature. "You don't know all," he had protested to the man who recruited him. State law forbade legislators from choosing one of their own for the Senate. He resolved the dilemma without ceremony, resigning the seat he'd just won. This angered voters and even hurt the anti-Nebraska cause; a Nebraska man won a special election to fill the vacant seat. But that couldn't be helped.

The senator up for reelection was a Douglas ally, James Shields, who knew Lincoln. In 1842 Lincoln had insulted Shields in a newspaper article, and the two men nearly met on a dueling ground before their friends negotiated a resolution. Now they were in direct competition. Shields wrote a friend to say he had supported the Kansas-Nebraska Act with great reluctance, which possibly helped to explain why he stayed out of state for much of the campaign. But he was eager for a second term, and a member of Congress warned Lincoln that "the friends of Shields are not without hope." Electing a senator was an inside game of unpredictable negotiations between lawmakers. Nobody knew what would happen when the House and Senate met together at the statehouse at three o'clock in the afternoon of February 8.

Lincoln needed fifty-one votes for a majority. He led on the first ballot with forty-four. Shields had forty-one, while a few others received votes, including five for an anti-Nebraska Democrat named Lyman Trumbull. Lincoln was friends with Trumbull, who once had lived near him in Springfield—part of "our little gay circle," as Mary called them. Trumbull was married to Julia Jayne, Mary Lincoln's close friend.

The sun set as legislators voted a second, third, and fourth time. Lincoln wasn't on the House floor, but was nearby to talk strategy with allies; there were places to huddle among the spectators who sat in the overhead gallery or stood in the lobby by the stairs. As the balloting went on some of his former supporters voted against Lincoln, who perceived what was going wrong. Shields was no longer his principal threat. The Douglas men above all supported Douglas, and if Shields couldn't win, any other Douglas Democrat would do. Some were covertly campaigning for a dark horse, the Democratic governor, who hadn't been in Congress for the

Nebraska debate and could fudge his position to appeal to both sides. He could win.

Lincoln concluded *he* would never win. A few anti-Nebraska Democrats would never vote for a Whig like him. He decided the most important thing was defeating Douglas—and if he could not reach fifty-one, then Lyman Trumbull could, because he was a Democrat and Lincoln could get Whigs to vote for him. Lincoln urged his core supporters to switch to Trumbull, who won on the next ballot. People cheered in the chamber and the lobbies until the Speaker pounded his gavel to restore order.

The next day's *Illinois State Journal* celebrated a triumph: Illinois had "rebuked" Douglas in a way that would be felt across the country. The Whig editor added a weather report on the bottom of one of the columns: "The flag flies beautifully over the State House. Wind from Nebraska." Lincoln had made this possible, though his friends felt the result was unfair. Judge David Davis, an adviser, said Lincoln never should have yielded to Trumbull, who had begun the day with a fraction of Lincoln's support. Mary Lincoln was so angry at Trumbull that she largely broke off contact with his wife, Julia.

Lincoln brooded privately, but received compensation. Because he couldn't run directly against Douglas, he had to challenge the senator's whole party—and this pushed Lincoln into party-building, helping to assemble the ad hoc coalition that eventually formed the bulk of the Republican Party of Illinois. His self-sacrifice in the Senate race assured that coalition's unity, completed its initial success—and left him in line for his next opportunity.

Lovejoy, 1811–1864.

Chapter 4

EXTREMIST: OWEN LOVEJOY

May 29, 1856

BUT LINCOLN WAS NOT YET A REPUBLICAN. WHILE THE NEW ANtislavery party became a force in national politics in 1854, conservative Illinois was slower to embrace it. Lincoln remained a Whig, and something more than loyalty kept him so. He declined to join the new party because its Illinois organizers were called abolitionists—widely seen as extremists.

The opposite of slavery was a multiracial republic with equal rights, which many white voters couldn't imagine. Even people who said *they* favored equality said other white people so opposed it that it would bring on a race war and the extermination of Black people. Abolitionists were fanatical social engineers who would cause the deaths of those they claimed to help. As late as 1863, a Democratic newspaper in Illinois reprinted a poem on its front page:

I'm not an abolitionist!
I glory in the thought

Write not my name with theirs who have
My country's ruin wrought . . .

And well I know the poor black man
Is loved far more by me,
Than by these men of evil name
And boasted sanctity.

This explained why many of slavery's critics followed a political tradition, reaching back at least to Thomas Jefferson, of saying that slavery must end, in some hazily defined way, at some future date, but not now. In 1854 Lincoln bowed to that tradition, saying only that slavery should be contained, and admitting he had no long-term answer. "If all earthly power were given me, I should not know what to do, as to the existing institution," he told the crowd in Peoria. This was due to public opinion: White voters like himself wouldn't accept the formerly enslaved "politically and socially" as equals. Even if there was no "justice" in this, a "universal feeling" could not be "safely disregarded." It was the speech of a politician reading the room, and transparently explaining his position by saying he'd read the room.

He mentioned an alternative to a multiracial republic, colonization—settling the formerly enslaved outside the United States. Henry Clay had led the American Colonization Society, and Lincoln sometimes addressed its Springfield branch. Some people emigrated to Liberia, established in West Africa as a destination, while others were intrigued by the idea, including family members of the famed orator Frederick Douglass. But Douglass and others opposed leaving the land of their birth, and even if they would go, Lincoln admitted that "there are not surplus shipping and surplus money enough in the world to carry them." The logic of his speech showed that colonization was irrelevant in any case. Nobody had a right to keep Black people enslaved simply because white society fretted about where to put them once freed. ("Is it not . . . a total destruction of self-government to say that he too shall not govern *himself*?") The "feeling" of the dominant group didn't matter if it violated individual rights. The correct position was to "allow all the governed an equal voice in the government," because "that, and that only, is self-government." He slipped racial equality into the same speech that called it impractical.

As he spoke across 1854, a member of the new Republican party perceived the radical sentiment in Lincoln's words. He was Owen Lovejoy, a square-jawed pastor with a sober countenance who ran a church in a town up toward Chicago. Lovejoy saw Lincoln as a potential ally who could help lift the antislavery movement into power—which Lovejoy was determined to do after laboring in that movement for seventeen years.

Lovejoy's antislavery conviction reflected both his faith and his family; he was carrying on the work of his older brother Elijah, a tragic figure of the movement. Elijah was the first of the pair to come from New England to the Mississippi River valley: he emigrated from Maine to Saint Louis, in the slave state of Missouri, in 1827. He worked as a newspaper editor, then entered the ministry, and finally combined his vocations as the editor of a religious journal. Elijah fearlessly told Missourians they fell short of his Presbyterian beliefs: He attacked tobacco use in his tobacco-producing state as well as the alcohol use woven into American culture. He also attacked the influence of Catholics in his traditionally Catholic city. But it was only when he criticized slavery—saying a man whose wife was sold away from him had "blood as red and warm as your own"—that some in Saint Louis were shocked, and he was briefly forced to leave the paper. After he returned in 1836, events drove him to speak out again: White men seized a Black murder suspect, tied him to a tree, and set him on fire. Elijah criticized their vigilante justice, so a mob came to wreck his printing press. He had it repaired in time to criticize a court proceeding that failed to convict the killers, so the mob smashed his press again. Concluding that Saint Louis was unsafe, he repaired the press and had it shipped a few miles up the Mississippi River to Alton, in the free state of Illinois, where a mob intercepted the press at the wharf and threw it in the river.

Moving to Alton nonetheless, Elijah ordered another press, and another after that was destroyed. He used each new press to print editorials more radical than the last. At first he hadn't favored outright abolition, but by 1837 he was demanding it. The mayor of Alton deputized twenty men to protect Lovejoy's last press against attack, but a larger group besieged the building where they guarded it, and shot and killed Elijah when he stepped outside.

Elijah's younger brother Owen was in Alton, and afterward knelt by his brother's body and vowed to continue the fight. Owen was twenty-six at the time. With a surviving brother as coauthor, he wrote a book praising Elijah and got John Quincy Adams to write its introduction; Adams called Elijah "the first American martyr to the freedom of the press, and the freedom of the slave." Owen became a pastor in the state where Elijah had been killed, making Hampshire Colony Congregational Church of Princeton his base. When some congregants objected to his antislavery sermons he told them, "I am going to preach that kind of gospel until you like it, and then I shall preach it because you do like it." Outside church he was struck by eggs and clods of dirt, but he never allowed himself to be driven from his pulpit. He operated his wood-frame home as a station on the Underground Railroad, helping people reach points north after they escaped from slave states. Arrested in 1843 for harboring a woman, Owen went to trial and was acquitted. Though there was no doubt he had sheltered her, the judge told the jury they could not convict Lovejoy unless the woman was proven to be enslaved.

He preached disobedience of unjust laws. For one sermon his text was a quote attributed to the apostle Peter: "We ought to obey God rather than men." He protested "the sentiment that I cannot, must not, obey the commands of God, because the Constitution of the United States and the Laws of Illinois forbid." Radicals said things like this all the time. The Whig senator William Henry Seward had said something similar during the debate over the Compromise of 1850, declaring that he believed in "a higher law than the Constitution." Seward was criticized for a virtual act of rebellion against the supreme law, and afterward moderated his tone—but criticism didn't deter Lovejoy. He was equally rebellious toward religious leaders. He told an antislavery convention that "the most potent influence" supporting slavery was "the sanction given it by the church in the name of our Holy Religion," and that no progress could be made "until this sanction shall be withheld." He was a living example of why even political leaders who opposed slavery commonly rejected abolitionists: his beliefs led him from a narrow critique of slavery to a broad attack on the entire power structure.

Before long he was seeking a place in that power structure. In 1844 he agreed to serve as a presidential elector for the Liberty Party, the abolitionist third party that ran its own candidate and spoiled the chances of Henry Clay. In 1846 and 1848 Lovejoy ran for Congress and failed, even though he lived in a part of the state that was settled by antislavery Northerners. In 1852 Lovejoy participated in forming another political party. It was called Free Democracy, and it included Joshua Giddings as well as Frederick Douglass. They drew limited support.

But in 1854 Lovejoy saw the country changing, and declared his candidacy in the state legislative district encompassing Princeton. He was an anti-Nebraska candidate, and at the start of October he traveled to Springfield with other men to organize the Republican Party of Illinois. He was at the statehouse on October 4 when Lincoln faced Stephen

Douglas there, and Lovejoy personally invited Lincoln to attend their organizing convention the next day. Lincoln declined. His friend Herndon claimed to have advised Lincoln to leave town to avoid being associated with the extremists, and Lincoln kept a plan to attend court elsewhere the day after his speech.

Republicans held their convention in the state senate chamber—smaller than the room that was crowded for Lincoln and Douglas, yet "the space was ample," said Paul Selby, one of twenty-six who attended. Many were from New England, the heart of antislavery sentiment, and Owen was among "the leading spirits on the floor" as they approved a governing structure for the new party. They adopted resolutions saying that "freedom is national and slavery local and sectional." They also ignored Lincoln's refusal to join them, and named him to the party's state central committee.

The 1854 elections challenged Lincoln's estimate of what "the great mass of white people" would support: Lovejoy won his state legislative race without any compromise of his views. An antislavery newspaper in Washington printed a letter exulting that the "brother of him who fell at Alton" had "never shunned to declare the truth." Once sworn in to the state house of representatives he spoke for an hour and forty-five minutes against slavery. He urged the restoration of the Missouri Compromise, as Lincoln and others did, and attacked the Fugitive Slave Act as unconstitutional. "I am not ashamed to avow myself a believer in the higher law," he declared. "I cannot and will not obey the requisition of that Fugitive Slave bill!"

LINCOLN DIDN'T ADVOCATE FOLLOWING A HIGHER LAW. HIS SKEPticism about the likes of Lovejoy had been evident for many years. As early as 1838 he had given a speech that showed he knew the story of Owen's martyred brother, but he referred to it in a revealing way.

Addressing a young men's group in Springfield, Lincoln described the Black man who'd been burned alive in Saint Louis—the crime that earned Elijah the first attack on his printing press: "This Government cannot last" by allowing mobs to "throw printing presses into rivers, shoot editors, and hang and burn obnoxious persons at pleasure." But having made an obvious reference to Elijah's death he didn't mention Elijah by name, nor his opposition to slavery. He spoke only of lawless violence. One way to read this speech was that Lincoln tailored his talk for a proslavery audience, criticizing only those acts he could lead them to deplore. Another reading was that Lincoln was uncomfortable with abolitionists, who placed their beliefs above the law. His theme was that the rule of law protected the republic from self-destruction. That was why he opposed mob violence in 1838, and why he accepted the Fugitive Slave Act in 1854. "Stand with anybody that stands *right*," he said in the later year. "Stand with him while he is right and *part* with him when he goes wrong. Stand *with* the abolitionist in restoring the Missouri Compromise, and stand *against* him when he attempts to repeal the fugitive slave law." He even warned against citizens who "resist the execution" of that law, equating them with Southern extremists who could endanger the stability of the Union. Yet Lovejoy and the other Republicans seemed untroubled when they named him to their central committee.

A few weeks later Republicans asked Lincoln to attend a meeting of the party committee in Chicago. Lincoln replied that he hadn't received the notice in time. "While I have pen in hand," he added, "allow me to say I have been perplexed some to understand why my name was placed on that committee. . . . I suppose my opposition to the principle of slavery is as strong as that of any member of the Republican party; but I had also supposed that the *extent* to which I feel authorized to carry that opposition, practically; was not at all satisfactory to that party." They'd heard his speech in October, so they couldn't misunderstand his position. "Do I misunderstand theirs? Please write, and inform me." At the start of the letter he seemed annoyed. By the end he seemed intrigued.

In 1855 Owen had one of the hundred votes in the Senate election, and Lincoln's allies didn't expect him to receive it. One friend assessed lawmakers who might give support, but then shrugged: "As to Lovejoy, you can judge as well as I can." Two days later another friend reported, "My brother, who is elected . . . is an abolitionist of the Lovejoy stamp," and was so devoted to abolitionism that "it would be worse than useless for me to attempt to do anything" to change his mind.

But a week after that, news arrived of a changing mind. Lincoln received a letter saying a political ally "has hopes for Lovejoy!!" Lincoln had been asking for radical support—if one didn't ask, one didn't get. One of his friends appealed to Lincoln's former congressional colleague Joshua Giddings of Ohio—and Giddings, in turn, promoted him to Lovejoy.

On February 6 Lovejoy gave his fiery speech against the Fugitive Slave Act. On February 8 the clerk called the roll to start the Senate election, and Owen voted for Lincoln. So did the "abolitionist of the Lovejoy stamp." Later they turned to Trumbull. In each case they voted pragmatically for the anti-Nebraska candidate who seemed most electable—and for people Lovejoy wanted in his party. He was following Lincoln's own advice to "stand with anybody that stands right." Lincoln did not agree with *him* on the Fugitive Slave Act, but they agreed on restoring the Missouri Compromise.

Lincoln stayed in touch. On August 11 he wrote Owen with a note of caution: "My dear Sir. . . . Not even *you* are more anxious to prevent the extension of slavery than I; and yet the political atmosphere is such, just now, that I fear to do any thing, lest I do wrong." He no longer spoke of their differing approaches, assuming they were on the same side. Instead he questioned whom their allies should be. An anti-immigrant movement had won many elections in 1854, and was uncomfortably close to Republicans. Lincoln didn't want to join them.

On August 24 he wrote Joshua Speed: "I think I am a whig, but others say there are no whigs, and that I am an abolitionist." In the next few months he left the Whigs behind, which was easier because their fading organization had been captured by the nativists.

IN FEBRUARY 1856 ANTI-NEBRASKA EDITORS MET IN DECATUR TO plot strategy for that year's election, and a politician joined the editors: Lincoln. Snow lay on the ground outside the hotel parlor where they met, having fallen so heavily the night before that trains were delayed and several editors were late. Even the editor of the *Illinois State Journal* failed to complete the forty miles from Springfield, but Lincoln had come early enough to make it. He helped the editors frame anti-Nebraska resolutions, which avoided extremes and included careful language that seemed to distance the party from nativism. He also helped to frame the editors' call for a Republican convention in May. They talked of nominating a candidate for governor, and Lincoln again deferred gratification; rather than suggest himself or a former Whig ally, he said the most electable choice was a former anti-Nebraska Democrat, William Bissell, a friend of Lincoln's onetime rival James Shields.

The night before the convention in Bloomington, a five-story hotel called the Pike House filled with delegates. "The verandahs, halls and doorways" were "crowded with a dense mass," said a journalist arriving on the train. Owen Lovejoy was there, working to win over conservative delegates; a journalist noted his "athletic personality" and said he was "making love to the abolitionist haters." Lincoln gave an impromptu speech outside the hotel. A newspaper described him saying that he "didn't expect to make a speech then," but "notwithstanding, he kept on speaking," and talked of Kansas. He said "a man couldn't think, dream or breathe of a free state there, but what he was kicked, cuffed, shot down and hung."

Lincoln, normally disciplined, was letting loose with unplanned graphic remarks. He was commenting on the news, and hadn't had time for reflection on the latest attempts to install a proslavery government in Kansas. In years past the Bloomington delegates would have known nothing of this—news would have dripped gradually out of Kansas—but the telegraph sped dispatches to newspapers, and the papers themselves came faster. In the 1850s an Illinois editor exulted that his small town was now "as near the center of the world as it is possible to get," because big-city newspapers arrived by railroad, "smoking from the press" on the very morning they were published. Two railroads passed through Bloomington beginning in 1853, connecting it with Chicago and Saint Louis.

The *Chicago Tribune* on May 20 featured the headline WAR IN KANSAS and said officials were arresting "every prominent Free State man in Kansas on a charge of TREASON!" Later the paper described the shooting of antislavery men. Proslavery gunmen attacked the antislavery town of Lawrence, destroying a newspaper press and setting fire to a building called the Free State Hotel. Further news came from Washington on May 22: An antislavery senator, Charles Sumner, gave a speech on Kansas and offended a proslavery congressman, Preston Brooks, who beat Sumner senseless with a cane. "Some eyewitnesses state that Brooks struck as many as fifty times on the head of Mr. S," said a newspaper out of Rock Island, Illinois. All this news reached Bloomington in time for the convention, placing its delegates among the first people in history called upon to make considered political decisions within a never-ending news cycle. Republicans wanted a calm and inclusive message, which would be impossible if the speakers vented their anger. A reporter in Bloomington scrawled a note to his distant editor: "Most intense excitement prevails in news of outrages."

On May 29 the convention came to order in Major's Hall, where delegates nominated William Bissell, Lincoln's choice for governor. Then came three main speeches. The first was from Orville H. Browning, a lawyer and a friend of Lincoln who delivered a sober conservative speech, reading words by Lincoln's hero Henry Clay. Two more speeches remained: Lovejoy followed by Lincoln, one radical and one conservative.

Lovejoy's recent rhetoric had been as extreme as ever; he'd told a Republican meeting in Pittsburgh that it was "time to light the fires of the revolution," and that he was ready to bring his rifle to Kansas "and take aim in the name of God." The news cycle invited more of this. But when Lovejoy rose to speak, facing Lincoln, who was waiting his turn, he emphasized his moderation. His half-hour address offered a disclaimer, as described by a newspaper: "Mr. Lovejoy stated that he had never proposed and never would propose any political action by congress with respect to slavery in the states where it now exists. He opposed its extension—that was all. He referred to the fact that his political opponents had always misrepresented him."

It's tempting to see Lincoln's lawyerly hand in this—Lincoln the storyteller, who said only what he wanted to say. *Of course* Lovejoy would have liked to end slavery in the states where it existed. But he couldn't end slavery through Congress, because it was a state issue, so it cost him nothing to promise he "never would propose" action *by Congress*. Lovejoy had been saying things like this for years—but saying so in just that way, before this crowd, reassured skeptics who hadn't heard or believed it before. A journalist said that many were "agreeably disappointed."

Next, Lincoln the conservative rose "amid deafening applause," and *his* rhetoric grew intense. His law partner Herndon was there: "I attempted for about fifteen minutes as was usual for me then to take notes, but at the end of that time I threw pen and paper away and lived only in the inspiration of the hour." Even journalists stopped trying to transcribe. "I shall not mar any of its fine proportions or brilliant passages by attempting even a synopsis of it," one wrote afterward. It became known as Lincoln's Lost Speech, and today a plaque marks the spot where he said whatever he said—a speech so memorable that nobody remembered. Only one reporter managed a partial record, according to which Lincoln said he was "ready to fuse with anyone who would unite with him to oppose the slave power." This was the message of unity Republicans needed. But he said more. Republicans were running a presidential candidate for the first time that year, and Southern states were warning that they would leave the Union if Republicans won. Lincoln said Republicans should defy this threat: "The Union must be preserved in the purity of its principles as well as in the integrity of its territorial parts." The Union must stand for something.

He also invoked his audience's interests: Did *they* want to be slaves? Slave-state papers, he maintained, had been expressing a "sentiment in favor of white slavery." When he sat down to applause at seven o'clock the convention was supposed to end, but "the large hall was still densely packed and the people refused to go." He'd so fired them up that they wouldn't leave until more leaders gave more speeches.

Lovejoy had moved toward Lincoln's conservatism and Lincoln toward Lovejoy's radicalism, at least in tone. This might be the real reason why the Lost Speech was lost: Lincoln, jolted by the electric news cycle, felt he had gone too far. A journalist insisted when it was over that "Mr. Lincoln must write it out and let it go before all the people," as he did with other speeches. He didn't, despite the clamor for it. In Herndon's opinion Lincoln was "newly baptized and freshly born," absorbing some of Lovejoy's fervor. But on reflection, he didn't want the wider public to see what he had said.

An account of the convention appeared in the *New York Tribune*: "Men of all shades of former political opinion—Democrats, Whigs, Free Soilers, Abolitionists—came together cordially . . . in the best spirit of conciliation to put down the common enemy. The news of Lawrence stormed and Sumner beaten by a Southern coward, had just come in. . . . Yet the delegates in convention acted with moderation and prudence."

At the start of July, a Republican meeting nominated Lovejoy for Congress. He overcame fierce criticism; one hostile newspaper called him "the notorious abolition disunionist," and even the friendly *Chicago Tribune* said Lovejoy faced "unfounded charges" and a reputation for extremism that risked his defeat. Lincoln was horrified, telling a friend that "it turned me blind when I first heard" that Republicans chose Lovejoy instead of a more moderate Lincoln ally, "but after much anxious reflection, I really believe it is best to let it stand. This, of course, I wish to be confidential." On July 4 he joined Lovejoy for a mass meeting at Princeton, and a newspaper said ten thousand attended: "They came singly and in crowds, on horseback, in long processions in wagons and carriages, and by regiments on the [train] cars. Flags, banners, and bands of music headed the moving masses."

In October the two were again on the list of speakers for a crowd of twenty thousand in Joliet. They joined Senator Lyman Trumbull, now a Republican. Greeley's *Tribune* said, "The prairies are on fire for Frémont and Freedom." That wasn't true: John Charles Frémont, the first-ever Republican presidential candidate, was on his way to losing Illinois and the national election. But Lincoln's choice for governor became the first non-Democrat to win the office in more than twenty years. Owen Lovejoy won his seat in Congress, where he served until his death in 1864.

Because Lincoln lived a little longer than Lovejoy, he had an opportunity to sum up the man whose partnership he had at first rejected. "He was my most generous friend," Lincoln said, and "every step" in their relationship "has been one of increasing respect and esteem. . . . While he was personally ambitious, he bravely endured the obscurity which the unpopularity of his principles imposed." Lincoln, also ambitious, had chosen a more cautious route. But his alliance with Lovejoy helped both men establish the power base on which they built all that followed.

Gillespie, 1809–1885, as seen in a contemporary book.

Chapter 5

NATIVIST: JOSEPH GILLESPIE

September 12, 1858

THE DEMOCRAT WHO DEFEATED JOHN C. FRÉMONT FOR THE presidency was James Buchanan, who promised at his inauguration on March 4, 1857, that the question of slavery in the territories would be "speedily and finally settled" by the Supreme Court. He'd been privately lobbying the justices for such a settlement, and two days later the Court delivered. It ruled against Dred Scott, who'd sued for his freedom because his owner had taken him into free states including Illinois. Chief Justice Roger Taney denied Scott had the right to sue; "the enslaved African race" had no rights when the Constitution was ratified in 1787, and therefore none in 1857. Even their descendants who had been freed could never be citizens. He added that slavery could not be prohibited in the territories, a finding unnecessary to the case. It was also needless for Taney to argue with the Declaration of Independence, but he took the opportunity to revise the document on which Lincoln and many antislavery figures before him relied. Taney asserted that "all men are created equal" didn't include Black people. Peering into the past, he guessed the original meaning of the words of dead men, which turned out to match his political preference.

Taney's opinion spoke to slave owners who saw their interests threatened by demographic change. Slave states that once dominated the Union were outnumbered in population and democratic power, so the Court nailed the old order in place, placing slavery beyond the reach of majority rule. Critics said such a blatantly political judgment needn't be followed. Connecticut lawmakers said Taney's "extrajudicial opinions are not law," while Black citizens continued acting as citizens, voting in the few states that allowed it. The ruling did have defenders; Stephen Douglas gave a speech at the Springfield statehouse warning that anyone who resisted it would be "enemies to the constitution." But in the audience, his head above all others as he listened, stood Abraham Lincoln—who delivered a rebuttal two weeks later in the same room. He told the crowd he would "offer no resistance" to the ruling, but because it was colored by "partisan bias" and "facts which are not really true," it was "not resistance" to say that it had failed to "establish a settled doctrine for the country."

He also said Douglas "dreads the slightest restraints on the spread of slavery," although events showed this was not quite true. President Buchanan went so far to impose slavery in Kansas that even Douglas could not agree; the people must decide. He broke with his fellow Democrat, and the divide in his party left him more vulnerable than ever as he approached reelection. State elections in 1858 would decide control of the legislature, which in turn would choose the next senator—and Lincoln planned to challenge him. Lincoln's path had been cleared; by stepping aside in the previous Senate race and then working to organize the party, he had earned overwhelming support. His fellow Republicans resolved in advance that if they won a legislative majority they would elect him.

The party ratified this at their convention on June 16, 1858, when delegates used the statehouse for a "spirited" meeting, according to Greeley's *Tribune*.

The main speech came from Lincoln. "Gentlemen of the Convention," he said to men crowded among the legislators' desks, "we are now far into the fifth year" since the passage of the Kansas-Nebraska Act, which had failed to stop the conflict over slavery. The conflict "will not cease until a crisis shall have been reached, and passed. 'A house divided against itself cannot stand.'" The nation would become "all one thing, or all the other." Slavery would be put on a "course of ultimate extinction," or "its advocates will push it forward, till it shall become alike lawful in all the states."

He cast the Dred Scott decision as more than a bad ruling. It was part of a conspiracy to spread slavery everywhere. Another ruling would follow, asserting the equal rights of people to take slave property across state lines. His friend and ally Leonard Swett felt the speech sounded extreme—"wholly inappropriate"—but Lincoln believed it "ultimately would find him in the right place." The image of a house divided set the agenda for the campaign, repeated by Lincoln and attacked by Douglas, and served Lincoln's political needs: slavery was so dangerous his coalition must unite on it, disregarding their differences.

Illinois Republicans were no longer mainly abolitionists, and the growing party with its range of beliefs complicated Lincoln's math. He not only had to build a majority, but to build *majorities* of voters in enough state legislative districts to win control. He filled eight pages with notes on the votes he needed from each county in the coming campaign. Some parts of Illinois were more conservative than others, and Republicans needed people whose views Lincoln considered repugnant.

THE AREA THAT MOST CONCERNED HIM WAS AROUND ALTON. IT WAS on the Mississippi River, which formed the whole western boundary of Illinois, weaving six hundred miles from the northern state line down to Cairo. Steamboats nosed up to the riverbank at Alton, and the river was vital to understanding the place. Its commerce flowed south with the current toward the slave states, which shaped its conservative politics and culture. Its proximity to the slave state of Missouri explained why the abolitionist Elijah Lovejoy fled to Alton from Saint Louis in 1837—and also explained the mob that killed him.

By the 1850s a new influence tugged at Alton: a railway station near the waterfront. The Saint Louis, Alton, and Chicago railroad advertised an "air line route" to "all eastern cities," with a change of trains at Joliet, Illinois. Alton became a crossroads of north and south, old and new. Warehouses, stores, and churches clustered near the riverside, making a prosperous urban center graced by the latest technology; the Alton Steam and Gas Pipe Works offered natural gas chandeliers for sale. Two daily newspapers were published in town; it had been a long time since a gang at the Alton docks had thrown Elijah Lovejoy's printing press in the river. But Alton's past could still give Lincoln pause.

To prevail on this problematic ground, he leaned on a friend just outside Alton. Joseph Gillespie lived in Edwardsville, the Madison County seat, in a house facing the public square. He was a dignified, clean-shaven lawyer with the last of his gray hair sticking out near his ears, and he'd known Lincoln since his head of hair was full. As a young man he'd volunteered for the Black Hawk War as Lincoln did, and in 1840 he won election to the state legislature, where his service with Lincoln in the Whig minority made them brothers-in-arms a second time. Once Lincoln jumped out of a window in a vain effort to deny the majority Democrats a quorum—and Gillespie leaped too. Springfield's Democratic paper mocked "this gymnastic performance of Mr. Lincoln and his flying brethren," and Gillespie was one of the brethren. "Mr. Lincoln," Gillespie once said, "had an astonishing memory. . . . He could recall every incident of his life particularly if anything amusing was connected with it," and he remembered Gillespie. They shared information about legal clients and, in 1849, when Lincoln was looking for a federal appointment, he asked Gillespie to help by appealing to connections in Washington.

Gillespie climbed from the lower house of the legislature to the upper, becoming a state senator representing the three-county district that included Alton. When Lincoln ran for the US Senate in 1855 he asked Gillespie for support, and paid him a compliment: "I know, and acknowledge, that you have as just claims to the place as I have; and therefore I do not ask you to yield to me, if you are thinking of becoming a candidate yourself." Gillespie didn't become a candidate, instead voting for Lincoln. He wasn't the keenest judge of Lincoln's ambition (he thought Lincoln was "not very aspiring"), but supported him loyally.

They remained friends even though Gillespie was a Know-Nothing. Anti-immigrant societies had been spreading across the country, gaining their nickname because members said "I know nothing" when asked about them. They had secret meetings, handshakes, and rituals, though their objective was no secret: to keep power in the hands of the native-born. Many, like Gillespie, were Whigs who resented Democrats for courting immigrant voters. It was unfair, they said, that immigrants could sometimes tip an election against natural-born citizens; equal voting rights for immigrants was unequal treatment of natives. A nativist tract decried "the interference of naturalized citizens, especially the Irish, with our elections;" citizens of foreign birth should be allowed to work but rarely to vote, and never to hold public office. Another book said immigrants must be regarded as "children," who could not possibly understand that their adopted republic was like no other nation in the history of the world. In Gillespie's county, a local paper said "the Native American doctrine" was prevalent in a suburb called Upper Alton—*Native American* meaning native-born white people. If a local Know-Nothing organization existed it was sub-rosa, though one could know its adherents by their headgear. An Alton hat store advertised soft hats and cloth caps in the "Know Nothing" style. The store also sold "Wide-Awake" hats, the common name of a broad-brimmed felt style that some Know-Nothings had adopted as part of their uniform. Some called themselves "Wide Awakes," suggesting those who woke to the threat in their midst.

By the 1854 election everyone knew about Know-Nothings, who endorsed some candidates and targeted others, capturing governor's offices and legislatures in several states as the old parties came apart. Reaching for power, they emerged from the shadows to hold public meetings and claim a respectable place in society. A book in their defense cast them as victims, "grossly misrepresented" by "partisan presses;" they were no bigots, merely Americans who had been "provoked" to confront the "evils" of foreigners in politics. Many officeholders survived by embracing the nativist cause, and Gillespie was typical, joining what a newspaper called a "fusion of Whigs, Abolitionists and Know-Nothings" in Illinois. When attacked by Democrats as a Know-Nothing it didn't hurt him. He won reelection to a four-year term in the state senate in 1854, presumably supported by voters who went to the polls in their Know-Nothing hats. In 1855 he was honored by a statewide council of anti-immigrant organizations in Springfield, which promoted "the cultivation of a purely American sentiment and feeling."

He was a son of Irish immigrants. His parents married in Ireland's County Monaghan and sailed for New York in 1807, just two years before their son Joseph was born, which meant he embraced a definition of

Americans that didn't include his own parents and barely included himself. But there was a distinction that Gillespie could use to justify his thinking: his family were Scotch-Irish, a largely Protestant group. The Know-Nothings targeted *Catholic* immigrants. The 1855 council that honored Gillespie made this clear when it resolved, "The Holy Bible shall be freely introduced and read" in public schools. It was common to assign readings from the Protestant version of the Bible, which Catholics resisted because they had a differing version. The council further vowed to fight "the corrupting influences and aggressive policy of the Romish Church," a reference to conspiracy theories that the pope sought to control the United States through Catholic immigration.

Lincoln surely followed news of this meeting, because a few weeks later the Know-Nothings were on his mind. In two private letters he said he opposed them as much as slavery. If nativists captured national power, "I should prefer emigrating to some country where they make no pretence of loving liberty—to Russia, for instance." Illinois nativists were "mostly my old political and personal friends; and I have hoped their organization would die out without the painful necessity of my taking an open stand against them." Yet it was hard for Lincoln to write them off, because their 1855 conclave also called to restore the Missouri Compromise. Many Know-Nothings opposed slavery's expansion, and Lincoln said Republicans needed their votes: "Until we can get the elements of this organization, there is not sufficient materials to successfully combat the Nebraska democracy."

Some nativists agreed they must unite with Republicans, and in 1856 performed a sleight of hand. Gillespie attended another meeting of nativists, now called the American Party, and was named a presidential elector—the Americans had nominated former president Millard Fillmore. The same meeting nominated a candidate for governor, but the gubernatorial candidate refused the nomination and went over to the

Republicans. He said a "union" against slavery was essential, and he looked forward to the Republican state convention. Gillespie helped to organize that convention. Having co-opted the nativists, Republican leaders managed to hold on to them while opposing one of their ideas: Republicans said they were "against political proscription on account of birth or religion." They could explain that they needed such a statement for party unity—because German immigrants were also part of the coalition. Winning was everything.

Lincoln kept an old newspaper clipping that showed the results of the presidential and governor's races in 1856 in Illinois. The presidential ballot had a Know-Nothing candidate who split the antislavery vote, and Republicans lost. The governor's ballot didn't have a Know-Nothing candidate, and Republicans won. In 1858 Know-Nothings again would be the difference between victory and defeat.

DOUGLAS LAUNCHED HIS CAMPAIGN ON JULY 9, STANDING ON A hotel balcony in Chicago. Addressing a crowd in the light of brightly colored pyrotechnic devices called Bengal fires, he quoted from Lincoln's House Divided speech. "He advocates, boldly and clearly, a war of sections—a war of the North against the South—of the free states against the slave states—a war of extermination." Black people would have "the rights of citizenship on an equality with the white man," and people would intermarry. Douglas instead supported the Dred Scott decision's definition of America: "This nation is a nation of white people, a people composed of European descendants, a people that have established this government for themselves and their posterity."

Lincoln attended, and when the senator finished people called for him to reply. He said he wouldn't take advantage of a crowd assembled for Douglas, but would speak in the same place the next evening—a delay that let Republicans raise their own crowd on July 10. Had his House Divided speech called for war between North and South? "I did not say that I was in favor of anything in it. . . . I did not even say that I desired that slavery should be put in course of ultimate extinction. I do say so now, however," he added to applause. "Let us discard all this quibbling about this man and the other man—this race and that race and the other race being inferior, and therefore they must be placed in an inferior position. . . . Let us discard all these things, and unite as one people throughout this land, until we shall once more stand up declaring that all men are created equal."

It was his strongest statement yet on racial equality, and he paid a price: his friend David Davis warned that among settlers from Kentucky, "it is industriously circulated that *you favor negro* equality." As an antidote, Davis proposed a meeting jointly addressed by "yourself and Gillespie," where his more conservative friend could give cover.

He needed that cover when Douglas accepted his proposal to hold seven debates across the state. Their joint meetings formalized a pattern that was now years old: Lincoln spoke wherever Douglas did. Now they took turns from the same stage—Lincoln's high voice and Douglas's booming one carrying far into the audience, whose boisterous members sometimes shouted back—an innovative format that drew thousands of spectators, even attracting steamboat excursions from out of state. Douglas's presence made it a national event, and newspapers printed transcripts of the Lincoln-Douglas debates across the country. Lincoln told the giant crowds that Douglas was part of the proslavery conspiracy, and Douglas said Lincoln was insufficiently racist. "Lincoln has evidently learned by heart Parson Lovejoy's catechism," Douglas roared at the first debate outside Chicago, which Owen Lovejoy attended. Douglas was right: the logic of Lincoln's speeches led to equality. Yet Lincoln insisted on controlling the story, saying only what he wanted. At a later debate he disavowed any desire for social or political equality with Black people; his sole ambition was restricting slavery. Challenged still later to explain his contradictory statements, Lincoln dodged by saying he saw no contradiction.

To win a majority of the one hundred seats in the legislature, Lincoln believed he needed all three seats in the Alton area—two seats in the state house of representatives and Joseph Gillespie's state senate seat. "We must struggle for . . . Gillespie's district," he wrote in his eight-page campaign strategy. So it was ominous when a newspaper said the Douglas forces considered Alton "all-important," and nominated a man who "was at one time a Know-Nothing" to oppose Gillespie. Lincoln warned Gillespie that Democrats were "making very confident calculation" of unseating him; Gillespie must win over local Republicans plus "four fifths" of the nativists. Gillespie replied that he couldn't. Democrats "will carry off at least one half of the American party if not more"; prominent nativists "will go to Douglas with might and main. . . . I shall take the stump and do all that lies in my power. I have all along feared Douglas with the American party in this part of the state."

Lincoln answered, "We must not lose that district. We must make a job of it, and save it. Lay hold of the proper agencies and secure all the Americans you can, at once." In this context "agencies" meant anything that produced a desired effect. Should he use persuasion, personal ties, propaganda, payoffs? Lincoln left that to Gillespie's judgment.

On September 11 Lincoln gave his personal help, traveling to Madison County to speak a few steps from Gillespie's home in Edwardsville. "This government," he told the crowd, "was instituted to secure the blessings of freedom." He said slavery "is an unqualified evil to the negro, to the white man, to the soil, and to the State." Gillespie stood with him—yet Lincoln apparently said nothing that pandered to nativists. He wanted their votes, but was silent on their ideas. The next day, September 12, he was scheduled to speak about thirty miles away in Greenville, and Gillespie offered to take him there. Their long buggy ride gave them a chance to more fully discuss the sleight of hand that Lincoln was desperately trying to perform.

As with car rides of later generations, they could talk easily as both faced forward without eye contact: Gillespie was busy with the reins on the dirt road. In this way he warned that Lincoln wasn't giving crowds the right message.

What was Lincoln failing to say? In a brief account, Gillespie said he wanted to hear more of the colorful "anecdotes" that Lincoln told so well. Have more fun with the crowd! But Lincoln declined, saying he preferred to focus on his cold, relentless logic against slavery.

Gillespie likely also urged Lincoln to support his beliefs about foreigners. A few weeks after the buggy ride, Lincoln complained about Gillespie's habit of doing that. Lincoln said he "loved" Gillespie and "respected him highly," but "could not endure" it when he started talking about immigration. Gillespie himself admitted to doing this frequently enough that Lincoln told him off. Lincoln exclaimed he "looked with disfavor" on nativist ideas because the "love of liberty and free government was not confined to this country." Immigrants were the equals of anyone else in America; "our beneficent institutions" were the result of fortunate circumstances and the ideas of the Age of Enlightenment—not "superior intelligence," not ancestry or race.

The buggy reached Greenville, where Gillespie the nativist stood on stage with Lincoln again. Lincoln apparently repeated the speech he'd been giving everywhere.

Republicans in Madison County thus were handicapped by their Senate candidate, and had to find their own ways to lure Know-Nothing voters. A week after Lincoln left Madison County, those local Republicans formed an alliance with the American Party, holding a joint convention in Edwardsville to endorse what they called the People's Ticket—essentially the Republican ticket, including Gillespie and others associated with the nativist cause. Lincoln felt so "anxious" about this meeting that he wrote Gillespie a reminder: "Please do not fail to go."

One newspaper said "Upper Alton Americans are unanimously in favor of Gillespie," and "almost worship him as their leader." But the paper added that the same nativists admired Douglas, suggesting they were in doubt about how to vote.

The seventh and final Lincoln-Douglas debate was scheduled for mid-October in Alton.

THE CANDIDATES HELD THEIR SIXTH DEBATE AT THE MISSISSIPPI River port of Quincy, then caught the same steamboat downriver toward Alton on October 14. The boat was a newly built behemoth 250 feet long, with space on a lower deck for hundreds of tons of produce, and berths above for 170 passengers, all powered by the latest steam technology. It's tempting to imagine the candidates talking politics in comfortable chairs in the parlor—a newspaper in 1858 said the boat was "furnished and fitted up in a most attractive and elegant style"—but Douglas needed to rest. He was losing his voice. If the candidates were going to sleep it had to be on the boat, which steamed southward all night.

At five o'clock in the morning the boat nosed up to the left bank, where Lincoln and Douglas crossed the gangplank and walked the inky streets of Alton. Lincoln checked in to the Franklin House, and Douglas the Alton House, where each had time for breakfast and an hour or two to himself. Later, as the day dawned overcast with a threat of rain, both received callers at their hotels. Gillespie was surely among Lincoln's callers; a newspaper said he was in Alton that day. The visitors also included

Gustave Koerner, a politician who had presided over the state Republican convention and the House Divided speech at the start of the campaign. He found the candidate in the Franklin House sitting room.

Lincoln immediately rose and said, "Let us go up and see Mary." Mrs. Lincoln had come down from Springfield and was in their room. "Now, tell Mary what you think of our chances! She is rather dispirited," Lincoln instructed. Koerner tried to boost her spirits, saying he was "certain" of Republicans winning a majority of votes in the state and "tolerably certain" that they would control the legislature. But Koerner began to think it was not Mary but Abraham who was "a little despondent." There were many reasons Lincoln might have been feeling down—the travel, the stress of debating, his depression—but it might have involved the presence of Koerner himself, who personified Lincoln's political difficulty. He was an immigrant.

Koerner had a remarkable story: Born in Frankfurt, he joined an armed uprising as a young man, suffered a wound from a soldier's bayonet, then fled to America. He settled with other Germans near Belleville, Illinois, just outside Madison County, and ran successfully for the state legislature. In 1852, as a Democrat, he was elected lieutenant governor. But on the very night of his nomination he was reading *Uncle Tom's Cabin*, the antislavery novel by Harriet Beecher Stowe, and before he finished his four years in office he severed ties with Democrats over slavery. Now he was a Republican, but in his new party he was unelectable. A Republican couldn't win without Know-Nothings. He never won another election, thanks to the same kinds of voters whose support Lincoln wanted.

Koerner didn't seem to recognize the possible significance of Lincoln's action when they met at the hotel—instantly ushering Koerner upstairs to see Mary. This took them out of the public sitting room, reducing the chance that an Alton nativist would see them together.

Koerner went away into crowded streets, where banners for Lincoln and Douglas stretched overhead. A ceremonial cannon boomed in front of Douglas's hotel. A train arrived bearing hundreds of people from as far away as Springfield and Chicago: the Springfield Cadets poured out of the cars and marched down the street accompanied by a cornet band. At City Hall, where five thousand spectators gathered in front of a specially built debate stage, Lincoln's opponent was visible in a knot of people; Koerner found Douglas looking "bloated" and "haggard," his voice a whisper. He was surrounded so tightly by admirers that a Saint Louis man stood beside Douglas with his left hand on the senator's right shoulder.

In each debate one candidate spoke for an hour, the other for an hour and a half, and the first had a half-hour rebuttal. Douglas spoke first this time, taking the stage to "long and loud bursts of applause," but didn't begin well. "Judge Douglas's voice has suffered badly by this out-door speaking," a journalist observed. "He speaks slowly, and gives every syllable an emphasis, but it seems as if every tone went forth surrounded and enveloped by an echo, which blunts the sound." Forcing himself to project, he delivered what Koerner judged a strong speech, rebutting Lincoln's House Divided. "This government *can* endure forever divided into free and slave states as our fathers made it, each state having the right to prohibit, abolish or sustain slavery just as it pleases." People cheered.

With his shattered voice he would have paused as the audience caught up to each half-heard phrase.

Why can we not thus have peace?
Why should we thus allow
A sectional party
To agitate this country
To array the North against the South
And convert us to enemies instead of friends?

"The Abolition party really think that under the Declaration of Independence the negro is equal to the white man, and that negro equality is an inalienable right. . . . With such men it is no use for me to argue. I hold that the signers of the Declaration had no reference to negroes at all when they declared all men to be created equal."

They did not mean negro,
Nor the savage Indians,
Nor the Fejee Islanders,
Nor any other barbarous race.
They were speaking of white men.

His invocation of Pacific Islanders was as close as Douglas came to endorsing the nativist creed that ran beneath the Alton electorate like a subterranean river. He could go no further, given the Irish Catholics in his coalition. But it was enough. Members of the crowd shouted "It's so," as others cheered.

He concluded: "I am told my hour is out. It was very short."

Lincoln was introduced next. "Although sun-burnt," Koerner said, he seemed "as fresh as if he had just entered the campaign." The despondent man from the hotel was gone, replaced by a performer who was "as cool and collected as ever." He stood onstage receiving applause for "several minutes," according to a reporter, looking out at "the waving of hats and handkerchiefs." Doubtless some of the waving hats were of the Know-Nothing style.

He didn't say a word that nodded to xenophobes, not a word that Koerner would resent. He stuck to one unifying issue. He did assure his conservative audience that if they supported him their lives would not change: They could restrict slavery in the territories, support the principle of equality, and even put slavery on the road to extinction without having to think about racial equality in their day-to-day lives; that was a decision for later. He said the nation's founders had set a standard for "free society," which would be "never perfectly attained" but could be "approximated" in ways that added to "the happiness and value of life to all people, of all colors, everywhere." Slavery violated that standard, and Lincoln said he wasn't extremist to wish that slavery "might sometime, in some peaceful way, come to an end." Douglas "says he 'don't care whether it is voted up or voted down' in the Territories," but people *should* care, because slavery was wrong.

That is the real issue.
That is the issue that will continue in this country
When these poor tongues of Judge Douglas and myself shall be silent.
It is the eternal struggle
Between these two principles—right and wrong—throughout the world.
They are the two principles
That have stood face-to-face from the beginning of time;
And will ever continue to struggle.
The one is the common right of humanity
And the other the divine right of kings.
It is the same principle in whatever shape it develops itself.
It is the same spirit that says,
"You work and toil and earn bread, and I'll eat it."

Douglas summoned the last of his voice to reply. "Agitators are enabled now to use this slavery question for purposes of sectional strife," he said. And then the Lincoln-Douglas debates were over. A train returned people to Springfield and Chicago. Someone walked from car to car taking a poll: 167 for Lincoln and 137 for Douglas. But these were northern Illinois voters, and Lincoln was not confident.

The train he rode home stopped at a town called Naples, and he had time to stretch his legs by walking three blocks from the station. Along the way he "met about fifteen Celts, with black carpet-sacks in their hands." He learned these immigrants had come to "work on some new railroad," but he doubted his own information. "What I most dread," he wrote a Republican ally, was that they were out-of-district voters imported by corrupt Democrats. He offered "a bare suggestion": Could an undercover agent insinuate himself amid such fraudsters, and induce them to vote Republican? It was as if, having refused to indulge the Alton crowd with paranoid visions of foreigners, he had by some dark art absorbed their vision. No evidence emerged that the men were anything but railroad workers. The matter never came up again.

On Election Day, November 2, Republicans received a majority of votes statewide. But not all seats in the legislature were up for election, and Democrats maintained control. Gillespie lost, as did the Alton-area Republican House candidates. Had Republicans won the three races in the Alton area, they would have held forty-nine of the hundred seats in the state legislature—near enough to a majority that a few cracks in Douglas's Democratic coalition might have made Lincoln a senator. Instead Douglas was assured of returning to Washington.

Because he wouldn't embrace nativist ideas, Lincoln had upheld his moral sense at the cost of another blow to his ambitions. He likely also contributed to Gillespie's defeat, but they remained friends and continued sharing political intelligence. Though their enterprise had failed, Republicans gained strength by pulling all the nativists they could into their tent, and the overall numbers mattered: People noticed when Lincoln's side carried the popular vote in a traditional Democratic state. If Republicans could do the same in a presidential election, Illinois's electoral votes would greatly increase their chances of winning. On the eve of the 1858 election a small Illinois newspaper had become the first in the country to propose that Lincoln should run for president, and after the results were known, a few other papers suggested the same.

WEED, 1797–1882, AS PHOTOGRAPHED BY MATHEW BRADY.

Chapter 6

FIXER: THURLOW WEED

May 24, 1860

A MAN WASN'T SUPPOSED TO SEEK THE PRESIDENCY; THE OFFICE must seek the man. The people conferred the nation's highest honor, and a would-be leader mustn't abase himself by campaigning for it. There were no presidential primaries, just national party conventions where delegates gathered to choose nominees. Still, men did seek the presidency, often desperately and for years, privately lining up convention delegates or attracting public attention in ways that technically did not count as campaigns. Lincoln took the latter approach when he accepted an invitation to give a paid speech in New York in early 1860. It was a chance to let the city's influential elites have a look at him.

In a lecture hall at the Cooper Institute he rose to address the crowd, a long-limbed country lawyer whose first line seemed startlingly humble: "The facts with which I shall deal this evening are mainly old and familiar; nor is there anything new in the general use I shall make of them." He then reviewed history to show that most of the nation's founders had favored limitations on slavery or looked to its eventual end—and the meaning of his opening line became clear. Because these were "old and familiar" facts, there was nothing radical about limiting slavery now. He could frame his calls for change as mere obedience to tradition. He made his progressive party sound conservative; he never rejected the founders, nor ceded their symbolic power to the other side. He knew many Southerners spoke of seceding from the Union rather than let Republicans govern, but he dismissed these "menaces of destruction to the Government," since Republicans weren't proposing anything new. He urged his listeners to "dare to do our duty as we understand it."

The *New York Herald*, always cynical, sneered at the speaker's ambition ("He makes his bid for the nomination this evening," the paper wrote as he arrived), but multiple papers including the *Herald* printed the speech from the first word to the last. The *Herald* even noted "uproarious applause," and quoted Horace Greeley of the rival *Tribune*, who spoke onstage after Lincoln. "My eloquent Western friend," said Greeley, had shown "how effort and honest aspirations may bring a man from the humblest ranks of society and place him at last in connection with the highest." Lincoln went on to New England—and, of course, it was not a presidential campaign swing; he was helping Republicans in local elections. He improvised new speeches based on stories he read in the newspapers. Learning that shoe factory workers were on strike, he shouted out his support in Hartford, Connecticut. "I am glad to know that there is a system of labor where the laborer can strike if he wants to! I would to God that such a system prevailed all over the world." The North must be on guard, he said, or "white free labor that *can* strike will give way to slave labor that *cannot*!" He generated such excitement that young Hartford men turned their political group into a pro-Lincoln organization. They appropriated a name that until recently had belonged to nativist groups: the Wide Awakes.

Lincoln returned to Illinois and worked with supporters to create a springboard to the national convention. Illinois Republicans chose their national delegates at an earlier state convention—and his nativist friend Joseph Gillespie was presiding, making it easy to stage-manage events. One of Lincoln's relatives arrived carrying two fence rails, supposedly among three thousand he and Lincoln had split together in 1830. He was "the Rail Candidate for President," according to an inscription. Cheers erupted. Lincoln just happened to have "stepped in to witness the proceedings," and consented to give a short speech. He was now fixed in the public mind as the Rail-Splitter; but the rail, or real, action came in a grove outside the hall. Lincoln and his allies, plotting strategy while lying on the grass, contrived to send Illinois delegates to the national convention with instructions to vote unanimously for their home-state favorite. This assured his name would be placed into nomination, though he would face several candidates who were more accomplished.

He planned this longshot effort with two key advisers: Judge David Davis and Leonard Swett, who expected to attend the convention while he stayed home pretending not to campaign. Both were devoted to Lincoln, though neither had any illusions about their influence. "I have sometimes doubted whether he ever asked anybody's advice about anything," Swett said, to which Davis added, "He never asked my advice" and "never took my advice." Lincoln was his own campaign manager, and in this way differed from the leading contender for the nomination. Senator William Henry Seward of New York had a manager, Thurlow Weed, to whom he delegated the grubby work of securing the presidency. Seward was so detached that this most famous of all nominating contests did not really pit Lincoln against Seward, but against Weed.

Weed looked like a man who would be interesting to meet and dangerous to cross. When he sat for a portrait in Mathew Brady's New York studio, his expression was best described as a glare. He had an oversized face with a strong chin. His long, lean body was covered by a three-piece suit with watch and chain. People called him New York State's "dictator," which was hyperbole—he was hardly the only power in the richest and most populous state—but as the leader of New York Whigs and then Republicans, he was a broker between other powers. He spent a lot of time riding trains through the Hudson River valley, which led from Albany down to New York City—the state capital and the capital of finance. He could channel money from New York railroad corporations to state legislators who regulated them and also help lawmakers attend to the needs of deserving railroads. Along the way he could ask the railroads for campaign donations to William Henry Seward, his inseparable friend and ally. Each man was presumed to speak for the other: Seward once wrote Weed that if either published a book, the other would get credit for it—and Seward suggested, revealingly, that Weed should be the one to do the work. Some people saw Seward's dependence on Weed as a sign of weakness, but Seward understood how much he gained from Weed's services.

Early in Weed's political career he'd run for office himself, but he found greater satisfaction in electing and influencing others. He was one of a new kind of leader who rose with democracy: the party boss. His power base was the media: he ran an Albany newspaper called the *Evening Journal*. The candidates he recruited included Seward, a young lawyer of medium height, red-haired, and sometimes diffident when addressing crowds. Weed perceived his strengths: ceaseless energy, intellectual curiosity, a sense of history, and comfort with the moral ambiguities of politics. Also he listened to Weed. Seward had grown up with a domineering father, then married into a family with an overbearing father-in-law, and was accustomed to accommodating strong personalities.

Weed engineered Seward's nomination for governor as a Whig in

1838 and collected enough from business figures to spend thousands of dollars during the election that Seward won. Governor-elect Seward then told Weed to assemble his cabinet. Naming a cabinet was the essence of politics, where careers and alliances could be made, and this was when people began calling Weed a dictator—but it was a strange dictatorship, in which he was also an errand boy. Seward instructed Weed to order the suit for his inauguration, and specified which kind. When the governor-elect's wife, Frances, resisted moving to Albany, Weed traveled over the primitive roads to Seward's distant home to persuade her to come. She consented, but expressed concern that Weed might be working himself to death.

He thrived instead. Supplementing his daily newspaper in Albany with a weekly journal of ideas, he hired Horace Greeley, then an ambitious young editor. Greeley was so successful that he moved to New York City to start his daily *Tribune*, becoming a seminal figure in American journalism. They were a triumvirate, the firm of Seward, Weed, and Greeley; and in 1849, at Weed's direction, the state legislature sent Seward to the United States Senate.

Time frayed Weed's empire. Weed and Greeley fell out in the 1850s, when Greeley campaigned for prohibition and Weed didn't want to lose the votes of drinking men. Greeley tried to run for office and Weed didn't help. Greeley made ominous moves, shopping for presidential contenders not named Seward; but Weed and Seward proceeded in tandem, and Seward positioned himself at the head of the new Republican party. In 1856 Seward wanted the presidential nomination but Weed persuaded him to wait; Seward had been fair to immigrants and Catholics, a handicap when nativists were strong. Seward grumbled but agreed to allow time for the nativist wave to fade. In 1858 he said in Rochester that an "irrepressible conflict" was brewing over slavery: "The United States must and will, sooner or later, become either entirely a slaveholding nation or entirely a free-labor nation." It was a less concise but more erudite version of Lincoln's House Divided speech that same year.

In 1860 Seward considered the Republican nomination rightfully his. There were other contenders, such as Salmon P. Chase, the first Republican governor of Ohio, but Weed was raising money no rival could match. Accused of helping railroads gain profitable New York City streetcar franchises in exchange for campaign contributions, Weed defended himself in an article that did not quite deny the charge: "During the more than thirty years that we have been associated with this Journal . . . no pecuniary consideration—no hope of favor or reward—has tempted us to *support* a measure which did not commend itself to our judgment and conscience, or to *oppose* a meritorious one." So he denied asking a "favor or reward" to support bad legislation, without addressing whether he asked a "favor or reward" for what he considered *good* legislation.

But as he was pulling levers for Seward, Greeley was pulling levers too. Greeley was connected with the men who'd brought Lincoln to speak at the Cooper Institute. And nobody could miss it when Greeley stood on stage afterward to praise him.

DEMOCRATS HELD THE FIRST OF THAT YEAR'S PRESIDENTIAL NOMINATING conventions, meeting in Charleston, South Carolina, where they fatally split over slavery. Southerners were determined to block Stephen Douglas, the leading contender for the nomination, despite his efforts to accommodate them. His 1858 debates against Lincoln haunted Douglas; Southern leaders rejected his view that the people of a territory could vote slavery up or down. The South's whole dilemma was that its voters were outnumbered, and slavery must never be up for a vote. Delegates from eight states seceded from the convention, preventing it from nominating anyone. Mainstream Democrats eventually met elsewhere and nominated Douglas, but the insurgents held their own meeting and nominated the sitting vice president, John C. Breckinridge of Kentucky. Yet another candidate, John Bell of Tennessee, was nominated by the remnants of the old Whig and Know-Nothing parties. Their opponents' divisions gave Republicans an excellent chance to win, which everyone knew by the time people began converging for the Republican convention in Chicago.

Murat Halstead, part owner of the *Cincinnati Commercial* in Ohio, witnessed the excitement of the convention even before he arrived to cover it. He was delayed en route as his train took on passengers coming out of New York—so many that they filled thirteen cars. They were "Irrepressibles," sent by Thurlow Weed to shout for Seward, the prophet of the irrepressible conflict; they planned to pack the Wigwam, a Chicago hall built for the occasion and large enough for ten thousand people. "The number of private bottles on our train last night was something surprising," Halstead wrote. They arrived in Chicago well-oiled to play the role Weed had scripted.

Weed was already searching for Seward's running mate. "I want a nominee for Vice from a Southern state," he wrote Seward—maybe Edward Bates, a Missouri Republican who wanted the presidency himself. But as Republicans rolled toward Chicago, Weed was absorbing ominous news. A delegate from New Jersey wrote to praise Seward's strength in a way that showed his weakness: "Some of us are strongly in favor of Mr. Seward for the nomination and are willing to take the chance tho' we cannot give any encouragement as to carrying this State for him." Seward would lose New Jersey in a general election. His history of criticizing slavery, dating back to his "higher law" speech of 1850, made him seem radical.

The idea of Seward the radical was misleading. His rhetoric was radical on occasion, but he didn't think radical action was required. Free labor was stronger than slavery and inevitably would prevail; the North's dynamic economy had produced a population that far outnumbered the South's. "A free republican government like this," he said, could not resist "the progress of society," which assured that slavery was "exceptional, local, and short-lived." Because he had faith in its eventual doom, he was willing to compromise along the way. He even said he could accept Douglas's popular sovereignty. Antislavery settlers in Kansas outnumbered proslavery men and would crush slavery as soon as President Buchanan gave up his futile effort to impose it. A brief passage of time revealed that Lincoln, not Seward, was less flexible about slavery in the territories and thus more radical. But Seward's image was what mattered.

Delegates approved a platform that seemed ideal for Seward. It quoted the Declaration on equality and said the "normal condition of all the territory of the United States is that of freedom." It also affirmed "the right of each State" to slavery and threw in seemingly unrelated planks. Republicans supported tariffs, internal improvements, and a railroad to the Pacific; they also wanted to make it easier for Westerners to settle on public land. In truth these planks did relate to slavery, because each appealed to a free-state interest: The tariffs for Pittsburgh ironworks and New England textile mills; the land and development policy for Westerners; the railroad for the new states on the Pacific. The North and South had competing economic systems, and the platform supported one as much as it opposed the other. Seward, the champion of free labor with Weed the New York money man by his side, personified the way Republicans sought to overlap moral and material interests to win.

Yet when Murat Halstead wandered among delegates at the Tremont Hotel, he heard many arguing that Seward was the wrong spokesman for the platform. "It was reported, and with a well-understood purpose, that the Republican candidates for Governor in Illinois, Indiana, and Pennsylvania would resign, if Seward were nominated." The gubernatorial candidate in Indiana "asserted hundreds of times that the nomination of Seward would be death to him." Not only did conservatives consider him radical; radicals considered him unreliable, and Westerners felt the heartland's resentment of a leader from the East. Lincoln supporters played on these feelings. His advisers David Davis and Leonard Swett mingled with delegates and argued that their man was the most electable. Pennsylvania delegates were committed on the first ballot to a home-state senator, Simon Cameron, but Davis and Swett asked them to switch to Lincoln on the second ballot if it looked like Cameron had no chance.

Weed and other Seward men radiated confidence when Halstead saw them. "They entertain no particle of doubt about his nomination in the morning. They have a champagne supper in their rooms at the Richmond House tonight, and have bands of music serenading the various delegations in their quarters." Halstead described the New Yorkers as "a party of tolerably rough fellows," ranging from a champion boxer and nativist leader to "Thurlow Weed (called Lord Thurlow by his friends)." Weed promised that upon Seward's nomination enormous funds were lined up for the fall campaign. But at least one New Yorker worked against Weed's purposes: Horace Greeley moved through hotel lobbies and dining rooms, having somehow managed to become a delegate from the brand-new state of Oregon. He wasn't supporting Lincoln yet, but wasn't helping Seward either, promoting the Missourian Edward Bates. Against his pernicious influence the Seward men could manage only a prank. They were passing out silk badges with Seward's image and name, and "some wag pinned one of them to Horace Greeley's back."

What most hurt Seward was his experience as a statesman. The culture of equality didn't value expertise. Politicians lived in the shadow of Andrew Jackson, whose principles of equality included the idea that government jobs were not hard and anyone deserved an equal chance to do them. It was offensive, even aristocratic, to imagine an experienced man was more capable than another; a man could be what he claimed to be for as long as he could pull it off. Conventions routinely nominated inexperienced candidates who caught the popular imagination. Frederick Douglass wrote in his newspaper that Lincoln was better positioned than Seward *because* Lincoln's friends "cannot claim for him a place in the front rank of statesmanship. . . . Our political history has too often illustrated the truth that a man may be too great a statesman to become President." Weed himself had turned aside Seward in 1856 because his long record was inconvenient; why wouldn't others do the same in 1860? The *Chicago Tribune* surmised that Weed's powers of persuasion failed to move the delegates because they didn't trust his judgment: "It was believed that his devotion to the senator from New York was as blind and unreasoning as devotion could be."

The *Tribune* promoted Lincoln in an article headlined THE WINNING MAN and praised "his position between the extremes of his party," having chosen his words so carefully that "no living man" could raise a "valid objection" to his public statements. He was as "radical" as he could be while respecting the rights of the South, which amounted to "wise conservatism." He could not have asked for anything better than to be called both radical *and* conservative, his reward for framing his antislavery stance so it was consistent with tradition.

Seward led all candidates on the first ballot in the Wigwam, but fell short of a majority with Lincoln in second place. On the second ballot the Pennsylvanians let go of Simon Cameron and voted for Lincoln. By the third ballot Lincoln took the lead—and when a man rose to announce that four Ohio delegates had switched their votes to Lincoln, he had a majority. Murat Halstead described a pause in the room as thousands took a breath, and then "there were thousands cheering with the energy of insanity." A crestfallen Seward supporter climbed on a table and called for the vote to be made unanimous.

THE NEXT MORNING, MAY 19, WEED WOKE ALONE IN HIS CHICAGO hotel room, "annoyed and dejected." Someone knocked, and he opened the door to see Davis and Swett, Lincoln's advisers, who wanted Weed's help to carry the general election. Weed shook his head. "I informed them very frankly that I was so greatly disappointed at the result of the action of the convention as to be unable to think or talk on the subject." He said he would travel west to see some land he owned, then go home. After that he should be ready to "do my duty for the Republican cause and for its nominees." Davis and Swett considered this. "They then urged me to return home via Springfield, where we could talk over the canvass with Mr. Lincoln."

Weed said he'd think about it, and caught a westbound train across the prairie to Davenport, Iowa. He spent the ride privately raging over the ways he'd been betrayed. He wrote Seward, filling four pages with an agitated scrawl even harder to decipher than most of his letters were, although a few phrases leaped out. "Greeley was malignant. . . . The Traitors from New York were few in number, but most violent."

But Weed knew what must be done. He'd been invited to help the nominee; it wasn't in his interest or Seward's to refuse. In his letter about "traitors," he added: "Lincoln's confidential friends ask me to go to Springfield," and Seward would have known as well as Weed that it was their chance to salvage some of what they had lost. Within a few days he was rolling back to Chicago, then changing trains for a southbound journey on May 24. Davis and Swett brought him to Lincoln.

There was no ideal place to meet. Lincoln's shabby law office was inadequate. Just before Weed's arrival the governor of Illinois wrote Lincoln, offering to let the nominee use the governor's reception room at the statehouse, but Lincoln would not yet have received the offer. He sometimes met a visitor at his hotel, but likely welcomed Weed into the Lincoln home at the corner of Eighth and Jackson Streets, where Willie and Tad, ages ten and seven, ran through the rooms.

Springfield's Democratic paper announced Lincoln was meeting the man who controlled New York State through "secret intrigues." The paper said Lincoln would not dare deny the dictator a "share of the spoils. Weed will win. Lincoln will promise." Weed would want a place for Seward, either as secretary of state or ambassador to London. News of their inside dealing was so jarring that the pro-Lincoln *Chicago Tribune* reflexively denied it: "That's a lie. Thurlow Weed has not been to Springfield." The real-life Lincoln and his image were at odds: the Lincoln in the *Tribune* was too pure to meet the dictator, while the Lincoln who lived in Springfield was not.

In the Springfield room where Weed really was, it was clear what each man wanted. Lincoln needed help to carry New York, and a working relationship with eastern economic interests. Weed wanted some of the benefits that he would have enjoyed from a Seward presidency, such as the power over federal patronage in New York. Both had reasons to want Seward in a Lincoln administration. By his own account, Lincoln was already thinking of this.

They could relate to each other because of the way they'd grown up. Weed had no more formal education than Lincoln did, having been born in the Catskill Mountains to a family so poor his father landed in debtors' prison. "When he was eight years old Thurlow felt the necessity of doing something towards his own support," one of his descendants said, and he went to work for a blacksmith. Next he signed up as a cabin boy on a Hudson River sloop, and finally worked on a farm before finding his calling in newspapers. The two men also could relate as politicians. "I found Mr. Lincoln sagacious and practical," Weed said, with "such intuitive knowledge of human nature, and such familiarity with the virtues and infirmities of politicians, that I became impressed very favorably with his fitness for the duties which he was not unlikely to be called upon to discharge." In truth Lincoln wasn't deeply familiar with many political figures outside Illinois, but he deduced enough to impress his visitor. He may also have given Weed an impression of his sagacity through the flattering expedient of agreeing with whatever Weed said. In any case Lincoln kept the dialogue going. "This conversation lasted some five hours" until the train arrived on which Weed was to depart. Lincoln soothed the wound of Weed's defeat with a generous helping of attention and time.

Weed let the hours pass without saying all that was on his mind. He was clever enough not to mention the levers of power that he would like to control. Lincoln wrote afterward that Weed "showed no signs whatever of the intriguer. He asked for nothing; and said N.Y. is safe, without condition." He was soon writing letters to Weed, offering political intelligence and opinions.

Writing one of their mutual acquaintances, Lincoln said he found Weed to be a man of good character, and that he didn't believe tales of Weed's corruption. The mutual friend passed on this reassurance to Weed, as Lincoln probably knew he would. By saying this Lincoln was also sending a subtle warning that he had *heard* tales of corruption. And he would not give Weed what Seward had, the power to choose who received which government job. Later Lincoln wrote Weed, "As to the matter of dispensing patronage, it perhaps will surprise you to learn, that I have information that you claim to have my authority to arrange that matter in N.Y. I do not believe you have so claimed; but still so some men say." Lincoln said he would make his own decisions, with a principle of justice for all.

His meeting with Weed began the effort to unite competing interests behind his cause. He might differ with Weed's tactics but couldn't do without him—which was true of the whole coalition he needed to win the presidency and to govern. He was privately listing people he meant to invite into his cabinet should he win. He wanted Chase, the antislavery zealot, as well as Bates, the more conservative Missourian. He would find a place for Cameron, who was thought to be corrupt but whose state had ensured his nomination. And he needed Seward, who like the others thought he should have been president. He made these choices with little regard for managing the crisis that would loom should he win, and much regard for the requirements of his party. But this was not irrational; a democratic leader needed political support as much as competence. If these men pulled in their own directions, Lincoln would have to manage them—and he did have experience in managing people who differed.

SEPARATION

Lincoln, November 1860,
in the first known portrait as he grew a beard.

Green, 1791–1875.

Chapter 7

CONSPIRACY THEORIST: DUFF GREEN

December 28, 1860

MOST SLAVE STATES DIDN'T EVEN PUT LINCOLN ON THE BALLOT in 1860, and Southern leaders warned that a Republican victory would cause their states to secede. Democrats made this part of their message—a vote for Stephen Douglas was a vote to save the Union!—but Lincoln made it through the general election without addressing the threat at all. He didn't speak on any issue, observing the tradition that presidential nominees rarely said anything. On August 8 he felt obliged to attend a Republican rally at the Springfield fairgrounds, where crowds mobbed his carriage, pulled him from it, and carried him over their heads to the stage—and even then he said only a few words. "It has been my purpose, since I have been placed in my present position, to make no speeches," he said, adding only that he didn't think the "tumult" of the rally honored him personally: "Four years from this time you will give a like manifestation to the next man who is the representative of the truth on the questions that now agitate the public."

He kept silent not only out of propriety but because he felt his words would be misused. Once he received a warning that Wall Street speculators planned to trigger a financial panic in the event of his election, but when asked to head off this plot by making reassuring statements, Lincoln replied in exasperation. "What is it I could say which would quiet alarm? Is it that no interference by the government, with slaves or slavery within the states, is intended? I have said this so often already, that a repetition of it is but mockery, bearing an appearance of weakness, which perhaps should be avoided." Saying anything would only be "encouraging bold bad men to believe they are dealing with one who can be scared into anything."

His allies brushed off the danger. Seward campaigned for him in Saint Paul, Minnesota, and instead of dwelling on the republic's possible destruction he spoke of its expansion. Someday the United States would control the hemisphere, he said—even Alaska. Of secession he cried, "Who is afraid? Nobody is afraid."

Many were afraid, and the campaign's feverish energy reflected it. The Wide Awake movement that had started in Connecticut became a nationwide phenomenon—young men marching for Lincoln in torchlight processions. When Seward campaigned for Lincoln in Chicago the city put on a giant parade; the *Tribune* claimed the Wide Awakes alone numbered ten thousand, and seventy-five thousand came into the city on "Monster Excursion Trains." Newspapers estimated Republican rallies with twenty thousand people in New York, ten thousand in Philadelphia. Douglas, breaking tradition by openly campaigning across the country, drew Democratic crowds in the tens of thousands. He shouted to the masses in Chicago: "This country is in more danger now than at any other moment since I have known anything of public life." In October he showed that he believed this. He concluded he couldn't win, and began campaigning for the Union instead of himself—traveling in Southern states where he might draw votes away from the proslavery Democrat Breckinridge.

On Election Day, November 6, Lincoln went to vote, and a reporter watched him walk across Springfield. A crowd near the courthouse gave him "such a cheer as no man ever received who has not the hearts as well as the voices of his people. Every vestige of party feeling seemed to be suddenly abandoned. Even the distributors of the Douglas tickets shouted and swung their hats." He voted the straight Republican ticket, after tearing off the top of the ballot so as to cast no vote for president. That evening he sat "almost alone" in the telegraph office, following election returns. By two o'clock the partial results on the clicking telegraph made it clear he had won, sweeping all the free states including Illinois. He went home to Mary and to bed, but didn't get much sleep: "I then felt the weight of the responsibility that was upon me."

He gave no victory speech.

In the days that followed, the president-elect received visitors during office hours. Anybody could find him in the corner reception room he'd been given inside the statehouse; he often opened the door himself. He welcomed Henry Villard, a New York newspaper reporter, to sit in. ("He never overlooked a newspaper man who had it in his power to say a good or bad thing of him," his law partner Herndon said.) Neighbors and tourists wanted to congratulate him or gawk; some men came in "muddy boots and hickory shirts," though women usually dressed up. Lincoln would ask people's names and "start a running conversation" as they lingered in the crowded room. Once as Villard watched, a "live disunionist" came—a man from Mississippi with "a blue cockade displayed upon his hat," the emblem of secession. He said he didn't object to Lincoln personally, but to his party. The president-elect sent him away with an autographed book of the Lincoln-Douglas debates.

What he didn't tell visitors was anything about the crisis. Villard said of Lincoln, "Every newspaper he opened was filled with clear indications of an impending national catastrophe," and people were urging him to "abandon his paralyzed silence . . . and pour the oil of conciliatory conservative assurances upon the turbulent waves of Southern excitement." On

November 20 Lincoln relented slightly, allowing Senator Lyman Trumbull to insert some remarks into a speech; people in the know would understand he was speaking for Lincoln. Trumbull said the president-elect had no designs to attack slavery where it existed, but the result only vindicated Lincoln's reluctance. Voices North and South scorned this as weakness or dishonesty.

Answering a sympathetic Southerner who urged Lincoln to speak, he asked, "Is it desired that I shall shift the ground upon which I have been elected? I can not do it." Even to repeat the Republican platform "would make me appear as if I repented for the crime of having been elected, and was anxious to apologize and beg forgiveness."

On December 20 a convention in South Carolina ratified its ordinance of secession. The *Charleston Courier* said "a united Commonwealth" had declared the Constitution to be "abrogated, repealed and annulled, so far as the State of South Carolina was concerned." South Carolinians seemed to expect no consequences; they immediately turned to questions like how to resume commerce with the country they had just left and whether they could persuade the United States to continue delivering the mail. In Springfield the *Illinois State Journal*, the paper closest to Lincoln, mocked South Carolina's declaration in a column headed FOREIGN NEWS. South Carolina "has cut the ropes—she has become an independent nation—she has actually *passed a resolution*! . . . They have severed the band that bound them to this glorious Confederacy with the scissors of revolution!" On Christmas Day the paper was quoting Andrew Jackson, who had confronted South Carolina's effort to nullify federal law in the 1830s. Jackson said states could not "absolve themselves" of their "most solemn obligations." Privately Lincoln told Thurlow Weed, another of his visitors that season, "No state can, in any way lawfully, get out of the Union, without the consent of the others," and the president's duty was "to run the machine as it is."

A FEW DAYS LATER A MAN IN WASHINGTON, DC, DECIDED TO MAKE his own pilgrimage to Springfield, "hoping that I could, by a personal appeal," persuade Lincoln to endorse a compromise that might save the Union. Duff Green thought Lincoln would listen because they were friends, and because he had boundless confidence; he'd been dealing with presidents for decades. There was hardly an event of the past thirty-five years about which Green hadn't had something to say, and he wanted Lincoln to heed the lessons of those years and accommodate the feelings of the South.

Green was a Kentuckian with irrepressible energy, though he was sixty-nine, used a walking stick, and grew a gray beard halfway to his belt. He'd been involved in politics since the early 1820s, when he bought a Saint Louis newspaper and supported the presidential aspirations of John C. Calhoun, who became Green's friend and ally and eventual relation by marriage. He then moved to Washington to publish a different paper, the *United States Telegraph*, and it's worth reading his earlier writings in light of his later passion for slavery. He wrote that a republic "based on equality of life, liberty and property" could never fall, and reprinted an article asserting "that every man is entitled to an equality of civil rights." When the Baltimore and Ohio railroad sought an exemption from tariffs on imported iron, Green opposed special treatment for corporations, saying the government was "based on an equality of rights, under which it was intended, that all should equally participate." He urged the abolition of debtors' prisons, "this system of refined cruelty." It was natural that in 1828 he supported the presidential candidate Andrew Jackson, who allied with his friend Calhoun. He published an address from a pro-Jackson convention in Maryland: "The *fundamental principle* on which our whole system rests, is the POLITICAL EQUALITY of the citizens," which led to "the doctrine, that *the will of the majority shall prevail.*" Jackson believed in majority rule because he felt the presidential election had been rigged against him in 1824; he expected a majority in 1828.

After Jackson won, the *Telegraph* became the official Democratic organ, but Green valued his autonomy too highly to last as a party spokesman. "His independence was responsible for most of his troubles," said his biographer, "for independence to Green precluded any and all compromises." Those who disagreed with him were not merely wrong but immoral, unprincipled, or part of a Catholic conspiracy. He felt "that man is selfish, that he is more under the influence of animosity than of friendship," and that party leaders were vile schemers who meant "to gratify their personal animosities in disregard of the public interest." This wasn't far from Lincoln's belief that people acted in self-interest, but Green applied the insight in darker ways. He soon alienated Jackson and went over to the opposition. His newspaper so insulted a Jacksonian congressman that the lawmaker found Green on the street, hammered him with a cane, knocked him into a gutter, and broke Green's arm, collarbone, and several ribs while also dislocating one of his legs. From his hospital bed Green dictated an editorial that repeated his original insults. Even people who loathed his words praised him as a symbol of the freedom of the press.

He was less independent than he seemed: he kept his newspaper in business by borrowing from the Bank of the United States, even as his editorials demanded its destruction. Green eventually relaxed his opposition to his creditor, deciding the bank was the victim of a conspiracy by New York financiers. He was fond of conspiracy theories. After he left the *Telegraph* he started another paper in Baltimore that waged a holy war against the Catholic Church. He speculated that European Catholics were conspiring to take over the country through American Catholics, who reported back to the foreign minister of the Austrian empire.

As the years advanced he saw conspiracies against slavery, which were conspiracies against his interests. He was a slave owner. His notions of equality didn't include Black people. "Slavery has always existed," Green said, "and will continue forever. We go further, and assert, that slavery as it exists in the South, is the best form in which it can exist." He urged Southern teachers to promote slavery in schools and started a publishing house to print books defending the Southern point of view. In 1856 he started a newspaper in Tennessee that combined his preoccupations into a single unified conspiracy theory, asserting that foreigners who swelled the population of the North were casting illegal votes in a bid to overturn slavery. "The immigration from Europe for the last five years alone, has poured upon our shores at least one million of foreign fanatics, who are, by process of forged naturalization papers already voting away our dearest rights."

Though his newspapers often failed—unsurprising when he alienated so many readers, advertisers, and politicians who paid for them—he made more stable investments. He owned Duff Green's Row, the line of houses facing the US Capitol, living in one house and renting out others, including the boardinghouse where Lincoln lived during his term in Congress in the late 1840s. He sometimes took his dinner at the boardinghouse table, and naturally made friends with Lincoln, who was practically part of his family. Green's nephew married a sister of Mary Todd Lincoln, and Green himself had married an aunt of Lincoln's Springfield ally Ninian Edwards. Just as naturally, Lincoln asked his fellow Whig for political help. But Green found his friend's antislavery views inexplicable, and Lincoln's nomination in 1860 didn't reassure him about the Republican Party. During the campaign Green produced an article addressed

"To the People of Pennsylvania and New Jersey." He said "the negro and the white man" were so different that it would "prevent an equality between the two races," and added that Republicans conspired to shut men like him out of power.

> *Is it not a strange feature of this delusion that the men, who insist that they themselves, are no better than the slaves (for they say all men are born free and equal, and therefore these slaves being their equals should be free, because they are equals). I say, is it not strange that such men should insist that we, the masters of these slaves, are so much degraded by being masters, that we are unfit to participate, as their equals, in the administration of government? We ask no more than to be treated as equals.*

When the South had been at the head of Jackson's majority, majority rule was paramount, and equality demanded it. Now that the South was outnumbered, majority rule was a crime against equality. Equality no longer meant an equal share of power for each voter but rather equal rights, and equal rights meant the right to slavery. To lose a single presidential election was to lose the right to "participate" in the "administration of the government," again a denial of equality. The South in power was equality; the South out of power was inequality.

Still, Green hoped the Union could be saved. Deciding that more words from him would make no difference in the campaign, he fell silent and, he said, "reserved my influence to be exerted on Mr. Lincoln in case of his election." His opportunity came after Lincoln's victory, when two congressional committees began meeting to seek a compromise to placate the South. The most concrete measure was associated with John J. Crittenden, a Kentucky senator, who proposed no fewer than six constitutional amendments enshrining slavery. Learning of Crittenden's proposal, Green walked to the executive mansion and waited on James Buchanan. He offered to serve as an emissary to Buchanan's successor, bringing him to support the compromise. By Green's account Buchanan "urged me to go to Springfield, and authorized me in his name not only to urge upon Mr. Lincoln the necessity of his coming to Washington, but to assure him that he would be received with all the respect due to the President elect, and that he, Mr. Buchanan, would most cordially unite in the measures necessary to preserve the Union."

HIS TRAIN ARRIVED IN SPRINGFIELD ON DECEMBER 28, AND HE ESCAPED the notice of reporters such as Henry Villard. One of the Springfield railway stations, on the Great Western line, stood less than a ten-minute walk from Lincoln's home, and as a distant relative by marriage Green surely was received into that house. In a note afterward he asked the president-elect to "remember me to your amiable lady," suggesting that both Lincolns greeted the white-bearded envoy of James Buchanan, who was also an envoy on behalf of the South, and also from the dead hand of the past.

When the conference was over Green returned to Washington and publicized his efforts. He informed the *New York Herald* of a cordial meeting: The paper said Green "speaks of Mr. Lincoln with much respect, and believes that he sincerely wishes to administer the government in such manner as to satisfy the South." Lincoln "will not favor emancipation in the District of Columbia, nor in the forts or dockyards of the Southern States." Lincoln surely did tell him so; he'd said the same thing in a private letter days earlier. But, Green added, "having resided so long in a non-slaveholding State, Mr. Lincoln has taken an active part in opposing what he terms the extension of slavery into the Territories, and believed that this constituted one of the chief issues in the late canvass, and is therefore firmly and unequivocally resolved to make no concessions on this point unless it be adjusted by an amendment to the constitution."

This wording showed their divergent views of the world. Green regarded Lincoln, his fellow Kentuckian, as a man who had crossed the Ohio into an alien belief system. Having "resided so long in a non-slaveholding state" (not a *free* state; that was not Green's perspective), Lincoln opposed "what *he terms* the extension of slavery" (not the way Green would describe it; he believed in a man's equal right to take his slaves anywhere). Green inferred more of Lincoln's thinking from a newspaper he picked up while in town. "Mr. Lincoln, so far as his views are indicated by the journal supposed to be advised by him, believes that secession is rebellion, and is resolved to use force to suppress and punish it." He probably had in hand the *Illinois State Journal* from December 27, which reprinted a Unionist politician's letter saying "that secession is revolution or rebellion." Again this was not a belief that Green shared: "The South believe the federal government [is] a compact between independent sovereign States."

Green tested his host's patience with an exposition of his philosophy. "By man's transgression 'came sin and death,' [and in this corrupt state] the stronger preys upon the weaker; and thus, when two races of men are brought in contact, there is no alternative but war and extermination, or subjection and protection." White people were stronger than Black people, in Green's view, and human nature determined that they would use this strength; therefore white people must destroy the darker race or else benevolently rule. Slavery was a blessing.

If Lincoln replied with his own views of human nature, Green didn't record it. The practical question was narrower: How could Lincoln persuade the white South that he would not interfere with them? Green reminded Lincoln that he'd won the presidency with a minority of the popular vote, about 40 percent in the four-way contest, though he had won more votes than any other candidate and a majority of the electoral vote. Abolitionists wanted "absolute control" of the country "under the pretence that they are a majority, and therefore authorized to enforce their party platform by the sword." The South refused to "become a subject province, conquered by the ballot box." He spoke for the oppressed minority of Southern slaveholders. "In reply to the inquiry of what will satisfy the South, Mr. Green placed in his hands a copy of Mr. Crittenden's resolutions." Lincoln must merely put slavery beyond the reach of the federal government forever. This wasn't so hard, Green suggested. Didn't Lincoln always say he had no plans to interfere with slavery?

The constitutional amendments in the Crittenden compromise banned Congress from interfering with slavery within a state, and also banned any future constitutional amendment to overturn that amendment. Another amendment would restore the old Missouri Compromise line, which seemed like a concession to the North. But that line would extend farther than it originally had, dividing the land conquered from Mexico and leaving New Mexico as potential slave territory.

Green thought the president-elect accepted the Crittenden proposals. "Mr. Lincoln did not say so," but Green inferred that Lincoln would "not only acquiesce, but rejoice if the Congress and the States will, by the adoption of Mr. Crittenden's resolutions, restore confidence and avert disunion."

Did Lincoln really accept? He did, in fact, write a statement that would signal this. Lincoln drafted it after their meeting was over.

Gen. Duff Green. Springfield, Ill. Dec 28th 1860.

My dear Sir—I do not desire any amendment of the Constitution. Recognizing, however, that questions of such amendment rightfully belong to the American People, I should not feel justified, nor inclined, to withhold from them, if I could, a fair opportunity of expressing their will thereon, through either of the modes prescribed in the instrument.

Congress or a convention could propose amendments that states could ratify; Lincoln wouldn't interfere. Lincoln didn't feel he was giving up much, since the amendment process didn't involve him anyway. He added a crafty condition: Green couldn't publish this letter unless he found six Southern senators willing to hold off their plans for secession.

But having written this letter, he didn't give it to Green. He mailed it to his ally Senator Lyman Trumbull in Washington: "Duff Green is out here endeavoring to draw a letter out of me. I have written one, which I herewith inclose to you, and which I believe could not be used to our disadvantage." He told Trumbull not to deliver it if Republicans felt it would do harm. Trumbull held it. That killed Green's mission. Green, frustrated, said he was "despairing of any action by Mr. Lincoln or by Congress unless the people impel them by an immediate and forcible expression of their wishes."

It's likely that Green so passionately lobbied his old friend that Lincoln finally promised to write something, then cautiously sent it in such a way that Green would never receive it. Trumbull's decision was consistent with Lincoln's own views. Two and a half weeks *before* writing his letter for Duff Green, he told Republicans in Congress what policy he expected them to pursue: "Entertain no proposition for a compromise in regard to the *extension* of slavery. The instant you do, they have us under again; all our labor is lost, and sooner or later must be done over. . . . The tug has to come & better now than later." He also wrote Thurlow Weed to say extending the Missouri Compromise line to the Pacific "would lose us everything we gained by the election." Drawing a line across the far West and allowing slavery south of it would give slave states an incentive to conquer more of Latin America, replaying the annexation of Texas.

Some in Washington felt Republicans resisted compromise out of political rather than patriotic motives. In the Senate in January, Douglas said Republicans were wrong to cling to their platform: Better that "all platforms be scattered to the winds" than that "the Union be destroyed and the country plunged into civil war." He felt Republicans "placed party first," in the words of his biographer, because their opposition to slavery expansion was all that united them. Douglas was a biased observer, but Henry Adams thought the same. The descendant of two past presidents was a Republican congressional aide: "So far as the Republican Party is concerned, secession if properly managed is rather a benefit than a misfortune. Anti-slavery was the only ground on which it could act with anything like unanimity. In ordinary times the tariff bill would have broken it down, and even under the tremendous pressure of disunion, the struggle over the Cabinet shook it to its very centre." An emerging faction in Congress, the Radical Republicans, saw no point in compromise; the crisis could end only with slavery's destruction. The Radicals came to include lawmakers Lincoln knew well—among them Joshua Giddings, Owen Lovejoy, and Lyman Trumbull, the very man Lincoln entrusted with his letter.

On a deeper level the dispute wasn't subject to compromise. Parallel revolutions in public opinion made that impossible. The North's slow revolution had crystallized public hostility to slavery, while the South's slow revolution exalted it. Slaveholders once had admitted the practice contradicted the country's principles, that it was a tragic inheritance, a corrupting force, which Jefferson himself said must end. They blamed the British of colonial times for introducing it; but as it grew more lucrative, and also came under threat from the North, many practitioners stopped apologizing. One scholar concludes that from the 1830s onward, slavery "took on the characteristics of a formal ideology with its resulting social movement." In the 1850s the Virginia intellectual George Fitzhugh said slavery had been the norm throughout history, and urged wealthy Southerners to vacation near home to avoid being contaminated by fashionable ideas against it: "Southern thought must justify the slavery principle, justify slavery as natural, normal, and necessitous." He didn't think racism was a firm enough foundation; Southerners must proclaim that even white slavery was desirable. In his book subtitled *The Failure of Free Society*, Fitzhugh said free labor turned white workers into "pauper banditti" while making a few capitalists rich. The poor would be better off in a paternal system that firmly directed them. "Make the laboring man the slave of one man, instead of the slave of society, and he would be far better off. . . . Free society is a monstrous abortion, and Slavery the healthy, beautiful and natural being which they are trying to adopt." Lincoln knew of Fitzhugh's notions; when he roared in his Lost Speech of 1856 that Southern newspapers were promoting white slavery, he doubtless was thinking of articles in major papers, like the *Charleston Mercury*, that were celebrating Fitzhugh's book.

This was the gap that Duff Green wanted Lincoln to bridge, and he came as near as anyone to persuading Lincoln to try. Lincoln's interest, if narrowly defined, might have called for him to seek compromise, drawing out discussion and deterring some states from seceding. But he wouldn't do it. His moral sense would not allow it. His position was already a compromise, which had evolved out of political necessity and his understanding of the Constitution. He could give no more to the South without embracing their idea of the world.

As the New Year arrived he prepared to travel to Washington with the crisis still unresolved. Green soon made a journey of his own. When he next wrote a letter to Lincoln three years later, he was living in Richmond, the capital city of the rebellion.

Florville, 1807–1868.

Chapter 8

OUTCAST: WILLIAM FLORVILLE

Late 1860

Lincoln's looming departure from Springfield prompted him to reflect on the city where he had lived almost a quarter century—passing "from a young to an old man. Here my children have been born, and one is buried." Here, too, was the only house he'd ever owned. The city had grown around the house, from twenty-five hundred people in 1840 to nine thousand, a transformation for which Lincoln could claim some authorship, having supported the transfer of the state capital there. His law office in a commercial building downtown had a view of the stone statehouse, which he had been among the first lawmakers to use, and where he had delivered his House Divided speech. Now he went to that office to turn over his legal affairs to his junior partner William Herndon—a slovenly, intellectual, exuberant friend who managed to admire Lincoln like a big brother while also supposing himself to be the more learned of the two. Lincoln generously told Herndon to leave his name on the Lincoln & Herndon sign over the door, and quietly advised him not to drink so much.

Walking to a shop nearby, Lincoln also visited William Florville, his barber. He'd been giving Lincoln shaves and haircuts for years while Lincoln handled his legal needs, meaning each served the other with his professional skill. Each was a husband and father; Lincoln knew Florville's son, William L. Florville, born in 1840 and an aspiring barber himself. Florville knew Lincoln's sons and considered Willie "a Smart boy for his age, so considerate, so manly." They knew a lot about each other's affairs.

A photograph of the barber showed a prosperous man in a three-piece suit with his own hair cut short. Over the years he worked at different locations near the statehouse, and one of his newspaper ads offered advice to political candidates: "Nothing is so necessary as a smooth face." To judge by his chatty ads he was the kind of barber who kept the banter going in his shop, and he took pride in his work: "I will always use the best instruments and keep them in excellent order," and he promised "a continued effort to please."

He was a man of the world: Florville was the English simplification of his name, which had been Fleurville when he was born on the north coast of Haiti. His native land once had been a French colony where enslaved laborers harvested sugarcane until they collapsed in the sun, but Florville had always been free. He was born in 1807, soon after Haiti won independence in a brutal war. He grew up in a nation convulsed by political divisions and partly isolated: President Thomas Jefferson did not extend diplomatic recognition to the Black republic. France also withheld recognition, demanding that Haitians pay reparations for the crime of winning their freedom. Florville's parents had died by his teenage years, and in 1823 his godmother took the orphan in hand as they joined the flow of Haitian refugees who fled to the United States.

In Baltimore the young man became an apprentice to a barber. Hoping to use his French language he migrated to the former French possession of New Orleans, which might have been congenial but for the slave markets: a free Black man could be kidnapped and sold. So in late 1831 he ventured north and settled in Springfield. He became part of its tiny free Black community, which grew to about two hundred people by 1860. He married Phoebe Rountree, a younger woman from Kentucky, and they raised a family. He played clarinet in a band and supported an effort to find a schoolmaster for Black children. He hosted Springfield's first-ever Catholic mass in his home, and said he closed his shop on Sundays to spend the Sabbath on "those duties which properly belong to that day."

When giving shaves and haircuts to Lincoln and other customers he used an oversized mirror, which his descendants later kept on their dining room wall. He hung art on the shop walls; an ad promoted his "large collection of paintings and engravings to amuse and entertain the troubled in mind"; the art would so "enliven" customers' spirits that "the gloom of despair will vanish like the dark cloud before the glory of the sun." Lincoln, who frequently suffered from melancholy, had found a barber who understood him.

In 1841 Lincoln had a disastrous episode in his courtship of Mary Todd: he broke up with her for more than a year before they reunited. He was so despondent that his best friend, Joshua Speed, took the precaution of removing razors from his presence. Maybe his barber knew, because one of his advertisements referred to such a danger. "The *Razor* is not to be trusted in the hands of any but the skillful barber. The papers tell of men, most every day, who are in the habit of shaving themselves, committing suicide with this dangerous instrument. To prevent such a fate . . . call on Billy and he will take off the beard with such ease, and cut the hair with such skill, that his patron will forget that he ever had the *blues.*"

If Florville ever had the blues, it wasn't because of his finances. When he moved his shop he put former locations up for sale and entered the real estate business. By the 1850s he had acquired several town lots in Springfield and Bloomington. He received the Bloomington property from a customer in exchange for an agreement to shave him for the rest of his life; Billy kept his side of the bargain and shaved the man a final time upon his death. For legal services he relied on Lincoln, although he mostly needed clerical work of the sort that Lincoln, who sometimes filed papers in his hat, didn't always keep straight. Once Lincoln confessed to a friend, "I am in a little trouble here," because basic information had been left off paperwork to confirm that "our 'Billy the Barber'" owned the Bloomington lots.

FLORVILLE'S ADS SUGGESTED HE HAD A SENSE OF HUMOR AS LINCOLN did and was amused by his place near the seat of power. He proclaimed he was the head of his own government, with a cabinet to advise him as he made a policy statement through a "proclamation" or a "Notice Extraordinaire." He called customers "my faithful subjects," who came to him during "audience hours" behind his "Palace door" and were expected to "pay into the treasury" for his services. He referred to his son the aspiring barber as "the Heir Apparent," leaving no sign if he intended the first word as a pun. One of his proclamations invited the patronage of leaders in the actual government:

> **Proclamation Extraordinary**
>
> I, BILLY, the Barber, would make known to the Senators, Representatives, Clerks, Judges and officers, and the Sovereigns themselves, that I am prepared to take off their beards almost by slight of hand, and clip their hair in the most fashionable style.

A republic had no king, and the people were "the sovereigns." Nothing could be more American than the way Florville proclaimed this truth, but in a wry tone, while also turning it to commercial advantage.

Florville himself was denied sovereignty, since Illinois reserved the vote for white men alone. Though he lived near Lincoln he was legally in a different world, governed by the Illinois Black Laws, which also said Black people couldn't serve on juries or testify in court. When he settled in Illinois he was required to file evidence of his free status with a county clerk.

Moving to Illinois reduced his risk of being sold into slavery but couldn't eliminate it, because the law presumed he was enslaved unless he could prove otherwise. In 1840 the sheriff of Macoupin County encountered a Black man he didn't know. The man was superbly dressed in a satinet coat and vest along with a black beaver hat, and "he says he is free, that he bought his freedom," but the sheriff was unconvinced. He locked up the man named Andrew Leeper "as a runaway," and placed an advertisement in the newspaper: "The owner of said negro (if any) will please come forward." The sheriff repeated this ad for many weeks, suggesting Leeper spent many weeks in jail; his fate is unknown. This problem diminished as Illinois courts become more hostile to slavery and presumed people to be free, but progress was halting. In 1848 Illinois voters approved a new constitution that authorized additional Black Laws banning Black people from moving to the state.

What did Lincoln make of these laws? His record was deeply ambiguous. When he said in debate with Stephen Douglas that he didn't favor "the social and political equality of the white and black races," he was accepting the reality of the Black Laws. This resembled his acceptance of slavery in the South while still striving for equality where he could; but he didn't loudly say the Black Laws were wrong. Occasionally he suggested they were wrong, as in an 1854 speech when he said that keeping free Black people "among us as underlings" seemed no better than slavery. His principles showed the Black Laws must be wrong, because "no man is good enough to govern another man, without that other's consent," but in 1858 he also said he "never manifested any impatience" about changing the laws. That implied he would like to repeal them but found slavery more urgent. Calling for reforms would dissipate his strength against slavery, giving ammunition to Democrats who said he favored racial equality.

Some of Lincoln's allies followed their convictions to their logical conclusion and tried to have the Black Laws repealed. Richard Yates, a onetime member of Congress, spoke against them, as did Owen Lovejoy. But the results were so appalling as to make Lincoln's inaction seem wise. When Yates ran for reelection in 1854, Democrats attacked his "proposal to put Negroes on an equal footing with white men"—and Yates lost even as other anti-Nebraska men won. Lincoln's ally Norman B. Judd presented a petition to the state legislature calling for Black people to gain the right to testify in court. But he failed to find votes to pass even this modest loosening of the Black Laws, and the Democratic majority decided they might as well tighten them instead.

Lincoln remained supportive of colonization, which gave him a defense against the charge of racial equality, though he knew colonization wasn't practical. This put him at odds with much of the Black community of his city. In 1858 the local Colonization Society met and proposed, not for the first time, that the legislature should pay to relocate the state's free Black population to Africa. Some people were interested—a Springfield man once had traveled to Liberia to explore the possibilities—but others weren't, and organized their own meeting at Clinton's Hall, a concert venue. "We have been unable to ascertain that any intelligent man of color" wants to move to Africa, they said in a resolution that referred to the Declaration of Independence. "We take [the] Declaration as the Gospel of freedom; we believe in its great truth, *that all men are created equal*. . . . We know ourselves to be men, and we claim our rights." Billy the Barber likely opposed colonization, having been born overseas and having chosen the United States. But he didn't let this difference of opinion spoil his relations with his friend and customer.

IN AUGUST 1860—THE SAME MONTH THAT THE PRESIDENTIAL campaign was heating up, and Republicans at the state fairgrounds hoisted Lincoln over their heads and carried him to the stage—Springfield's Black residents organized a ball. It was a social event, where young men and women dressed up elegantly and danced. The Democratic paper in town covered this celebration, using a racist term in the headline and stereotypes in the text: "There was an extravagant display of crinoline and white shining teeth." The main part of the article described a "Bloody Finale": Two young men got into a knife fight. One was William L. Florville, the son and namesake of Lincoln's barber, then about twenty years old. The newspaper identified the younger Florville as a "general business man at the aristocratic establishment of Madam Nash." Apparently someone complained to the newspaper, and the next day's paper contained a correction affirming that he didn't work at what sounded like a brothel. "Florville is a young man who bears an excellent character, and we deem it an act of simple justice to him to remove the false impression." The paper had confused Florville with the other Black man in the fight.

Two and a half months later Lincoln won the presidential election, and as befitted this change in his life he began to change his appearance. He bought a new suit and hat—which caused some neighbors to say he was "putting on airs"—and visited his barber. He gave instructions for sculpting a beard that he was just beginning to grow. This was sometime before November 25, when he was photographed with whiskers for the first time.

Considering the fame of that beard, his session in Florville's chair is poorly documented. The strongest confirmation that there even was such a meeting is an inference from facts: Florville shaved him, and he grew what was called a Shenandoah beard along his jawline, which required delicate shaving around the mouth and below the nose. Lincoln's barber thus had something to do with this brilliant political imagery, eventually represented on everything from pennies to Mount Rushmore. But nothing he said about it was preserved. The only account of their conversation has Lincoln saying of his whiskers, "Billy, let's give them a chance to grow!" But even if Lincoln said those words they don't give the whole story. Lincoln recently had rejected a beard. During the campaign a girl named Grace Bedell had written him from New York State, saying she could get her older brothers to vote for him if he grew a beard: "You will look a great deal better for your face is so thin." He replied, "As to the whiskers, having never worn any, do you not think people would call it a piece of silly affect[ta]tion if I were to begin it now?" He may have been giving voice to the opposing argument on his way to a decision. His barber would have been the person who helped him decide.

When he reached the capital, the care of Lincoln's beard passed to another Black man. But at least twice in later years, when people from Illinois visited, Lincoln began reminiscing about his Springfield barber. One visitor was the Republican governor of Illinois, who returned to Springfield and told Florville his name had come up. Florville then wrote the president a letter. He expressed an "irresistible feeling of gratitude" that his old friend remembered him. With a gesture of humility worthy of Lincoln himself, he said he hoped "it might not be improper for one so humble in life and occupation, to address the President of the United States." Yet he also felt confident that "if it is read by you . . . it will be read with pleasure as a communication from Billy the Barber."

Lincoln was overwhelmed with letters from people wanting favors, but Florville asked for nothing. He reported on the condition of the Lincoln house in Springfield, and on the Lincolns' dog. He also said "the truly great man" regarded "the poor, and down trodden of the Nation" with a respect equal to "those more favored in Color, position and Franchise rights. And this you have shown, and I and my people feel grateful to you for it." Lincoln had given his friend equal treatment, even if he had never campaigned against the Black Laws. What could be said was that his antislavery stance was leading to a revolution with implications far beyond slavery, making the repeal of the Black Laws inevitable.

One of the first acts by the bearded president that showed his openness to greater equality involved Florville's native nation. Lincoln opened diplomatic relations with Haiti, which no fewer than thirteen of his predecessors dating back to Jefferson had failed to do across more than half a century. "If any good reason exists why we should persevere longer in withholding our recognition," he said, "I am unable to discern it." Congress passed a bill to fund a diplomatic mission, and Lincoln appointed the first US diplomat to Haiti. He could do this because it was right; because the Southerners who would have blocked it had resigned from Congress; and because it didn't threaten the voters back home.

Seward (1801–1872), center, giving his view to Lincoln. Gideon Welles is between them.

Chapter 9

EDITOR: WILLIAM HENRY SEWARD

February 23, 1861

BEFORE ASSUMING THE PRESIDENCY, LINCOLN HAD NO EXECUTIVE experience beyond running his two-person law firm. He needed veteran advisers and expected from the time of his nomination to offer the top post in his cabinet to William Henry Seward. This created his first problem in personnel management. Lincoln knew how disappointed Seward was to lose the Republican presidential nomination. Everyone knew. Seward made the mistake soon after the convention of talking at his home with Henry J. Raymond, the founder of the *New York Times*, and raging that Horace Greeley had betrayed him. Raymond turned the rant into an acidic *Times* article. It said Greeley engineered Seward's defeat, having "special qualifications, as well as a special love, for the task." Lincoln's nomination was "purely an accident"; Greeley would have been happy with anyone but Seward. This triggered a spectacular public feud with Greeley, who used his newspaper to air the grievances he'd kept private for years. Seward told his wife he'd been subjected to "humiliations," and while he managed to campaign for Lincoln he barely concealed his feelings. In Detroit he stood on a balcony and told a crowd of Wide

Awakes, "Believe me sincere, when I say, that if it had devolved upon me to select from all the men in the United States a man to whom I should confide the standard in this cause . . . that man would be Abraham Lincoln." He had to say "believe me sincere" because they didn't.

He nonetheless established relations with the man who defeated him. They met when Seward's train stopped at Springfield during the campaign, and they also exchanged letters. In one, Lincoln made a deft choice of words: "It now really looks as if the Government is about to fall into our hands." *Our* hands. After the election Lincoln asked him to join the administration, and Seward wrote his wife, "I will try to save freedom and my country." That revealed Seward's expansive opinion of his destiny, but was justified by the terror in Washington, where he was finishing his Senate term. He viewed President Buchanan as a hostage to his secessionist advisers. "Treason is all around and amongst us," he said on December 29. John B. Floyd of Virginia, the secretary of war, was that day pressing the president to withdraw federal troops from Fort Sumter in Charleston Harbor, abandoning the last rock of South Carolina under federal authority. Buchanan refused, bolstered by other cabinet members. Floyd resigned in protest and became a Confederate general.

Seward tried to serve as a stabilizing force. When he scheduled a speech for January 12 the Senate gallery filled beyond capacity, and even when a man in the crush of spectators dropped a pistol, which discharged, Seward calmly went ahead. He said he would "meet prejudice with conciliation, exaction with concession which surrenders no principle, and violence with the right hand of peace." He even grew vague about slavery in the territories. In private he told a Virginia friend that he might favor the doomed Crittenden compromise—saying anything that would keep Virginia in the Union and buy time.

"I am the only hopeful, calm, conciliatory person here," he wrote his wife. His critics found him inconsistent—sometimes lacking courage, other times showing too much. A man who loved to entertain, inviting powerful men to his home for multicourse dinners, he said more than he should over a glass of wine. He even talked loosely of a war with European powers that would unite Americans in patriotic fervor. His policy differed from Lincoln's in both substance and style: Seward spoke and wrote in long, elaborate sentences, which suited his elaborate efforts to mollify Southerners and generally talk his way around the crisis. Lincoln's sentences were shorter and direct, which equally suited his purpose. He'd been nominated on the Republican platform and meant to follow it. He'd been elected to the presidency and meant to assume it. As secessionists seized federal courthouses, arsenals, and forts, he privately wrote a letter that sounded like a forecast of war: "If the forts shall be given up before the inaugeration [sic], the General [Winfield Scott, commander of the army] must retake them afterwards."

Many expected Seward to be the true head of government, with Lincoln as a figurehead. But Seward began to learn who was in charge when he wrote Lincoln with advice. He suggested Southern Unionists might be invited to join the cabinet in a gesture of unity, and also urged Lincoln to quickly choose secretaries of war and the navy to prepare for the country's defense. Lincoln didn't. He gave serious thought to a Southern cabinet secretary—but who would decide the administration's slavery policy, Lincoln or the Southerner? As for other secretaries, "I shall have trouble with every Northern Cabinet appointment," he advised Seward on January 12, "so much so, that I shall have to defer them as long as possible, to avoid being teased into insanity, to make changes." He knew, but didn't say, that Seward was among those likely to drive him insane. Lincoln was considering men Seward opposed, including Salmon P. Chase of Ohio, one of Seward's rivals for party leadership.

He started for Washington by train in February. Speeches became unavoidable—crowds gathered for him everywhere—but even now he avoided definite statements. From a hotel balcony in Indianapolis, he posed his policy as a hypothetical question. If the government "simply insists upon holding its own forts, or retaking those forts which belong to it," would that really count as the "coercion" of a state? If the federal government couldn't hold its own property then "the Union, as a family relation, would not be anything like a regular marriage at all, but only as a sort of free-love arrangement."

In Westport, New York, he climbed off the train to greet Grace Bedell, the girl who had suggested he grow a beard. Reaching Philadelphia, he had the honor of raising a flag over Independence Hall, where the Declaration of Independence had been signed. He said the idea of equality in that document gave "hope to the world for all future time." He added, "If this country cannot be saved without giving up that principle—I was about to say I would rather be assassinated on this spot than to surrender it."

His listeners didn't know Lincoln had been told of a plot to kill him. A private detective reported that people in Baltimore planned to attack him as he passed through the city. Lincoln had virtually no security: three army officers he'd invited on the train and a self-appointed bodyguard, his friend and fellow Illinois lawyer Ward Hill Lamon. Years later, Lamon concluded that "there was no conspiracy," but at the time he "implicitly believed in the reality of the atrocious plot." Lincoln agreed to an unannounced change of itinerary, leaving his family and the rest of his party behind. Coded telegrams were sent to Washington to signal the change, then a railroad executive arranged for wires to be cut so that nobody could spread the word. Accompanied only by Lamon and a railroad detective, Lincoln stealthily boarded an overnight train, trying to sleep in a berth too short for him to stretch out. The Capitol came into view through the car windows around six o'clock on the morning of February 23.

BY HIS OWN ACCOUNT SEWARD MET LINCOLN AT THE STATION. BY other accounts the only person who met Lincoln was the Illinois lawmaker Elihu Washburne, so it seems likely that Seward turned up a little late. He caught up with the president-elect by the time he checked into the Willard Hotel, on Pennsylvania Avenue two blocks from the White House, and their breakfast together was the beginning of a days-long conversation. Seward escorted him to the White House, where they called on President Buchanan. Then they returned to the Willard, where Lincoln received callers—members of Congress and members of a peace conference. General Scott came to greet the future commander in chief, as did Francis Preston Blair, a shrewd and energetic counselor to presidents dating back to Andrew Jackson. A small man with a large personality, Blair was an early organizer of the Republican Party, and of interest to Lincoln because he was from the slave state of Maryland; Lincoln wanted any support he could get from slave states. Blair brought his son Montgomery, whom he wanted in Lincoln's cabinet.

At day's end Seward invited Lincoln home for one of his hours-long dinners, where they began to sketch out Seward's responsibilities. According to Seward's son and aide Frederick, Lincoln said foreign relations were "one part of the business" that "I think I shall leave almost entirely in your hands." This remark has been taken as Lincoln's confession that he knew little of the world, but its intent may have been different. Foreign relations *were* the job of the secretary of state, which hardly needed to be said. Seward was thinking of himself as the head of the cabinet, with authority to intervene in other departments; Lincoln may have been hinting that Seward should mind his business.

The next morning was Sunday. Seward walked Lincoln to Saint John's Episcopal Church across a park from the White House. The pastor delivered a sermon based on 1 Corinthians 7:31, part of a passage urging believers not to make big changes in their lives, "for the fashion of this world passeth away," and it was better to focus on God. A single man should not marry, as a wife would compete with God for his attention. But a man who already was married might as well stay married, and a man who was engaged should go through with it. Having counseled against breakups and distracting changes, the pastor "made several allusions to the present state of the country, and to the change in Administration which was about to take place."

Lincoln sat in Seward's pew, and afterward retired to Seward's house for a two-hour conference. There, Lincoln made a gesture that showed his trust in him. He gave Seward a draft of his inaugural address, which he had written out and had printed before he left Springfield.

That evening Seward marked up the draft. Other men who had seen it suggested changing a word or two, or none at all; Seward made notes all over the document and wrote a cover letter. He told Lincoln the address was strong except for the beginning, the middle, and the end, which were completely unsuited to the situation in Washington. "I, my dear sir, have devoted myself singly to the study of the case here—with advantages of access and free communication with parties of all sections. I have a common responsibility and interest with you, and shall adhere to you faithfully in every case. You must, therefore, allow me to speak freely and candidly."

Lincoln's beginning said he'd been elected on the Republican platform, "the Chicago platform," and he intended to follow it. To Lincoln this seemed obvious, but Seward felt the Chicago platform was exactly the problem because Southerners universally rejected its call to restrict slavery. Announcing his determination to follow this platform was doubling down, like a man who repeats his words when told they give offense. It would "give such advantages to the Disunionists that Virginia and Maryland will secede," and "the dismemberment of the Republic would date from the inauguration of a Republican administration."

The middle of Lincoln's draft said he would use "all the power at my disposal" to "reclaim" federal property and forts. Seward suggested something more vague. (Another adviser, Orville Browning, suggested the same.) He was also alarmed by the ending, in which Lincoln directly addressed the South:

> *In* your *hands, my dissatisfied fellow countrymen, and not in* mine, *is the momentous issue of civil war. The government will not assail* you, *unless you* first *assail* it. *You can have no conflict, without being yourselves the aggressors.* You *have no oath registered in Heaven to destroy the government, while* I *shall have the most solemn one to "preserve, protect, and defend" it.* You *can forbear the* assault *upon it;* I *can* not *shrink from the* defense *of it. With* you, *and not with* me, *is the solemn question of "Shall it be peace, or a sword?"*

Was this a time to rattle swords? "The argument is strong and conclusive," Seward said, "but something besides or in addition to argument is needful—to meet and remove prejudice and passion in the South, and despondency and fear in the East. Some words of affection—some of calm and cheerful confidence." He suggested two alternative endings, the shorter of which read this way on Seward's page, with a few words scratched out:

> *I close. We are not we must not be aliens or enemies but fellow countrymen and brethren. Although passion has strained our bonds of affection too hardly they must not, I am sure they will not be broken. The*

> *mystic chords which proceeding from so many battle fields and so many patriot graves pass through all the hearts and all the hearths in this broad continent of ours will yet again harmonize in their ancient music when ~~touched as they surely~~ breathed upon ~~again~~ by the ~~better angel~~ guardian angel of the nation.*

Lincoln received these and many smaller edits without offense. If his ego writhed under Seward's criticism, he kept it to himself. He didn't have to be the one who was right all the time, but did need to give a good speech. He deleted the reference to the Chicago platform. It went without saying anyway. The promise to "reclaim" forts went away, leaving a milder vow to keep those still in federal possession. He broadly accepted Seward's new ending, but rewrote Seward's rewrite, making the sentences tighter and more poetic:

> *I am loath to close. We are not enemies, but friends. We must not be enemies. Though passion may have strained, it must not break our bonds of affection. The mystic chords of memory, stretching from every battle-field, and patriot grave, to every living heart and hearthstone, all over this broad land, will yet swell the chorus of the Union, when again touched, as surely they will be, by the better angels of our nature.*

A sentence of fifteen words became six ("We are not enemies, but friends"), losing nuance but gaining power. "The mystic chords of memory" was memorable alliteration even if a listener might wonder what it meant; and Lincoln took Seward's scratched-out "better angel" and made it a sentiment both lyrical and democratic. Seward looked to heaven for salvation. Lincoln placed responsibility on the people, who must find it within human nature to save themselves.

In reviewing these famous edits, it's common to observe that Lincoln showed he was more brilliant than Seward. Lincoln's secretaries John Hay and John Nicolay said so in a biography of their leader: "Whatever the inaugural gained in form and style in these final touches came as much through his own power of literary criticism as from the more practiced pen of Mr. Seward." This is both correct and unfair to Seward. It was Lincoln's job to make the words sing, and Seward's to serve as his editor.

Hay and Nicolay may not have fully understood the role of an editor. (Their ten-volume biography of Lincoln exceeded five thousand pages.) Seward considered Lincoln's words on their own merits, thought of how the intended audience might receive them, and challenged them constructively. He didn't entirely set aside his own ego: he moved the speech nearer his preference for fuzziness, forbearance, and delay. But by taking his edits, Lincoln showed he understood an editor's role, and Seward's larger role as his adviser.

On March 4, Inauguration Day, a crowd gathered at the East Front of the Capitol. Behind the platform rose the Capitol's white columns, and above them a new dome was under construction beneath a cloudy sky. The president-elect prepared to speak, and in a gesture for the ages, Senator Stephen Douglas held his hat. His address drew cheers at every mention of the Union. Chief Justice Roger Taney administered the oath of office, and a reporter felt the author of the Dred Scott decision "looked very agitated, and his hands shook very perceptibly with emotion." At the final words of the oath the crowd roared once more, and the sound carried a short distance away, to where General Scott was personally supervising a battery of artillery in case anything went wrong. When the ceremony ended without incident, the cannons rumbled in salute.

Telegraph lines were still open to South Carolina, crossing what the Carolinians deemed an international border, and the *Charleston Courier* received the text of the address in time for the next day's paper. "We are grievously disappointed," the editors wrote, "not that we expected much." Lincoln refused to accept the reality of secession: "We find the President elect repeating the stale truisms of Northern schoolboys, concerning the indissoluble perpetuity of the Union. . . . It is our wisest and best policy to accept it as a declaration of war." Judging by those words, Seward's effort at a pacific tone had failed; but South Carolina didn't go to war. The troops who had aimed artillery at Fort Sumter didn't open fire.

From Rochester, New York, came a different reaction. Frederick Douglass, who edited a newspaper there, found the address "little better than our worst fears, and vastly below what we had fondly hoped." Lincoln "should have boldly rebuked" the South, and told slaveholders "their barbarous system of robbery is contrary to the spirit of the age." Instead he clouded his intentions. "No man reading it could say whether Mr. Lincoln was for peace or war." He didn't even say if he would uphold the party platform—Douglass caught what Seward had persuaded him to omit. Douglass also noted Lincoln's clandestine arrival: "He reached the Capitol as the poor, hunted slave reaches the North, in disguise, seeking concealment, evading pursuers, by the underground railroad." Lincoln's ruse resembled his policy: "More cunning than bold, evading rather than facing danger, outwitting rather than bravely conquering and putting down the enemy."

Mainstream papers were more positive. The *New York Herald* said "moderate men of both parties" favored the tone. No more states moved to secede. Virginia and Maryland remained in the Union, allowing time for the work of better angels.

AS SEWARD SUBORDINATED HIMSELF TO EDIT LINCOLN, HIS EGO emerged elsewhere, like a balloon squeezed on one side that expands on another. Lincoln revealed other cabinet choices, including Chase as secretary of the treasury. Seward decided a "compound Cabinet" wouldn't work, and wrote a note to the president.

> *My Dear Sir: Circumstances which have occurred since I expressed to you in December last my willingness to accept the office of Secretary of State seem to me to render it my duty to ask leave to withdraw that consent.*

This was Saturday morning, and the inauguration was Monday. Lincoln's secretaries were astounded that the resignation came "from the man who for several months had held intimate counsel" with Lincoln. Now he'd created a crisis.

Lincoln read the note at the Willard and said nothing. He managed it as Seward was trying to handle the South, playing for time. Saturday and Sunday passed without Lincoln mentioning Seward's resignation. If Seward wanted to negotiate for a different cabinet, Lincoln didn't. On Monday morning he finally wrote a note urging Seward to reconsider, but offering no concessions and requesting an answer by nine o'clock the following morning. Handing it to a secretary he said, "I can't afford to let Seward take the first trick." If Seward wanted out, Lincoln would appoint him ambassador to London. He reinforced this message in a long talk with Seward on the evening after the inaugural ceremony.

The next morning Seward said he would lead the State Department after all. He told his wife, "I believe I can endure as much as anyone; and may be that I can endure enough to make the experiment successful. At all events I did not dare to go home, or to England, and leave the country to chance." Lincoln had correctly understood Seward's opinion of himself: he wouldn't abandon the president because he felt he was indispensable, an opinion Lincoln likely encouraged in their long meeting.

Once the Senate confirmed him Seward recovered his exuberance, to the dismay of the rest of the cabinet. He wanted to control the other secretaries' access to the president. When some suggested that the president hold regular cabinet meetings, Seward waved them off. Unnecessary! Regular meetings would consume everyone's time! If Lincoln wanted his full cabinet he could tell Seward, who would summon them. He seemed to view them not as seven men who reported to the President but six who reported to Seward. His colleagues unanimously rejected this and biweekly meetings became the norm, but Seward involved himself in the business of other departments. Gideon Welles, the secretary of the navy, felt Seward was "acting at times from impulse, without sufficient forethought of consequences—fond of displaying power—frequently exercising questionable authority."

Seward even tested the president's authority, composing a memo titled "Some Thoughts for the President's Consideration." He told Lincoln the administration was "without a policy, domestic or foreign." He wanted to surrender Fort Sumter, allowing more time to defuse the crisis with the South. He wanted to demand that European nations stay out of the crisis, and to declare war on them if they didn't. He also wanted to communicate about the crisis in a specific way: "Change the question before the public from one upon slavery, or about slavery, for a question about union or disunion." Whatever policy Lincoln adopted, he must lead energetically or delegate leadership to "some member of his cabinet." Perhaps Seward. Though he said he wasn't seeking this.

Lincoln replied the same day. Did he really need a policy? "If this must be done, *I* must do it." But he had already given his policy in the inaugural address that Seward had edited. He wouldn't abandon Sumter. He did agree with Seward's call to focus on "a question about union or disunion." Slavery couldn't unite the loyal states but union could. Two weeks after Seward's memo the war began, and Lincoln focused solely on the Union—to the dismay of many in his party. Joshua Giddings, the old antislavery provocateur, thought his friend's effort to conciliate Democrats and slave interests merely blurred what Republicans stood for. But Lincoln sided with Seward, and if the rest of Seward's memo was impertinent, the president said no more. "Seward has a passion to be thought a master spirit in the administration," said Welles—a passion that Lincoln could disregard because he knew who was president. Seward was a useful editor, and Lincoln decided which edits to take.

UNION

Lincoln, 1864.

Jessie Benton Frémont, 1824–1902.

Chapter 10

EMISSARY: JESSIE BENTON FRÉMONT

September 10, 1861

WHEN THE CANNONS RINGING CHARLESTON HARBOR FINALLY opened fire on Fort Sumter on April 12, 1861, people across the country took sides. Four more slave states joined the seven that had seceded—among them Virginia, which brought the rebellion within sight of Washington. Lincoln said federal law was "failing of execution, in nearly one-third of the States." His answer was to rally the more numerous loyal states, asking for volunteers to serve in the army. Thousands from those twenty-three states answered the call, and their superior manpower should be enough to crush the rebellion—a military expression of the superior voting power that brought about his election. A democratic election could not be overturned so long as the majority was willing to fight.

To hold that majority he had to manage bitter political divides, especially in four loyal slave states, or border states: Delaware, Maryland, Kentucky, and Missouri. All but Delaware caused him trouble. He couldn't let Maryland secede, because that would leave Washington surrounded and indefensible. He ordered his commanding general, Winfield Scott, to monitor the Maryland legislature for signs of disloyalty, to prepare for the "bombardment of their cities" and, "in the extremest necessity, the suspension of the writ of habeas corpus"—arresting citizens without court hearings. The bombardment wasn't needed but the arrests were. In Kentucky, the government declared neutrality and some of Mary Lincoln's relatives joined the rebellion. But the president found Unionist support among friends and family there. He assigned Joshua Speed to distribute weapons to loyal citizens, relying on his best friend who differed with him over slavery. Soon Lincoln sent a loyal Kentucky military officer to help Speed: Major Robert Anderson had become a hero for his brave though unsuccessful defense of Fort Sumter and returned to his home state with a promotion to general.

Missouri was hardest of all. Loyal US Army officers shipped thousands of weapons out of the Saint Louis arsenal to keep them away from a disloyal state militia, which was directed by the disloyal governor. Though the loyal state legislature deposed him, he fled to southern Missouri and set up a pretender government that appealed for Confederate armies to invade. Federal troops held Saint Louis, a longtime military outpost, but additional soldiers were called for, along with a leader to mold them into an army.

On July 3 Lincoln received a visitor who offered to lead: John Charles Frémont, just returned from a stay in Europe. He may have been the most famous living American, a hero of the country's westward expansion. He was a onetime army officer who'd led trail-mapping expeditions in the 1840s; his reports of his adventures became popular books that lured settlers to Oregon and Mormons to the Great Salt Lake. He not only drew maps but changed the boundaries on them, taking part in the capture of California from Mexico. He became absurdly rich buying California real estate just before the Gold Rush, then was the first Republican presidential nominee in 1856. Now he was standing in Lincoln's second-floor office in the executive mansion, ready to volunteer for the expanding army.

Frémont was less impressive in person than in the newspapers. To the surprise of people who expected a wilderness giant, he stood about average height—well mannered, soft-spoken, almost withdrawn—but was an important political figure who had to be kept on the team. Seward once had thought of him as a possible secretary of war, and Lincoln had considered naming him minister to France. Now that he was offering to resume his uniform, the only question was where to assign him. Several armies were forming, including one that was soon to advance toward a rebel army near a railway junction at Manassas, Virginia. But Frémont preferred to command at Saint Louis, the former base for his expeditions. Lincoln agreed. Moving with a speed that fit the urgency of Missouri's crisis he wrote Seward at the State Department, "Suppose you step over at once," so they could confer with General Scott about "assigning a position to Gen. Fremont." *General* Frémont—Lincoln would give him a higher rank than he'd ever held during his army service. A review of that service would have revealed how sketchy it was: he'd commanded only small groups of men, disregarded orders, and wasn't even formally trained, having talked his way into the army because of his skill with maps. But he was famous—if he couldn't build an army, who could? That same day they named him commander of the Department of the West, entrusted with all military affairs across a region encompassing several states and territories.

By late July he was on a train for Saint Louis with Jessie Benton Frémont, his wife, who planned to serve as his secretary and adviser. She was part of a small elite of women who influenced national events through their proximity to powerful men in Washington. Even in that formidable group she was an elite of one, widely traveled and well educated, able to speak with diplomats in their languages and political wire-pullers in *theirs.* Her square face, framed by bob-length hair, came alive when she talked in a sitting room or over dinner. Seward called on her from time to time and found her "a noble-spirited woman" who had "much character" and was "very outspoken." Lincoln's secretary John Hay, seeing the Frémonts together, said John was "quiet earnest industrious, imperious," and Jessie "very much like him, though talking more and louder." Men weren't accustomed to women talking politics, so Hay may have felt she was louder than she was. But many men found her more forceful than her husband, who was more comfortable amid snow-capped mountains than human beings.

Once during an argument she wrote "Jessie Benton Frémont" on a paper and showed it to a man: "Do you know who I am?" Her late father, Thomas Hart Benton, had been a senator from Missouri for thirty years. As a girl she followed him to the Senate and the White House, where Andrew Jackson was the first of many presidents she knew. In her early twenties she acted as her husband's representative, meeting James K. Polk on his behalf while he was away fighting Mexicans. After the war she went to live with John in California—and still acted as his representative. Francis Preston Blair, the wily counselor to presidents, kept in touch with them in San Francisco by corresponding with her. Later Blair conspired with her to put John in the White House, and though they failed, Jessie's fame grew; women were active in the antislavery movement and made her a symbol of their cause.

In 1861 her friend Blair supported John's appointment to Saint Louis, thinking General Frémont would be an ally of his family: his son Frank P. Blair lived in Missouri, had been elected to Congress, and was trying to keep the state in the Union. The elder Blair thought Jessie should stay behind in Washington, where he would find a role for her. "It is not fit for a woman to go with an army," he said. But she loved Saint Louis, her late father's home city, and arrived with her husband on July 25. "Everything was changed," she said. "The many steamboats were laid up at the wharves, their fires out, the singing, cheery crews gone." The Confederate seizure of the lower Mississippi had disrupted traffic to New Orleans. "As we drove through the deserted streets we saw only closed shutters to warehouses and business places; the wheels and the horses' hoofs echoed loud and harsh as when one drives through the silent streets late in the night. It was a hostile city." It was a point of debate just how hostile—Saint Louis, unlike the rest of the state, had voted for Lincoln—but there had been riots in the city and rebel forces were active in the countryside.

The Frémonts had to manage without immediate help from Washington, which faced trouble nearer at hand: the Union army had advanced on Manassas, only to be routed by Confederate troops and sent fleeing back to Washington. A note from the chaotic capital warned, "I find it impossible to get any attention to Missouri." It was from Montgomery Blair, another of Francis Preston's sons, now postmaster general. Jessie wrote her best friend—Elizabeth Blair Lee, yet another Blair—describing a shortage of weapons, "troops on paper and a thoroughly prepared and united enemy thick and unremitting as mosquitoes." They needed to hold on until the Northern population could be mobilized.

Jessie had a wealthy cousin who said the Frémonts must stay in her vacant Saint Louis mansion, the Brant house, which became John's headquarters. It was the first of many mistakes, a violation of the culture of equality. Soldiers and civilians alike found the three-story residence pretentious, its rental at government expense from one of Jessie's relatives corrupt, and General Frémont inaccessible behind layers of guards. But Jessie felt the house was perfect for reviewing newly arrived troops, who marched up Chouteau Avenue past the front door. One regiment from Illinois called themselves the Frémont Rifles, and both the gray-bearded general and his younger wife came out to greet them. The men gave her three cheers as she tied a red, white, and blue bow on the regimental flag. For close to twenty years they had tended to their celebrity and didn't stop now; the expanding military infrastructure in Saint Louis included

Benton Barracks, and on the day the camp opened John turned up to inspect ten thousand recruits. Thousands of spectators came, and John stood on a platform "so that all could have the opportunity" of seeing him. It was reasonable to name a camp after Jessie's late father, a great Missouri Unionist, though another facility was "Camp Jessie." Newspapers said she was constantly by John's side: "She acts as his private secretary, writing many of his most important business letters, and taking notes of his conversation with officers."

It was another mistake for General Frémont to raise a personal bodyguard with hundreds of soldiers commanded by a Hungarian officer, which seemed as pretentious as the mansion. And it was a serious mistake when John alienated the Blairs. Frank Blair, the congressman, thought military contractors were taking advantage of John. John thought Blair was seeking advantage for his own business friends, and their relations grew worse.

On August 13 old Francis Preston Blair intervened from Washington. He wrote Jessie, his coconspirator in managing John: "Now I hope we may begin a correspondence—you and I—about the great things which are to make history hereafter and in which we are to be equally interested—you for your husband's exploits and I for my sons, as well as his." He proposed an arrangement based on their interests. "I mean to apply myself to do your bidding in every thing that concerns our copartnership . . . and . . . I shall expect you to exert your utmost influence to carry my points." He wanted the Frémonts to use their influence to have Frank Blair appointed a general of Missouri militia. This the Frémonts did not directly have the power to do, and they made little effort to do it. The Blairs decided John had no political sense, and if the Blairs believed this it was true by definition, since John needed to maintain good relations with such an influential family. Soon the Blairs were blaming John for military defeats: On August 10 a rebel army overwhelmed a smaller Union force at the Battle of Wilson's Creek, killing hundreds.

John had advised the commander to retreat before the battle, but had left it to the commander's discretion.

Missouri may have faced less danger than it seemed. Most residents favored the Union, new regiments kept arriving, and John gave an important command to a gifted officer, Ulysses S. Grant. But pressure mounted inside the Brant mansion, and John took a drastic step. Jessie was present shortly after daybreak on August 30 when John read aloud a proclamation he'd drafted, apparently with the help of abolitionists on his staff. John declared martial law in Missouri. Anyone found bearing arms within Union lines would be court-martialed and shot. The army would seize the property of disloyal citizens, and free any slaves they owned.

In describing this scene later, Jessie gave it a historic glow: Her husband read the momentous words in a quiet room, with just enough light from the window for the paper to be legible in the new day. It was an emancipation proclamation.

In Washington, his commander in chief learned about it by reading the newspapers.

LINCOLN KNEW FRÉMONT WAS SEIZING AN IDEA THAT HAD BEEN IN the air from the start of the war. The garrison at Fort Sumter had barely pulled down their flag when Frederick Douglass pointed out the obvious: "Fire must be met with water, darkness with light, and war for the destruction of liberty must be met with war for the destruction of slavery." His essay "How to End the War" urged freeing and arming the enslaved. This was not Lincoln's policy. Seward had advised him to make the conflict "a question about union or disunion," not slavery. This seemed essential to maintain Unionist support in the border states—and also in free states, which were recruiting hundreds of thousands of soldiers.

Volunteers were stepping forward to defend their country, which was in their interest, but might not feel the same way about fighting to end slavery. Hostile Democrats were already saying it *was* a war on slavery; now Frémont gave them proof. A correspondent in the capital reported that the news "struck the entire Cabinet and the President with utter amazement, as for the first twenty-four hours they remained in a quandary, like the crew of a wrecked boat dashed on the surf."

From Lincoln's perspective the problem grew worse, not better, when the proclamation triggered celebrations across the North. It was cathartic, after the Union's early defeats, to see the slave power get what it deserved. The *Chicago Tribune* said "joyful satisfaction" was "unanimous." A New York paper called the proclamation "the most important document that has appeared since the breaking out of hostilities," and said its wisdom "will be conceded by every just and loyal citizen." In Cincinnati the *Daily Press* said, "If the rebellion is to be put down, undoubtedly this is the way to do it." In the same paper an abolitionist confronted the possibility of "servile insurrection," the terror that servants would attack their masters. Rather than play down this primal fear, the writer approved: Frémont's order *would* turn slaves against their masters, which was good. In a Chicago church the Reverend M. D. Conway exalted Frémont in terms that hardly seemed appropriate for a mortal. "The nation cried for a leader—a man: lo, he is here! . . . He takes the step that Congress was too timid to take openly."

The pastor was referring to a recent act of Congress, the Confiscation Act. It authorized the seizure of rebel property for military purposes and established a process to strip rebels of any right to the future labor of the enslaved. Representative Thaddeus Stevens of Pennsylvania, a Radical Republican, said "one of the most glorious consequences of victory" was freeing the oppressed, and if the South "must be laid waste, and made a desert, in order to save this Union from destruction, so let it be." But to Stevens's disappointment the final legislation, drafted by Lincoln's friend Lyman Trumbull, was restrained. Congress wasn't ready to decree an end to slavery—so the law was silent on the future of "contrabands," as workers were called. They were free from their masters but not from their status as slaves, considered contraband or illicit property taken by authorities.

Some papers assumed Frémont's proclamation fell within this law, but the Chicago pastor knew it went beyond. Frémont was signing "deeds of manumission" declaring people "to be free, and forever discharged from the bonds of servitude." Frederick Douglass also understood: the servants of traitors would not be "confiscated property, but *liberated men*," thanks to an action "strong enough to convulse a continent." What Douglass didn't know was whether Lincoln would uphold General Frémont's action. The suspense was "truly painful."

It didn't take long for doubts about the wisdom of the proclamation to spread. A Joliet, Illinois, newspaper said progressive jubilation would cost the Union friends: "The very fact that it is endorsed by the *Chicago Tribune* . . . and all the Abolition journals in the country, will cause the Union sentiment in the South to revolt at its threatening aspect." The same paper took note of slave insurrections: "We do not believe this rebellion can be permanently put down by acts of barbarity."

A Louisville newspaper mocked Northern "ecstacies over Frémont's infamous proclamation," saying some Northerners wanted martial law in "all the border states." On September 2 a mass meeting in Kentucky said Frémont's policy "would, by turning loose upon the community a large number of free negroes, not only destroy the value of all slave property, but render all the slave States unfit for the residence of the white man." By September 13 the state's most prominent Unionist was alarmed. General Robert Anderson warned the president that Frémont's proclamation "is producing the most disastrous results" and if it was not "annulled, Kentucky will be lost to the Union." A whole company of army recruits "disbanded."

Anderson couldn't know that Lincoln was privately trying to take the edge off Frémont's move. The president had visions of disaster: "The very arms we had furnished Kentucky would be turned against us. I think to lose Kentucky is nearly the same as to lose the whole game. Kentucky gone, we can not hold Missouri, nor, as I think, Maryland. These all against us, and the job on our hands is too large for us."

He wrote Frémont a gently worded letter. Rather than overturn the entire proclamation, he said "two points" of it "give me some anxiety." He didn't want rebels executed, as Confederates would execute Unionists in reprisal. Also, the emancipation clause "will alarm our Southern Union friends, and turn them against us—perhaps ruin our rather fair prospect for Kentucky." He suggested that Frémont "modify as your own motion" the provision on slavery so that it went no further than the law. He could confiscate slaves; he just shouldn't free them. But despite Lincoln's reassurances ("This letter is written in a spirit of caution and not of censure"), Frémont responded badly when the letter reached Saint Louis. He *did* feel censured; he was being told he'd made an error. Changing the order himself should allow him to save face, but he saw it differently: Lincoln wanted to blunt his popular action, and he wanted Frémont to take the blame. He wrote a letter declining to modify his words: "If I were to retract on my own accord, it would imply that I myself thought it wrong." If the president wanted him to change his proclamation, "I have to ask that you will openly direct me to make the correction." Such pride had long marked John's career. Years earlier he'd been court-martialed for failing to obey a superior officer, and when granted clemency he refused it, because accepting it would imply that he thought he was guilty.

He didn't send this letter by telegraph or the mail, fearing someone might intercept it; the feud with the Blairs was making the Frémonts paranoid. John sent it by a messenger—his wife. Jessie had been looking for a reason to return to Washington as his emissary, believing she could talk sense to the president.

"I left by the night train with only my English maid," she said. "We had only common cars and I had to sit up two nights in the overcrowded train." When she'd been a girl a journey from Saint Louis to Washington took weeks by steamboat and stage, and her family was among the few who could afford to travel in style, reserving a whole stagecoach for themselves. Now rail travel was swift and available to the masses, which she experienced as a disappointment.

By the time she disembarked at the capital on the evening of September 10, two advisers were waiting for her at the Willard on Pennsylvania Avenue; she'd telegraphed for them to come. While conferring with them she sent a message to the executive mansion, asking when she could discuss important business with the president. The messenger returned with a card on which Lincoln had written: "Now." It was nearly nine o'clock. Her advisers said she should go after a night's rest, but she started for the door. "I thought it best to make no delay, and though my baggage had not been delivered and I was still in the dusty dress in which I was two days and nights, I walked across to the White House."

One of her advisers escorted her, a Judge Edward Cowles. A porter showed them down the high-ceilinged hallway, and they turned left into the Red Room to wait. A fire blazed in the hearth, and chairs were scattered about. She'd been visiting the Red Room long enough to recall when it wasn't red; the high walls had been yellow until Polk's time. "All my life I had been at home in the President's House," she said, "as well received there as in the family circle."

This time, however, they waited long enough for Jessie to become annoyed.

A SIDE DOOR SWUNG OPEN FROM THE STATE DINING ROOM, AND the bearded president appeared, at least a foot taller than his visitor. He pushed the door shut behind him, but Jessie thought an unseen hand propped it open again—as if a child was on the other side, or Mary Lincoln, who once had said, "I never allow the President to see any woman alone." In Jessie's telling, "the President did not speak, only bowed slightly." She introduced her companion, and as Lincoln "still said nothing, I gave him the letter, telling him that General Frémont felt the subject to be of so much importance, that he had sent me to answer any points on which the President might want more information. At this he smiled with an expression that was not agreeable." He neglected to offer his guests a seat. "Moving nearer the chandelier to read better," the president "read the letter standing." This was the letter in which the general declined to modify his proclamation unless ordered.

Jessie felt a hostility she'd never known from past chief executives: "The president's unusual manner was a reversal of the old order of things." She finally took a seat without being invited. Judge Cowles stepped back to the doorway that led to the Blue Room, where he "walked back and forth like a sentinel."

Lincoln looked up from the letter and drew up a chair next to Jessie. He said, "I have written to the General and he knows what I want done."

Jessie said she had come to explain his reluctance, and alluded to conspiracies. "The General feels he is at the great disadvantage of being perhaps opposed by people in whom you have every confidence."

"What do you mean? Persons of differing views?"

She meant the Blairs, of course, but Jessie moved on. It would be "long and dreadful work to conquer by arms alone," and political moves were essential. General Frémont's emancipation would power the war effort and help with international relations. England, France, and Spain were less likely to recognize the Confederacy's independence if it became a war between freedom and slavery.

"You are quite a female politician," Lincoln said, and added that her husband should never have issued the order. "He never would have done it if he had consulted Frank Blair," and now Jessie fully understood that the Blairs were the president's closest allies in Missouri.

Jessie asked when she might receive an answer to her husband's letter. Lincoln said he would respond another day, and the meeting was over. On the way out Judge Cowles told Jessie her husband was finished, and would soon be removed from command.

This was Jessie's version of the meeting, which was credible as far as it went. The words she attributed to Lincoln resembled things he would say. His manners were subject to interpretation, but Lincoln surely received her with less deference than she had experienced with past presidents who'd known her father. She'd caught him off guard: he was said to be "embarrassed in the presence of most women." His own account acknowledged he was unsure how to behave: "She . . . taxed me so violently with many things that I had to exercise all the awkward tact I have to avoid quarreling with her." He added one aspect of the conversation that Jessie left out. "She more than once intimated that if General Frémont should decide to try conclusions with me, he could set up for himself." He could challenge Lincoln for the presidency.

The next morning Jessie had a caller at the Willard: Francis Preston Blair. The Blair family patriarch was a tiny man of seventy with crooked teeth, a nearly bald head, and eyebrows so shaggy they nearly covered his eyes. "Who would have expected you to do such a thing as this, to come and find fault with the President?" Jessie felt so familiar with him that she didn't recognize the depth of his anger—"I laughed at first—laughed at him"—but Blair said John had "made the President his enemy!" She understood at the end of their two-hour talk that their friendship was broken. Blair loved her like a daughter but loved his sons more; and a counselor to presidents could not stay relevant by alienating presidents.

Blair's visit revealed how angry Lincoln was. She had seen Lincoln Wednesday evening, and by the time Blair found her Thursday morning he apparently knew everything. It would seem that Lincoln was so irked he'd summoned Blair that night or early the following morning. Lincoln told Blair everything that he avoided saying to Jessie with his "awkward tact." Blair passed on the message.

The president was not driven solely by his pragmatic concern for Kentucky. He felt the general had stolen his authority. "Fremont's proclamation . . . is *purely political*, and not within the range of *military* law, or necessity," he said. A general might seize a farm when necessity required, but couldn't take it forever. "The same is true of slaves. If the General needs them, he can seize them, and use them; but when the need is past, it is not for him to fix their permanent future condition." Doing that was "simply 'dictatorship.' It assumes that the general may do *anything* he pleases—confiscate the lands and free the slaves of *loyal* people, as well as of disloyal ones. And going the whole figure I have no doubt would be more popular with some thoughtless people, than that which has been done! But I cannot assume this reckless position."

When Lincoln answered Frémont's demand for a direct order, he dated it September 11, the day after he met Jessie. He didn't give it to Jessie to deliver, though she was waiting to receive it, and sent it to John by mail:

> *Your answer, just received, expresses the preference on your part, that I should make an open order for the modification, which I very cheerfully do. It is therefore ordered.*

If the word *cheerfully* alone did not signal Frémont's doom, the phrase *very cheerfully* did. Lincoln ordered the general to publicize the modification. He also released his letter to the newspapers, which were faster than the mail service; General Frémont first read Lincoln's order in the papers, just as Lincoln had learned of his proclamation.

Frederick Douglass was crushed. "The action of Fremont was the hinge, the pivot upon which the character of the war was to turn. It was whether the war should be against traitors only by the cunning technicalities of the crafty lawyer, or by the cannon and courage of the determined warrior." The crafty lawyer in the White House had prevailed and "placed a tame and worthless statute between the rebels and the merited chastisement which a brave and generous General had wisely prepared. . . . The weakness, imbecility and absurdity of this policy are sufficiently manifest without a single word of comment." But he couldn't stop himself from commenting that Lincoln's act was "pusillanimous and proslavery." In a headline, Douglass expressed a new divide in the Republican Party: FREMONT AND FREEDOM—LINCOLN AND SLAVERY. Frémont's reputation rose among the Radical Republicans, spurring talk of his presidential candidacy in 1864.

Lincoln didn't fire the general over slavery, instead waiting a few weeks for other grievances to pile up against him. In a follow-up letter to Jessie he assured her, "No impression has been made in my mind against the honor and integrity of Gen. Fremont," but this letter omitted Lincoln's impression of the general's competence. He said elsewhere that Frémont "is losing the confidence of men near him, whose support any man in his position must have to be successful." He asked an experienced soldier who served under Frémont to assess him, and received a straightforward reply: "I am now convinced he has no general plan." This was slightly unfair; John drafted a plan for attacking down the Mississippi, which was part of General Scott's overall strategy for winning the war. But it was true he'd never commanded an army and couldn't inspire subordinates who knew he outranked them because of his fame. Lincoln replaced him as commander of the Department of the West at the end of October.

For all his faults, General Frémont had identified the means for winning the war. The *New York Times*, though devoted to Lincoln, had no doubt. "The Proclamation of Gen. Fremont . . . only states the inevitable result of the rebel war, no matter what legal provision Congress may have made. . . . The slave will not only assert his own liberty, but will turn upon his master. This is history without exception or qualification. The war, if prosecuted, necessarily involves the destruction of the institution, whether we will it or not." The weapon Frémont used was the same one Lincoln employed one year later. Though his Emancipation Proclamation was more carefully drawn, the approach was similar: freeing the enslaved out of military necessity. In her meeting with Lincoln, Jessie Benton Frémont was not so much wrong as ahead of time. Lincoln had shown he would decide when it was time.

Lincoln and McClellan (1826–1885)
near the Antietam battlefield, 1862.

Chapter 11

STRATEGIST: GEORGE B. McCLELLAN

September 2, 1862

On July 23, 1861, the president pulled a paper across the table and began composing a memo. The Union army had just been defeated near Manassas—the Battle of Bull Run, which took its name from a nearby stream, though it evoked the style of the retreat. Apparently it wasn't going to be a short war, and Lincoln wanted to think through the transition to a long one. He listed nine initial steps based on General Scott's strategy. A naval blockade of rebel-held ports must be enforced, strangling Southern commerce. The restive city of Baltimore must be held with "a gentle, but firm, and certain hand." Troops at various points must secure their lines and train for the day when they could advance. The defeated army outside Washington must be "reorganized as rapidly as possible," and recruits who had signed up for short-term service—ninety days—must be mustered out and replaced with men who enlisted for longer periods. In April it had seemed reasonable to enlist ninety-day volunteers; Lincoln's service in the Black Hawk War of 1832 hadn't lasted even that long. But in this larger, more technologically advanced conflict against an enemy with similar weapons and training, ninety days was just long enough to organize one army and send it to lose one battle.

Once his forces completed the nine steps, Lincoln wanted to launch two offensives. An army at Cairo, Illinois, should start by advancing down the Mississippi River to take Memphis, Tennessee—the first step toward controlling the river all the way to the Gulf. The reorganized eastern army should advance on the railway junction at Manassas, disrupting the movement of rebel troops and supplies and taking a step toward the rebel capital, Richmond. That junction was what the army had been advancing toward when it lost at Bull Run; now he wanted Manassas to "be seized, and permanently held."

His aides already had sent a telegram summoning the man to do it: George B. McClellan. He was thirty-four, forty years younger than Winfield Scott, but seemed like a winner. In the war's first months he organized a few thousand recruits and led them into the mountain passes of western Virginia. His victories over small Confederate forces cleared the region for a Unionist government and the eventual creation of the separate state of West Virginia. Newspapers in search of Northern heroes dubbed him Young Napoleon, and this well-timed gust of publicity encouraged the president to promote him to command the army at the capital. If he could capture a whole region the size of a state, he surely could march thirty miles from Washington to Manassas.

McClellan was a prodigy, the son of an elite Pennsylvania family. He'd entered the University of Pennsylvania at thirteen, then moved on to the United States Military Academy at West Point, which waived its requirements so he could enroll a few months before the minimum age of sixteen. He was barely twenty when he fought honorably in Mexico, and later went into private life as chief engineer of a railroad before returning to uniform at the start of the war. Days after the president's memo Mc-

Clellan reached the capital and stood before Lincoln, the picture of a Victorian soldier—young, compact, and strong, with arresting eyes and a Vandyke beard. Lincoln confirmed his new command, which came to be called the Army of the Potomac.

McClellan seemed respectful to the president during additional meetings at the White House and War Department. Then he wrote his wife to say what he was thinking. "I find myself in a new & strange position here," he said, "Presdt, Cabinet, Genl Scott, and all deferring to me—by some strange operation of magic I seem to have become the power of the land." Given access to all the resources at the government's command, he swiftly began to reorganize the army. At West Point he'd written a paper praising Napoleon's skill at inspiring and caring for his men, and he proved a master at the same skill, building a competent force out of a few trained officers and thousands of raw recruits. He ordered soldiers to learn their craft through "frequent military marches," conducted "sometimes at night," forcing them to learn how to live in the open and rely on one another. He thought about details: Each soldier must be supplied with spare underpants, spare shoes, and forty cartridges for the rifle on his shoulder. He stockpiled wagons and artillery. He frequently inspected his units and showed he was proud of them. "No general had ever better cause to love his men than I have to love mine," he said.

But he didn't move on Manassas. He told the president the Union must "display such overwhelming strength, as will convince all our antagonists, especially those of the aristocratic governing class, of the impossibility of resistance." He calculated he needed precisely 273,000 men, far more than the War Department could send him, and even when his force grew beyond 100,000 he never considered it enough. Feeling that the fate of the country rested on his shoulders, he let his outward confidence give way to insecurity, and lashed out at the men who entrusted him with such responsibility. He took to calling Lincoln "the original gorilla." He told his wife he was in "a terrible place," because "the Presdt is an idiot, the old General in his dotage," a reference to Scott. "They cannot or will not see the true state of affairs." McClellan alone knew that "the enemy have from 3 to 4 times my force," a claim that was not accurate for any force the Army of the Potomac faced throughout the war. The definition of the war was that the Union had the numbers, as it had when the South lost the election. But McClellan's prodigious brainpower conceived of all that could go wrong; so instead of attacking the enemy he attacked his commanding officer, quarreling with Scott until the old man decided to retire. Lincoln asked McClellan to outline his plans for an offensive and the general declined, saying the president couldn't keep a secret. Once Lincoln and Seward visited McClellan's house in Washington, waiting an hour in his parlor for him to return home. McClellan came to the door, passed them and went upstairs to bed without stopping. Lincoln let the insult pass and kept his focus on his goal: thirty miles.

The general spent the first winter of the war without a major offensive. The newspapers were screaming for results, and the government was nearly going broke financing the army he wasn't using—paying debts not in coin but with an early form of paper currency, known as greenbacks. The one time a portion of the Army of the Potomac advanced it was defeated, triggering a reaction in Congress: lawmakers established the Joint Committee on the Conduct of the War, whose secret sessions began hunting for disloyal officers. McClellan himself was on the list of suspects. Lincoln finally wrote an order to begin a general offensive in early 1862; McClellan didn't. It was clear by then that he didn't want to advance the thirty miles. He preferred a giant leap southward—staging a grand amphibious operation, moving troops down the Chesapeake Bay to land on Virginia's eastern shore near Richmond.

Lincoln wrote a letter asking how this was better than marching overland. “If you will give satisfactory answers,” he said, “I shall gladly yield my plan to yours.” The nearest McClellan came to a reply was a windy letter that celebrated his building of the army. Lincoln finally acquiesced to McClellan’s plan, fearing that otherwise the general might never advance at all.

The army moved in the spring of 1862, more than one hundred thousand men and their equipment on an armada of wooden ships—down the Potomac and through the bay to Fortress Monroe, on the tip of the Virginia Peninsula, one of the few federal posts in the South that had never lowered its flag. The troops came ashore safely and established a battle line, thanks in part to McClellan’s organizational skill; had his operation succeeded it would have ranked with later American seaborne triumphs like the D-Day landing. To complete that success, however, the army had to march seventy-five miles up the peninsula to Richmond, meaning they weren’t much nearer than if they had simply occupied Manassas. Confederate troops made a show of resistance and McClellan didn’t advance. In a telegram from Washington, the president prodded him: “I think you had better break the enemies’ line . . . at once. They will probably use *time*, as advantageously as you can.” McClellan didn’t take this as an order.

Each day’s inaction increased the pressure to strike a blow at slavery, which Lincoln still considered unwise. In Congress, even his ally Owen Lovejoy vented his frustration, publicly comparing the president to the driver of a buggy pulled by a Radical Republican horse—but barely moving because Lincoln was trying to pull a slow conservative horse on a halter behind him. Lincoln was lucky that at least Lovejoy remained his friend. The *New York Tribune*’s Washington correspondent had long since mocked the president’s policy (“We are to pursue the war with vigor, with determination, and with our hands tied”) in an article that was presumed to speak for the radical leaders of Lincoln’s own party.

THESE FRUSTRATIONS IN EARLY 1862 CAME DURING THE SAME PEriod when the Lincolns' eleven-year-old son, Willie, grew sick and died. The president fell into depression and the first lady seemed unable to recover. She gave away her son's toys, saying she couldn't bear to see them. She even isolated her surviving son, Tad, ordering that his friends not come to the White House because they reminded her of Willie. She wore black for many months and disrupted Washington social life, ordering a halt to regular concerts outside the White House because she couldn't bear the music. Occasionally the president found relief, walking around the White House trailed by Tad, who wore a uniform provided by Lincoln's army guards. Once he left for an expedition. When the military planned to capture the Confederate naval base at Norfolk, Virginia, Lincoln took an astonishing risk, joining Chase and Secretary of War Edwin M. Stanton on navy vessels and moving down the coast to choose a landing point for federal troops. The troops captured their objective. But he returned from the adventure to find McClellan still hadn't captured Richmond.

News from elsewhere was at once positive and grim. Federal troops captured Memphis as he wanted. Ulysses S. Grant was also advancing southward into Tennessee, forcing an entire rebel army to surrender. But Confederates struck back at the Battle of Shiloh: Grant's army endured the two-day fight while suffering thirteen thousand men killed, wounded, or captured, the bloodiest battle yet. On the peninsula, McClellan finally advanced and the rebels, understanding his superiority of numbers in a way that he did not, gave ground until he was within a few miles of Richmond. Then they chose an advantageous moment to counterattack and stopped him. Afterward a new Confederate commander, Robert E. Lee, drove Union forces back for miles through a brutal offensive known as the Seven Days. The Army of the Potomac fought skillfully, making tactical retreats while punishing its attackers, but McClellan's offensive was finished. Lincoln spent these days in the White House reading grim progress reports and telegrams from McClellan, who told his superiors he wasn't responsible for his defeat. *They* were, for failing to send enough troops. He told Secretary of War Stanton, "If I save this army now, I tell you plainly that I owe no thanks to you or any other persons in Washington. You have done your best to sacrifice this army."

Lincoln ignored this to focus on the larger goal, which was in fact to save the army. He sent telegrams to soothe McClellan, and promised to send what reinforcements he could. He praised McClellan's "heroism and skill." He even informed McClellan that a Richmond newspaper had called his campaign a "masterpiece of strategy," which Lincoln himself did not believe.

At the start of July he decided to visit the general, boarding a navy steamboat for a journey down the Chesapeake and up the James River. It docked at McClellan's headquarters, at a place called Harrison's Landing, and McClellan stepped aboard in his blue uniform, greeting the president in his black suit. They retired to a parlor and McClellan produced a memorandum: suggestions for how Lincoln should prosecute the war. Lincoln read it in McClellan's presence then thanked the general but said no more, leaving McClellan to guess his thoughts. They went ashore so the president could review some of the troops, and now McClellan hid his thoughts, though probably not well. He wrote his wife afterward, *"I had to order* the men to cheer & they did it very feebly." Other witnesses thought the troops warmly welcomed the president, suggesting McClellan's observation was colored by his dislike for Lincoln.

The president asked McClellan's senior officers if the army could safely board ships and retreat. Most said it could be done, though they would be vulnerable while evacuating, with part of their strength on the water and part on land. Lincoln left without giving orders. He also didn't answer McClellan's memorandum on how to conduct the war. He never would, McClellan told his wife: "His reply may be, however, to avail himself of the first opportunity to cut my head off." McClellan always felt beset by enemies in his rear; only the army was on his side. After Lincoln left, the general spent a day among the wounded from the campaign, including one thousand on a nearby hospital ship—"poor, maimed, brave fellows"—which was a "harrowing" experience but also made him "proud," because "I realized how these men love and respect me."

The year of disappointments made it relevant that McClellan had a different concept of war than the president. In his early command in western Virginia he'd issued a proclamation saying his troops would not interfere with slavery: "We will, on the contrary, with an iron hand crush any attempt at insurrection." Saying the federal government would enforce state slave laws was just as political as Frémont emancipating people in Missouri. McClellan had come from an elite family in Philadelphia, and was a product of its elite schools; when he went to West Point he befriended elite cadets from the South—"Somehow or other I take to the Southerners"—and absorbed their views of society even though he remained devoted to the Union.

His opinions could be overlooked in 1861, when Lincoln made no move against slavery. But in 1862 Congress was preparing to pass a second Confiscation Act, stronger than the first: It said the government could not only confiscate people enslaved by rebels, but could free them. The war's growing brutality had worn down resistance to such a step. McClellan's views were unchanged, and he expressed them in the memorandum that he handed the president at Harrison's Landing. The war should be conducted "upon the highest principles known to Christian civilization," and should not be "a war on population, but against armed forces and political organizations." He favored protection of private property, and opposed freedom for the enslaved: "Military power should not be allowed to interfere with the relations of servitude." He favored gradual emancipation, but only after the war. His forces outside Richmond sometimes sheltered people escaped from slavery and paid them for manual labor, but McClellan felt they believed only in "idleness" and were "entirely unfit for sudden emancipation." This explained why Lincoln said nothing in response to the general's letter. Lincoln was thinking the opposite—how much more ruthless and transformative the war must become.

ON JULY 13 LINCOLN ATTENDED A FUNERAL. THE SECRETARY OF WAR had suffered the death of an infant child, and Lincoln folded his long legs into a carriage to ride to the service outside town. Seward and Gideon Welles joined him in the carriage, and Lincoln said he was thinking of publishing an emancipation proclamation. "He dwelt earnestly on the gravity, importance, and delicacy of the movement, said he had given it much thought and had about come to the conclusion that it was a military necessity," Welles said. Lincoln asked what they thought. Both approved, though Seward said it was such a "momentous" step that he wanted to think it over.

On Tuesday, July 15, Lincoln was in the White House when Orville Browning visited. A steward said the president was in the library with instructions that none should disturb him, but Browning, Lincoln's friend from their Illinois days and now a Republican senator, knew him well enough to ignore that. He found the president "weary, care-worn and troubled." Browning said he feared for Lincoln's health. Lincoln "held me by the hand, pressed it, and said in a very tender and touching tone—'Browning, I must die sometime.' I replied 'your fortunes Mr. President are bound up with those of the country, and disaster to one would be disaster to the other, and I hope you will do all you can to preserve your health and life.' . . . We parted I believe both of us with tears in our eyes."

On July 17 Congress passed the Second Confiscation Act. Browning urged the president to veto the bill, because freeing the enslaved would seem too extreme for the border states. Lincoln himself once would have agreed, but signed it. The border states were more secure now. They also had declined to help him out of his dilemma: He'd recently gathered their leaders at the White House and asked them to support a plan of compensated emancipation, in which the federal government would pay slaveholders to free their property. The border-state men wouldn't do it. So he decided to go forward with his Emancipation Proclamation, though he drafted it in a way that still took the border states into account. His Proclamation left alone the enslaved in loyal states, commanding freedom only in areas resisting federal authority.

He showed a draft to his cabinet on the twenty-second. Seward said the timing was bad because of McClellan's recent defeats, and suggested waiting for a victory so it wouldn't seem like an act of desperation. Lincoln agreed.

On the twenty-fourth Browning returned to the White House, and Lincoln spread out a map, running his finger down the Mississippi. The map illustrated the Black population along its riverbanks; he was almost certainly gesturing at a US Coast Survey map that indicated the slave population in each county as of 1860. Counties were shaded according to the percentage of residents enslaved, and the darkest hues were along the river, such as 79.8 percent of Tunica County, 86.7 percent of Bolivar County, and 92.3 percent of Washington County. Lincoln "spoke of the importance of having the Mississippi opened, and said, 'I will tell you—I am determined to open it, and if necessary will take all these negroes to open it, and keep it open.'" They were a tool he could use to achieve his strategic objective.

But to use that tool he needed emancipation, and for that he needed a victory. Lincoln told Browning "that if by magic he could reinforce McClellan by 100,000 men to day he would be in an ecstasy over it, thank him for it, and tell him that he would go to Richmond tomorrow, but that when tomorrow came he would telegraph that he had certain information that the enemy had 400,000 men, and that he could not advance without reinforcements."

Antislavery activists felt that Lincoln was the dilatory one. Frederick Douglass skewered him that summer, saying his failure to act against slavery was "passive, cowardly and treacherous." Greeley published an open letter to the president in his *New York Tribune*, saying Lincoln was "disastrously remiss" in failing to use his new authority to free the enslaved, "unduly influenced" by "fossil politicians" in the border states. Lincoln's best answer would have been the proclamation that he wasn't ready to publish. Instead he answered Greeley with an open letter of his own, aimed less at the editor than the wider public. From the disasters of the past year he distilled a statement of his policy: "I would save the Union. I would save it the shortest way under the Constitution." He said he was willing to do this by freeing all the enslaved, some of the enslaved, or none. "What I do about slavery, and the colored race, I do because I believe it helps to save the Union; and what I forbear, I forbear because I do *not* believe it would help to save the Union." Though he would later be misread as saying freedom was not his concern, he was seeking broad support for the proclamation in his pocket. He was assuring radicals that he would act at the right time, and assuring conservatives he would act *only* in the national interest.

Privately, he was trying to arrange the military success on which all depended. To oversee all Union armies, including McClellan's, he brought a new commanding general to Washington—Henry Halleck, whose forces had won victories in the West. Much of Halleck's success was due to his subordinate Grant; but he was a career soldier and scholar, author of a book on tactics that officers on both sides of the war had studied, and he turned his intellect on McClellan. Visiting Harrison's Landing, Halleck concluded McClellan "does not understand strategy and should never plan a campaign." It seemed to be time to replace him; but Halleck also heard that McClellan's senior officers were talking of changing the government in Washington. Ambrose Burnside, a general traveling with Halleck, exclaimed it was "flat treason, by God!" Removing McClellan could provoke mutiny.

Stanton, the secretary of war, was seeking a solution. In his office just down from the White House, the edgy, workaholic, long-bearded lawyer did his job behind a standing desk, where he'd become Lincoln's iron fist—cashiering incompetent officers, shouting at politicians who asked for favors, and ordering the arrest of Northern men who too sharply criticized the war. Stanton had taken the job in January as McClellan's friend, and seemed to share McClellan's view of slavery; but he also seemed to share the view of Radical Republicans in Congress, trimming his positions depending on who was in the room. Stanton's true north was power: impatient or abusive with those below him, he was respectful to those above. The man above him was Lincoln, and he soon shared Lincoln's frustration with McClellan. The general didn't help by showing Stanton the same disrespect as he did other civilians.

Stanton's plan seemed elegant. He didn't strip McClellan of command, instead taking away the soldiers who made up his army. He ordered its many divisions to withdraw from the peninsula, board their transports, and embark for the Potomac. They would pass out of McClellan's control, reinforcing a different army guarding Washington. McClellan was characteristically slow to obey, but troops began returning. By late August he himself returned to the Potomac and discovered he had no duties except to hurry the last of his troops forward to the other army, commanded by an officer in Lincoln's favor, General John Pope.

Pope was more of an antislavery man than McClellan—and also "a braggart and a liar, with some courage, perhaps, but not much capacity," according to Montgomery Blair, the postmaster general. He inspired no confidence in the men from the Army of the Potomac, telling veterans who'd lost thousands of comrades that he would show them how to fight. But he led them toward Manassas, as Lincoln had wanted for more than a year. They were near the old battlefield of Bull Run when Lee came up from Richmond to launch a brutal flank attack. The blue army retreated toward Washington, losing thousands killed and wounded.

Even worse was McClellan's reported conduct: a treasonous act of pique, failing to rush reinforcements to help Pope. His sympathizers insisted this claim was fiction, but McClellan had been slow at every step of relocating troops from the peninsula, with the effect that tens of thousands just missed reaching the battlefield in time. Lincoln was outraged. Cabinet members circulated a letter asking the president to fire him. Stanton was "so absorbed in his scheme to get rid of McClellan that other and more important matters are neglected," according to Navy Secretary Welles. Salmon P. Chase, once McClellan's biggest supporter, said "that he ought to be shot."

The defeated army was said to be streaming down the roads toward Washington with rebels in pursuit. The capital itself seemed in danger. "There is considerable uneasiness in this city," said Welles on August 31, though he considered it "mere panic." But on September 1 wounded men began streaming into the city, and word spread that Pope felt "distressed and depressed." He'd written a wild letter to the War Department, claiming McClellan loyalists had undermined him. He thought the army might come apart. By September 2 Pope's forces were taking shelter within the city's fortifications. Halleck, the general-in-chief, seemed overwhelmed: "I am entirely tired out."

The cabinet gathered for a regular meeting at the White House. They were waiting on Lincoln to join them when Stanton gave them stunning news in a choked voice, "trembling with excitement." McClellan was back in charge: he'd been asked to take over the defense of Washington.

MCCLELLAN HAD BEEN AT BREAKFAST THAT MORNING WHEN Lincoln appeared. It was a little after seven at his house, the same one where he'd insulted the president by going up to bed. The general wore civilian clothes; he'd informed his wife that he ripped his last summer uniform on his way off the peninsula, and he'd been going around in a flannel hunting shirt, though he still had a dress uniform somewhere. Lincoln was accompanied only by the prickly and stressed General Halleck. No one recorded if McClellan poured their coffee. Lincoln did the talking.

Of the accounts of this meeting, McClellan's letter to his wife that same day is the most credible. He couldn't contain his excitement: "Pope is ordered to fall back on Washn & as he reenters everything is to come under my command again!" Lincoln "expressed his opinion that the troubles now impending could be overcome by me better than anyone else." Responding to this appeal to his ego as well as his patriotism, McClellan seized the opportunity to recover his reputation. He faced "a terrible & thankless task—yet I will do my best with God's blessing to perform it. God knows that I need his help."

In a later account McClellan heightened the drama, claiming Lincoln and Halleck "asserted that it was impossible to save the city, and I repeated my firm conviction that I could and would save it." Lincoln surely didn't say that but was in a dire frame of mind. McClellan reassured him. He saw off his callers and immediately resumed work. He reestablished his headquarters where it once had been near the White House and sent the president two written updates that day. He put on his dress uniform, complete with a yellow sash and sword, and crossed the Potomac. He rode out to meet the returning troops—*his* troops. He met Pope on the road, and they briefly conferred. The men of a nearby brigade learned McClellan was resuming command, and roared in celebration.

Lincoln returned to the White House for his cabinet meeting, and saw the faces of his shocked advisers. According to Welles, the president "said he had done what seemed to him best and would be responsible for what he had done to the country. Halleck had agreed to it. McClellan knows this whole ground; his specialty is to defend; he is a good engineer, all admit; there is no better organizer."

His advisers were not persuaded. "There was a more disturbed and desponding feeling than I have ever witnessed in council," said Welles; "the President was greatly distressed." Edward Bates, the attorney general, felt that Lincoln might hang himself.

Chase said Lincoln's decision was "a national calamity." Stanton was horrified. Lincoln had no illusions about McClellan, saying the general had "the slows." But he challenged his cabinet: If they could name an officer who could rescue the army "as promptly and well, he would appoint him." Chase and Stanton seemed to think anyone would do, but backed down.

Around this time Lincoln began writing on a scrap of paper.

The will of God prevails. In great contests each party claims to act in accordance with the will of God. Both may be, and one must be wrong.

> *God can not be for, and against the same thing at the same time. In the present civil war it is quite possible that God's purpose is something different from the purpose of either party—and yet the human instrumentalities, working just as they do, are of the best adaptation to effect His purpose. I am almost ready to say this is probably true—that God wills this contest, and wills that it shall not end yet.*

McClellan felt no such agony. He visited many returning troops, and many cheered; their morale was transformed, as was his own. Shaping and inspiring an army was the work he did best; he could get his brain around all the details. He lost the slows. From two commingled armies—his own and Pope's—he selected troops to defend the capital, giving that stationary duty to the more damaged and depleted divisions. He chose 85,000 of the freshest men and placed them in the charge of his favored officers, forming a field army that could move against the Confederates. He still thought about danger in his rear—he told a friend he should have demanded Stanton's resignation—but let that go to focus on his work. His initial assignment was simply to defend Washington, but events made it necessary to range beyond. Reports suggested on September 5 that Lee's soldiers were crossing the Potomac northwest of Washington—an invasion of Maryland.

Lincoln went from the White House to read dispatches at the telegraph office inside the War Department next door. Walking with his secretary John Hay, he said McClellan's conduct had been "unpardonable," but he was "too useful just now to sacrifice." Lincoln needed a functioning army, and "we must use what tools we have."

On September 6, McClellan led the Army of the Potomac out of Washington to intercept Lee's army. "This evening some twenty or thirty thousand passed my house within three hours," Welles told his diary, adding a telling observation: "There was design in having them come up from Pennsylvania Avenue to H Street." By turning off Pennsylvania Avenue they passed McClellan's house, and "they cheered the General lustily, instead of passing by the White House and honoring the President."

On September 17, McClellan's forces battled Lee's across Antietam Creek, about sixty miles northwest of Washington. Confederate forces were divided and Union troops massively outnumbered them, perfect conditions to deal a crushing blow. McClellan knew it too: his men had captured a copy of Lee's plans. But his caution returned; he delayed attacking and held back a huge reserve in case of trouble. When the blue-uniformed troops finally advanced, three assaults pounded Lee's right, center, and left with such force that the rebel lines nearly collapsed. It was the deadliest single day of the war, with the combined armies suffering more than 3,500 dead and 20,000 wounded; but Lee desperately shifted troops from one threatened point to another—and McClellan's initial delay meant there was just enough time for Confederate reinforcements to arrive. Lee managed to end the day with his army bleeding but on the field, and began withdrawing across the Potomac the next afternoon.

Strategically Antietam was a Union victory, because Lee abandoned his invasion and suffered losses the Confederacy's smaller population couldn't sustain. McClellan had built a war machine so large and well trained it inflicted punishment even if McClellan was leading it. For Lincoln this was victory enough, and on September 22 he issued his preliminary Emancipation Proclamation. Rebels would be allowed time to come to their senses, then at the start of 1863 "all persons held as slaves within any state, or designated part of a state, the people whereof shall then be in rebellion against the United States shall be then, thenceforward, and forever free."

His action resembled Frémont's military emancipation one year earlier.

But the legal, political, and military situations were different. His Proclamation was not going to apply in a loyal border state, and he based his authority on the new, stronger act of Congress. Above all, the frustrations of the past year made him feel he must act: "When, early in the war, General Fremont attempted military emancipation, I forbade it, because I did not then think it an indispensable necessity." But at last, "I was, in my best judgment, driven to the alternative of either surrendering the Union, and with it, the Constitution, or of laying strong hand upon the colored element. I chose the latter."

His relations with McClellan soured after Antietam, when the general resumed his old ways and failed to pursue Lee's damaged army into Virginia. Gideon Welles thought McClellan "wishes to outgeneral the Rebels, but not to kill and destroy them." Lincoln wanted destruction. In November he relieved McClellan for good, replacing him with General Ambrose Burnside, the loyal general who'd warned of treason among McClellan's officers. Lincoln chose him even though Burnside was self-aware enough to say he was not competent to run a large army, and Burnside soon proved it, leading the army to defeat at Fredericksburg, Virginia. The many dead at Fredericksburg may have been the necessary price to keep the government safe from its own military: Burnside was an old friend of McClellan, so his appointment didn't trigger mutiny.

September 22, 1862, was the day Lincoln altered history—all but ensuring victory in the war and shifting the United States toward its eventual refounding as a multiracial republic. His determination to write the Proclamation grew partly from the agony of his struggles with McClellan; had the general been more successful, Lincoln might not have been able to justify it. Releasing the Proclamation became possible because Lincoln gave McClellan one last chance to command, and he responded just well enough. Welles felt that by acting "independent of his Cabinet," against the "sentiment of the people," and even against his own "personal feeling" to restore the tarnished general, Lincoln "proved his ability as chief." At Lincoln's direction, the Young Napoleon inadvertently cleared the way for an act of liberation that he didn't approve of at the time and probably never did. When he wrote his memoirs after the war, he never mentioned it.

Plains delegation at the White House, 1863.
Lean Bear, 1813–1864, is in the front row, third from left.

Chapter 12

SOVEREIGN: LEAN BEAR

March 27, 1863

THOUGH THE CIVIL WAR WAS TRANSFORMING THE GOVERNMENT, the economy, and society, it didn't interrupt the United States' westward settlement. Powerful interests demanded better communication across the two thousand miles between the Mississippi and California, and the 1860 Republican platform pledged to do it. A railroad would make the Pacific coast easier to populate and to defend, and also would open a route for trade across the ocean to China. In 1862 Lincoln signed the Pacific Railroad Acts, giving land grants to subsidize construction of the Union Pacific. He took a personal interest in this first transcontinental railroad, even answering a request that he determine its gauge, the measurement between the rails. (He chose a five-foot gauge, though the Union Pacific later adopted the standard four feet, eight and a half inches.)

Settlers were moving westward well ahead of the railroad, occupying land in the interior West that, when glanced at on a map, would seem to be the territory of the United States. This was deceptive. Notes on the maps hinted at reality, identifying the domains of people such as the Comanche or the Arapaho, who according to an 1832 Supreme Court ruling legally controlled the land until they surrendered sovereign rights through purchase, treaty, or war. To expand lawfully, the United States had to accommodate the tribes, and often negotiated treaties with them—then routinely violated them in ways that led to war.

This became Lincoln's problem in the summer of 1862, when Dakota people, commonly known as Sioux, went to war in Minnesota. Lashing out at settlers who were failing to honor a treaty, the Dakota killed women and children as well as men. Not all participated, and within two months a military expedition largely put down the outnumbered fighters. But Minnesota's governor demanded federal help, which risked diverting resources from fighting the rebellion.

Rather than a large number of troops, Lincoln sent one senior officer: General John Pope, who had to be shuffled somewhere after his disgrace at the Second Battle of Bull Run. Arriving late to the tense situation, General Pope did nothing to encourage calm, saying the Dakota must be treated as "maniacs or wild beasts." He approved when a Minnesota militia general put Dakota prisoners on trial before a military commission, which reflected the fury of the white community by sentencing 303 men to hang. This was a war crime. Prisoners of war should be kept safe until their freedom was negotiated, as Pope knew because it was the practice in the war among white men he'd just been fighting. Instead Pope complained that too many men were being acquitted. He demanded faster proceedings and more death. The Minnesota general violated military law by sending back cases of men who had been acquitted, telling the commission to make "revisions" to its findings.

White men sympathetic to the Dakota appealed to Lincoln, who ordered the trial transcripts sent to him and assigned two lawyers to review them. Minnesota lawmakers demanded that the executions go forward—Gideon Welles said they "threaten the Administration if it shows clemency"—but Lincoln threw out 264 death sentences in December 1862. General Pope had assured him all the condemned men had raped white women; evidence almost never supported this. Lincoln approved thirty-nine executions for men "proven to have participated in *massacres*, as distinguished from participation in *battles*." He was applying a principle of the laws of war: a common soldier was not culpable for ordinary acts of combat, but was responsible for atrocities against helpless people. One last man received a reprieve, and thirty-eight were marched to the gallows.

The only way to avoid further horrors of this kind was to improve relations with other tribes in the West; and with that in mind, the Bureau of Indian Affairs invited eleven Great Plains leaders to visit the president at the White House in early 1863. The government intended to awe these visitors, as presidents had done before. After the 1832 Black Hawk War in which Lincoln served, the captured leader Black Hawk was taken to meet President Andrew Jackson, then sent on a tour of eastern cities to see the power and population of the United States. He became a celebrity, met by curious crowds. The delegation that arrived on March 27, 1863, attracted similar interest: A newspaper said "the novelty of the occasion" inspired officials to invite diplomats and distinguished citizens. They crowded the East Room, the largest in the White House, eighty feet long with vast windows at each end. Seward, Chase, and Welles came, as did the ministers of France, Prussia, and Brazil. Ladies attended, among them Kate Chase, the glamorous twenty-three-year-old daughter of the treasury secretary.

Excitement increased as the delegation entered. The federal Indian agent and interpreter who'd brought them from the West wore black suits, while the native men dressed in the finery of the Plains. Two were accompanied by women identified as their brides, aged sixteen and eighteen, who seemed to have obtained fashionable ladies' hats. The onlookers crowded around them so tightly that most couldn't see, so the visitors relocated to a spot along one of the long walls. Had everyone stood back, a newspaper said, "every person might have enjoyed the privilege of seeing and hearing, but unfortunately there seems to be an incurable habit among the good people of our country in the house of the Chief Magistrate to press forward and not give an inch to those behind. The President's appearance was a signal for all the more violent pressure in this vicinity."

The delegates at the center of this crowd represented multiple tribes, and they included Lean Bear, whose name also translated as Starving Bear. He was around fifty, in a buffalo-hide buckskin war shirt. It was brain-tanned, with stripes and fringes decorating the sleeves. He wore his hair long and parted on his right, and he had a dignified expression that suited his role as a representative of the Cheyenne Nation.

His nation was centuries old, and had an eventful history. In the seventeenth century they lived in the Great Lakes region. Driven westward by wars with the Dakota, they moved to the Black Hills, until the Lakota people drove them farther west and south. By the early nineteenth century they lived and hunted buffalo near the Platte and Arkansas Rivers, which flowed out of the Rockies and across the Great Plains. The Cheyenne did business with a few French fur traders, and went to war with other Plains nations such as the Pawnee. This was the world in which Lean Bear was born in 1813.

He grew up learning to hunt and fight. It was a high honor to count coup of an enemy, charging near enough to touch. He lasted longer than some; a description in his forties called him "an old brave man" who had counted coup more than anyone, but had learned to fight carefully. "Go slowly," he advised younger men on the way into a battle, "we will get there in time." He raised a family, and brought his son to war. He rose in the Cheyenne governing structure, becoming a member of the Council of Forty-four, who made decisions together.

During his adulthood a change came over the Plains. By the 1840s convoys of white settlers passed each summer along the Oregon Trail, and each year's wagon trains were longer than the last. John Charles Frémont rode among the Cheyenne at the head of his party of explorers. After the conquest of California more settlers passed through, as did soldiers surveying routes for railroads. It became necessary for the United States to negotiate some arrangement with native nations, and federal representatives met Great Plains leaders at Fort Laramie in 1851. The resulting treaty was more honorable than most: The government demanded no native land, instead confirming the boundaries of seven nations including the Cheyenne and Arapaho. The United States gained the right to build roads and military posts to assure the safe passage of migrants, and would pay the nations $50,000 per year for fifty years. Had the terms been honored, the history of the Plains would have been different; but when the Senate ratified this treaty it unilaterally cut the annual payment to ten years, and settlers violated other terms before the ten years passed.

Cheyenne and Arapaho land included much of the modern state of Colorado, and when gold was discovered in the Colorado Rockies in 1858 it became inconvenient to let them keep it. White settlers founded Denver and other gold towns, driving the Cheyenne out of their homelands. The Treaty of Fort Laramie promised that the United States would protect "Indian nations against the commission of all depredations by the people of the United States," but the government failed. Instead a new negotiator summoned Cheyenne and Arapaho leaders to an outpost called Fort Wise and insisted on a new treaty, taking most Cheyenne land and limiting them to a smaller reservation. The negotiator held a signing ceremony on February 18, 1861, ignoring the secession crisis in the East. One US Army officer who signed as a witness was Lieutenant J. E. B. Stuart, who soon quit to become a Confederate cavalry commander.

The Cheyenne were promised money, houses, stock animals, and mills, and were told to adopt a lifestyle based on agriculture. But some objected to this radical change in their lives, arguing all forty-four members of their governing council should have attended the negotiation. Only six signed the treaty, including the senior leader Black Kettle. It also bore the X mark of "Avo-na-co," or Lean Bear. The veteran fighter had become a peace chief, believing in good relations with white men, even as a military society known as the Dog Soldiers talked of resistance.

In 1863 a federal Indian agent invited Lean Bear to join the delegation he was gathering to meet the president. Disregarding the late winter weather, they descended the Arkansas River into Kansas, then cut overland to Fort Leavenworth, outside Kansas City. A Missouri River steamboat took the delegates downstream, after which railroads carried them to their meeting with Lincoln.

In the East Room that day, the bearded president sat in a chair against the long wall. Delegates sat on the floor in a semicircle facing him, and behind them stood the wider semicircle of spectators, people straining to see around ladies' bonnets or over shoulders. Each delegate rose to shake Lincoln's hand—men from the Kiowa, Comanche, Apache, and Caddo nations as well as the Cheyenne and Arapaho. The interpreter didn't introduce the two young women, reportedly following the delegation's preference, though the women took their places in the semicircle, showing "gentle and amiable faces."

The president turned to the interpreter. "Say to them I am very glad to see them, and if they have anything to say, it will afford me great pleasure to hear them."

Lean Bear rose to speak, then asked for a chair, explaining to the interpreter that he felt "weak and nervous." People were surprised—*this* imposing man felt nervous? According to Cheyenne tradition, his ill feeling was an omen, warning him to avoid saying anything harmful to his tribe; he surely felt great responsibility. But when someone produced a chair and he arranged himself in it, he improved his position. He was now facing the seated president on equal terms, which he would not have been while standing.

Lincoln invited him to speak "with perfect freedom," and Lean Bear spoke a few sentences in the Cheyenne language, then paused for the interpreter before continuing. He was "a natural orator" who spoke in a "fluent and animated style." His speech was a masterpiece of subtle persuasion, beginning with a poetic expression of humility that Lincoln, master of humble expressions, would appreciate. He said "the chiefs who had come with him were of different tribes, but they were all glad to see the Great Chief of the white people and shake him by the hand, and speak their hearts to him. They had come a long way, and wanted his advice and counsel on many matters concerning their condition. [Lean Bear] would hear all the great chief had to say; and when he went away he would not carry it in his pocket," as a letter, "but in his heart, out of which it could not be lost."

Next he made an observation. "The President is the Great Chief of the white people; he [Lean Bear] was the great chief of the Indians." He was asserting his equality.

Finally he arrived at his message. It turned out he had not come to hear advice so much as to give it. "Many white people have come to settle" on Cheyenne land, he said. Lean Bear "always wished to be at peace with them. He feared these white men on the plains were not as ready to keep peace towards them. . . . He would always endeavor to prevent his people from doing any thing to incur their ill-will; and if there was trouble, it would not be owing to bad conduct on the part of the Indians."

Reporters took down slightly different versions of this speech, and one had Lean Bear making his point more sharply. "He asked the president to counsel his white children on the plains so there would be no more war between them and the whites, his purpose being to make traveling over the plains as safe to the whites as possible. He wished to live in peace for the balance of his life, on the buffalo, as his fathers had done, while that lasted, and again urged the President to counsel his white children, who were annually encroaching more and more upon their tribes, to abstain from acts of violence and wrong towards them." The most poignant phrase was "while that lasted"; he understood white hunters were killing the buffalo.

Having delivered his message, Lean Bear went on to say what he knew the president wanted to hear. Some native nations had sided with the Confederates in their rebellion, and Lean Bear assured Lincoln that the Cheyenne would not; they had no interest in the war among white men. Then he was finished and turned over the chair to an Arapaho leader, who gave a shorter and less substantive talk.

WHAT WAS THE PRESIDENT THINKING AS HE LISTENED? HE WANTED peace with these visitors, though he seemed aware that his government had not done much to deserve it. Lean Bear was gently informing him that white settlers were the real problem, and that it was in the interest of the United States to restrain them. Lincoln's task, however, was to persuade the Indians that it was in *their* interest to get along with the settlers.

He waited until his visitors finished speaking, then took his turn. He said the diplomats in the room had come from around the world. "We pale-faced people think that this world is a great, round ball, and we have people here of the pale-faced family who have come almost from the other side of it to represent their nations here and conduct their friendly intercourse with us, as you now come from your part of the round ball." Someone rolled forward a globe on a stand, and one Professor Henry stepped up to show them where Washington was, and where their homelands were.

Lincoln went on: "The pale-faced people are numerous and prosperous because they cultivate the earth, produce bread, and depend upon the products of the earth rather than wild game for a subsistence.... You have asked for my advice. I really am not capable of advising you whether, in the providence of the Great Spirit, who is the great Father of us all, it is best for you to maintain the habits and customs of your race, or adopt a new mode of life. I can only say that I can see no way in which your race is to become as numerous and prosperous as the white race except by living as they do, by the cultivation of the earth."

He was making a sales pitch that dated to the time of George Washington: native nations should abandon nomadic lives for modern agriculture, the basis of modern civilization. The United States would help those who wanted to make the transition. Indians could prosper and multiply—and because farms were smaller than hunting grounds, they would need less land, opening more for white settlement. Some nations had embraced this bargain; the Cherokee of the southern Appalachians had gone so far as to dress and worship as their white neighbors did, holding legislative elections while their leader, John Ross, talked of the Cherokee Nation joining the Union as a state. But as commonly happened, white settlers wanted all their land, not just some, and the Cherokee were pushed onto new land west of the Mississippi.

"It is the object of this Government to be on terms of peace with you," Lincoln said, "and with all our red brethren. We constantly endeavor to be so. We make treaties with you, and will try to observe them; and if our children should sometimes behave badly, and violate these treaties, it is against our wish. You know it is not always possible for any father to have his children do precisely as he wishes them to do."

This was the closest he came to expressing regret for the Colorado gold rush, the unfair treaty, and the tensions that followed. He was expressing what officials in Washington believed: There was no way to stop settlers who wanted land or gold. They'd have to send an army and might even face a new civil war. It was also true that officials sometimes counted on settlers to create new facts on the ground, overriding the legal and moral complexities of the nation's growth.

If it was impossible to stop the Colorado gold rush it should have been possible to compensate the Cheyenne and Arapaho nations for lost land. The 1861 treaty proposed to do this, paying for Denver land at $1.25 an acre. A federal report later concluded this was an absurdly low payment for urban real estate, but it was a payment. Lincoln signed the treaty—and the federal government never paid. After Lincoln sent the treaty to the Senate for ratification, senators arbitrarily cut that provision. Paying for stolen land by the acre might have set an uncomfortable precedent; it was customary to pay small lump sums for millions of acres.

The president rose to shake each visitor's hand, and delighted the two ladies by shaking theirs. On their way out the guests were taken through the conservatory, a greenhouse just west of the mansion, where later generations would find the West Wing and Oval Office. Amid the botanical wonders, a photographer took advantage of the midday light to pose the delegates for his camera. At some point Lean Bear and the other delegates received peace medals to wear around their necks—special gifts from the president.

BEFORE THE DELEGATES COULD START FOR HOME AN INVITATION arrived, proposing a side trip to New York. P. T. Barnum, the famous showman, said he'd like them to meet the public at Barnum's American Museum, where he lured paying customers to see animals, freaks, oddities, and scams. The delegates accepted and took trains up the coast. For several days they lived in a room next to the museum's lecture hall; Barnum provided them with "bread, raw meat and coffee," which they cooked to their own tastes. They slept on mattresses and rugs on the floor, and rose in the early morning to watch "the antics of the monkeys in the upper hall," or listen "to the performances of the musical seal in the room below." Later they came to the lecture hall to meet Barnum's customers. A newspaper said they drew enormous crowds, nearly as large as those for Tom Thumb, the most famous of Barnum's proportional dwarves, who'd created a sensation when he married Lavinia Warren some weeks earlier.

At last they started westward and recovered their horses at Fort Leavenworth. By summertime Lean Bear was among his people, who were struggling. The transition from hunting to farming wasn't easy. Lean Bear, Black Kettle, and other leaders continued to counsel peace, but some men raided the ranches of white men for food.

Early in 1864 a white rancher complained to authorities, who sent forty soldiers to recover his purportedly stolen horses. Without much investigation the soldiers confronted the first Indians they found. These men opened fire and drove away the soldiers—who retreated and called for reinforcements. They soon found a Cheyenne village, killing all the inhabitants they could. Colorado authorities began enlisting additional troops for war.

In May, Lean Bear and other Cheyenne were living in a camp, chosen in the hope that it was remote enough to keep clear of trouble, when they saw soldiers approaching. One in the group, Wolf Chief, described the incident: "A number of us mounted our horses and followed Lean Bear, the chief, out to meet the soldiers. We rode up on a hill and saw the soldiers coming in four groups with cannon drawn by horses. . . . We did not want to fight. Lean Bear . . . told us to stay behind while he went forward to show his papers from Washington which would tell the soldiers that we were friendly. . . . [He] had a medal on his chest given at the time the

Cheyenne chiefs visited Washington." Lean Bear rode near the soldiers, who didn't wait to learn the identity of the man with the peace medal on his chest, opening fire and killing him along with his son.

Warfare spread across hundreds of miles of the Plains, as Cheyenne Dog Soldiers and members of other tribes lashed out. Warriors attacked wagons carrying supplies to western settlements. "Over $300,000 worth of property has been destroyed and stolen by the Indians on the road east of Fort Kearney," a newspaper dispatch reported from Nebraska. "Our men report that flour, coffee and tea, and all kinds of groceries, are scattered over the prairie—the trains having been sacked by the Indians." On September 8 the *New York Times* blamed "the savage tide" on the influence of Confederates. But there had been no need for the rebels to stir up trouble when loyal citizens had done so much.

Some Cheyenne still saw the wisdom of peace, and tried to negotiate with Colorado's governor, who refused to talk with them; the governor said an extra regiment of soldiers had been recruited "to kill Indians, and Indians they must kill." Realizing the threat, a sympathetic army offer instructed about five hundred Cheyenne to make camp near the fort that he commanded. They were on Sand Creek, within the limits of the reservation. But the officer who protected them was later replaced. In the early morning hours of November 29, 1864, seven hundred soldiers quietly surrounded the camp, and Colonel John M. Chivington ordered his men forward. They massacred more than two hundred Cheyenne and Arapaho. They chased women and children into the streambed, killed them, and in many cases mutilated them. The male victims included War Bonnet and Standing-in-the-Water, two Cheyenne leaders who had been with Lean Bear on the visit to President Lincoln.

Chivington, a Methodist minister, felt that God sanctioned the massacre, but still lied about what he had done and claimed he'd won a heroic battle. He was exposed—the Sand Creek Massacre became one of the most infamous events in the West. A military commission documented Chivington's crimes, but he wasn't put on trial and was allowed to resign. Captain Silas Soule, who was present for the massacre and refused to allow his men to take part, gave testimony against Chivington and was murdered soon afterward in Denver.

The massacre didn't end the war, since it targeted people who weren't fighting. Warriors went on to kill numerous settlers and forced the army to divert eight thousand troops from battling the rebellion so they could restore order on the Plains. A federal report later found the war to have been "useless and expensive," costing some $30 million, with many federal troops killed in pursuit of Cheyenne warriors. In combat against hostile Cheyenne fighters—as opposed to massacres of civilians—a mere "fifteen or twenty Indians had been killed, at an expense of more than a million dollars apiece," in a war that was "dishonorable to the nation, and disgraceful to those who had originated it." It ended with yet another terrible treaty that was not followed, despite its already unequal terms.

Lincoln needed quiet on the Plains so he could focus on the Civil War, but he'd invited the wrong people to the White House. The delegates he asked for peace were not the ones responsible for the war.

A visiting card for Pendleton, 1825–1889.

Chapter 13

DISSIDENT: GEORGE H. PENDLETON

June 25, 1863

VOTERS IN THE 1862 ELECTIONS REBUKED LINCOLN'S PARTY. Democrats won many state and local offices and made dramatic gains in Congress, which were seen as a judgment of the war and a rejection of the Emancipation Proclamation. Democrats even recaptured the legislature in Lincoln's home state, and afterward staged a meeting in the same room where he'd given his House Divided speech. Those attending included John T. Stuart, Lincoln's first law partner, a onetime ally who'd gone over to the Democrats and won a seat in Congress. They said Lincoln was launching "a crusade for the sudden, unconditional and violent liberation of three millions of negro slaves," triggering "the most dismal foreboding of horror and dismay." The war had been in their interest, but now was in someone else's interest, a social engineering project that might harm them if freedmen came north in search of work. The new legislature acted to bar the door to Illinois, proposing a new state constitution that would enshrine some of the Black Laws.

Challenges to the administration grew so intense they triggered fears of treason. Confederates dreamed of luring Western states to unite with them, leaving the antislavery East to fend for itself, and the administration took this threat seriously enough to run a network of informants on purported conspiracies, filling the prisons whenever they felt national security demanded. Ordinarily the Constitution mandated the writ of habeas corpus—bringing a suspect before a judge to face charges—but the administration had been detaining suspected traitors without court hearings since the start of the war.

In 1861, while trying to keep open supply lines through Maryland, Lincoln suspended the writ in some cases. Chief Justice Roger Taney ordered a court appearance for a Maryland man imprisoned for setting railroad bridges on fire. But on Lincoln's orders, the army locked the man behind the brick walls of Fort McHenry and ignored the federal marshal Taney sent to the gate to retrieve him. Lincoln based his authority on his own reading of a sentence in the Constitution: "The Privilege of the Writ of Habeas Corpus shall not be suspended, unless when in Cases of Rebellion or Invasion the public Safety may require it." This passive sentence didn't say *who* could suspend the writ in case of rebellion. Taney concluded only Congress could, since the sentence appeared in a section enumerating the powers of Congress. Lincoln decided the president could, and he did. Even if he was wrong, he asked, "are all the laws, *but one*, to go unexecuted, and the government itself go to pieces, lest that one be violated?" Taney could have seen this coming. At the time of the Dred Scott decision in 1857, Lincoln questioned whether the Supreme Court was the final arbiter of the Constitution. In a speech, he read a quote from Andrew Jackson: "Each public officer, who takes an oath to support the Constitution, swears that he will support it as he understands it, and not as it is understood by others." Jackson had not actually defied a court ruling when he said this, but Lincoln followed Jackson's thinking into active opposition.

In 1863 Congress made the point moot by passing a law granting him the power he said he already had; but his critics still found it disturbing that one man could sweep away rights that were guaranteed any other time. A critic among Democrats, Congressman George H. Pendleton, wove constitutional arguments into his broader attack on the administration: "No free people should listen to this argument of State necessity. Its history is marked by the wreck of popular liberty and free institutions."

He was a challenging opponent. His photo showed a charismatic face—he could smile with his eyes—and his name announced him as a member of the political aristocracy, with links to the founding generation. His grandfather served in the Revolution and befriended Alexander Hamilton—eventually serving as Hamilton's second, negotiating the terms of his duel with Aaron Burr in 1804. Pendleton's father settled in Cincinnati and won election to Congress, and George H. followed him to Congress by the time he turned thirty-one. He solidified his place in Washington's elite when he married a daughter of Francis Scott Key, author of "The Star-Spangled Banner"; she was also a niece of Chief Justice Taney. Nothing illustrated his connections to power quite so well as his role in a Washington scandal: His wife's brother, Philip Barton Key, had an affair with the wife of Democratic congressman Daniel Sickles, who shot and killed Key in 1859. Pendleton was close enough to the events to be called as a witness at Sickles's spectacular trial.

When war came he was just thirty-six, with ambitions for higher office. First he had to navigate the rebellion, which divided his party; there were War Democrats and Peace Democrats. He called for peace in his characteristic short sentences ("Peace is the first step to Union. Peace is Union.") though he smoothly denied he favored surrender. "The Union and the Government ought to be maintained," he said in Congress in December 1860. "We intend, if possible, that they shall be maintained.... The centripetal forces of the Union are interest and feeling. Force cannot maintain it. Arms can not hold it together. Armies can not unite us." He sometimes voted for military appropriations and said he favored measures the government truly needed to sustain itself. His relative moderation suited his future ambitions, and fit the divided temper of Cincinnati, just across the Ohio from a slave state. But as Lincoln took more ruthless measures to end the war, Pendleton became more obstructive. Republicans called men like him Copperheads—poisonous snakes. Peace Democrats adopted the slur as their own, and wore copper badges. Some even wore butternut pins—the color of many Confederate uniforms.

When Congress considered a bill explicitly authorizing the enlistment of Black soldiers after the Proclamation, Pendleton was a crafty critic in House debate. He knew what made white voters anxious. If Black men fought alongside white men, "they will meet in the trenches; they will commingle on the battle-field; they will stand side by side in the assault. Their dead bodies will fall side by side in the battle, and be placed peacefully together in the same grave. And how, when they are placed together in moments of danger, how can they be kept separate at the camp fire and mess table? If that association is permitted, you know well enough the temper of the army to be assured that it will thin out the ranks of the white soldiers. They will not submit to association of this kind." Equality would undermine the Union, which was not in the interest of white people. Worse would come at the end of the war, when Black soldiers returned home after defending the Constitution. They naturally would expect equal rights under the Constitution. Why wouldn't Republicans admit they were planning a social revolution?

IN THE SPRING OF 1863 LINCOLN APPOINTED A NEW COMMANDER of a military district known as the Department of the Ohio. He needed somewhere to put General Ambrose Burnside, who had lasted only two months in command of the Army of the Potomac, so Burnside took charge of military affairs in most states of the Ohio River valley. He was a longtime army officer from Indiana, considered brave, honorable, and not brilliant—ultimately most famous for the bushy hair on his face, which people called sideburns. Soon after reaching his headquarters in Cincinnati he published General Order 38, proclaiming that people who aided the enemy would be tried as spies. He added restrictions on speech: "The habit of declaring sympathies for the enemy will no longer be tolerated." People with this "habit" would be put on trial or "sent beyond our lines into the lines of their friends. . . . Treason, expressed or implied, will not be tolerated." The notion of "implied" treason could mean anything, and citizens would be judged not in a civilian court but before a military commission.

Ohio Democrats took the lead in challenging Burnside. Their most outspoken leader was Clement Vallandigham, an ex-congressman seeking his party's nomination for governor. He spoke in the state capital at the end of April, "denounced General Burnside's order," and said he would resist. Vallandigham then spoke at a rally in Mount Vernon, Ohio, which attracted such attention that a procession to the event was several miles long. Standing beneath a canopy and a giant American flag, he attacked "an injurious, cruel and unnecessary war—a war not being waged for the preservation of the Union—a war for the purpose of crushing out liberty and establishing a despotism—a war for the freedom of the blacks and enslaving of the whites." He predicted that military marshals would soon be regulating speech across the land. He said he "spat" on General Order 38, basing his authority on "General Order Number One, the Constitution." Military conscription was beginning, and those who were drafted would not be fighting for the Union but in a "wicked Abolition war."

George H. Pendleton attended the same event and likely expressed similar sentiments, but phrased them carefully enough to attract little attention from the army officer in civilian clothes who monitored the event while leaning on the edge of the stage. Vallandigham wanted the attention. "The hissing Copperhead is evidently desirous of martyrdom, and Gen. Burnside will be entirely willing to begin with him," said a newspaper.

Days later Burnside ordered a company of soldiers onto a train at Cincinnati and sent them up the tracks to Vallandigham's home in Dayton. When they demanded entry to his house at three o'clock in the morning, someone inside fired a pistol. Fearing the gunshot might be a signal to summon help, the soldiers broke into the house, seized Vallandigham, and heaved him onto the train before a mob could form. Hundreds rioted in Dayton the next night and burned the office of a Republican newspaper. Vallandigham was tried before a military commission, with Pendleton as one of his lawyers, and was of course found guilty, but not before he managed to slip out a message to the public: "I am here in a military Bastille for no other offense than my political opinions." His defenders appealed to a federal judge for a writ of habeas corpus, but the judge denied it. He was sentenced to spend the rest of the war imprisoned at Fort Warren, on an island outside Boston Harbor.

Nationwide condemnation rained on Burnside and the administration, and not solely from Democrats; Republicans had been advocates of free speech before the war. Burnside pressed ahead, ordering the opposition *Chicago Times* to stop publication. But in Washington, his civilian superiors understood he was creating a firestorm more damaging than Vallandigham's original criticism—and that Vallandigham at Fort Warren would become "a constant source of irritation and political discussion." On May 19 Lincoln considered the matter with the cabinet. "It was an error on the part of Burnside," Gideon Welles said. "All regretted the arrest." But what to do? Releasing him would embolden people like him. Lincoln chose an alternative: a cavalry detachment escorted the prisoner to Tennessee and passed him over enemy lines, ignoring his protests that he was a loyal citizen. This was a deliberate effort to diminish him; compared with putting him in prison, it "would excite far less sympathy with the prisoner, and, in fact, seriously damage his prestige." It didn't entirely work. Vallandigham slipped out of the Confederacy, booking passage on a blockade runner that evaded Union warships. Within weeks he announced his arrival in Canada. By then, defiant Ohio Democrats had nominated him for governor, and he ran his campaign from a Canadian hotel, where Pendleton went to meet him.

Welles brooded on these events, and his thoughts apparently mirrored Lincoln's. The arrest had "created much feeling. It should not be otherwise. The proceedings were arbitrary and injudicious. It gives bad men the right of questions, an advantage of which they avail themselves. Good men, who wish to defend the Administration, find it difficult to defend these acts." The Ohioan should have been arrested only in a case of great necessity. The government had the right to do it, but it wasn't right.

Burnside, finally realizing the embarrassment he had caused, offered to resign. The president, who'd known him before the war and considered him so honorable that he'd now given Burnside *two* major commands he'd proven incompetent for, replied by refusing to abandon him. "When I shall wish to supersede you I will let you know. All the cabinet regretted the necessity of arresting, for instance, Vallandigham, some perhaps, doubting, that there was a real necessity for it—but, being done, all were for seeing you through with it." Receiving a critical message from New York Democrats, Lincoln responded with a public letter saying he was acting lawfully against "a clear, flagrant, and gigantic case of Rebellion." He said Vallandigham did more than give an opinion; he "was laboring, with some effect, to prevent the raising of troops, to encourage desertions from the army, and to leave the rebellion without an adequate military force to suppress it." But he also admitted, "I do not know whether I would have ordered the arrest of Mr. V." The president's allies praised the letter, though its recipients said he was claiming "more than regal authority."

Soon he had to defend the arrest in person. The Ohio Democratic convention that nominated Vallandigham for governor also appointed delegates to visit the president and demand his return. George H. Pendleton was its chairman. Lincoln would have to face the congressman who'd been present for Vallandigham's speech and would have his own memory of what was said. And Pendleton would be appealing to a president who didn't even approve the arrest.

Soon after the delegation disembarked from their train at the Washington depot, Lincoln received advice from an Ohioan. Chase, the treasury secretary, sent a brief note: "My dear sir. . . . Permit me to suggest that whatever is said to them or replied to them should be in writing. Salmon."

Chase didn't say why he suggested this. He may have hoped that whatever Lincoln wrote could be published to good effect. Communicating in writing would also prevent the Ohio Democrats from giving their own distorted version of whatever Lincoln said. But it's just as likely that Chase didn't trust what Lincoln might say, having already admitted his doubts. Lincoln followed this advice, donning his storyteller's mask. When the delegation came to the White House on the morning of June 25, the president gave them "nearly half an hour," according to one account. The visitors expressed "the injudiciousness and unconstitutionality of the proceedings in the case of Vallandigham—views which they declared to be shared by men of all parties in Ohio. The President said nothing more than courtesy required in response." Lincoln suggested that they write their objections and bring them the next morning.

The delegates brought their papers the next day. Lincoln held his tongue a second time, and promised a note in return.

HE SHARED A DRAFT OF HIS REPLY WITH THE CABINET DURING their meeting on Sunday morning, June 28. The main news of the meeting was a change in command of the Army of the Potomac. Pulling a telegram from his pocket, Lincoln said it was the resignation of Joseph Hooker, the most recent general to fail. Orders had already gone out to replace him with General George Meade, who had to immediately take charge of chasing Lee's army, which was launching a second invasion of the North, crossing Maryland into Pennsylvania. Within three days the armies would collide at Gettysburg.

But before telling the cabinet of this momentous change, Lincoln read aloud his answer to the Democratic delegation. Welles gave a review to his diary: "Save giving too much notoriety and consequence to a graceless traitor who loves notoriety and office, and making factious party men who are using him for the meanest purposes that could influence men in such a crisis conspicuous, the letter is well enough, and well conceived." Lincoln made an astonishing offer: He proposed to allow Vallandigham back into the Union. All Lincoln wanted was for Pendleton's committee to sign their names to a paper admitting some facts:

1. *That there is now a rebellion in the United States, the object and tendency of which is to destroy the national Union; and that in your opinion, an army and navy are constitutional means for suppressing that rebellion.*
2. *That no one of you will do any thing which in his own judgment, will tend to hinder the increase, or favor the decrease, or lessen the efficiency of the army or navy, while engaged in the effort to suppress that rebellion; and,*

3. *That each of you will, in his sphere, do all he can to have the officers, soldiers, and seamen of the army and navy, while engaged in the effort to suppress the rebellion, paid, fed, clad, and otherwise well provided and supported.*

He said causing "influential gentlemen of Ohio" to affirm these statements would be "of immense value" to the war effort, "more than compensating for the consequences of any mistake in allowing Mr. V. to return." Lincoln—the man who said, "Unless among those deficient of intellect, everybody you trade with makes something"—was proposing to trade for Vallandigham. He surely knew Pendleton wouldn't accept this, but also knew the letter would become public. His proposal was a smokescreen, a distraction from the overreach of the arrest.

His letter went to the committee, which rejected his terms. They said if the banishment were "legal" and "deserved," it "ought not to be revoked." That Lincoln would even consider revoking it came near to admitting it wasn't legal or deserved.

Pendleton went on to New York, where he spoke at a Democratic meeting at the Academy of Music on the Fourth of July. Before a "fashionable" crowd (the dress circle was reserved for "ladies and gentlemen accompanying them"), he gave a short, punchy speech. He announced himself as an "ambassador from the Democracy of Ohio, accredited to Abraham Lincoln." People hissed at the president's name. Pendleton denied that "the destruction of these constitutional guarantees and security of personal rights were necessary to a vigorous prosecution of the war." He called for peace. "Compromise is the first law of combination. . . . Partners in business compromise, governments compromise, husband and wife compromise, and the scheme of salvation was compromise by which God accepted in our stead the atonement of his son." People cheered.

The decision of who was right or wrong belonged to the people of Ohio. Tuesday, October 13, was election day there, and by nominating Vallandigham the Democrats had made him the issue. Welles told his diary that day, "The President says he feels nervous. No doubts have troubled me." Lincoln used the word *nervous* to mean depressed. By October 14, however, the telegraph had brought news that Vallandigham was decisively defeated. Welles found Lincoln changed. "I stopped in to see and congratulate the President, who is in good spirits and greatly relieved from the depression of yesterday. He told me he had more anxiety in regard to the election results of yesterday than he had in 1860 when he was chosen. He could not, he said, have believed four years before, that one genuine American would, or could be induced to, vote for such a man as Vallandigham, yet he had been made the candidate of a large party, their representative man, and has received a vote that is a discredit to the country. The President showed a good deal of emotion as he dwelt on this subject, and his regrets were sincere."

Lincoln felt he'd avoided making a bad situation worse. He accepted Burnside's mistake and played it through to the end, and one result was the end of Vallandigham's career. During his Canadian exile he had met Confederate emissaries, adding to doubts about his loyalty. When he eventually returned to the United States, Lincoln's administration made a wiser choice to ignore him. But Pendleton emerged with his stature enhanced, and became a contender for the Democratic presidential nomination in 1864. Burnside's overreach in Ohio became a weapon in Pendleton's hands.

Douglass, 1818–1895, in an illustration from his 1845 memoir.

Chapter 14

ACTIVIST: FREDERICK DOUGLASS

August 10, 1863

THE EMANCIPATION PROCLAMATION GAVE THE UNION A NEW source of manpower. That was its purpose, which Lincoln wrote into the final version issued January 1, 1863. While the last substantive line reflected its righteousness (it was "an act of justice," for which he asked "the gracious favor of Almighty God") the next to last line reflected its practicality: "Persons of suitable condition, will be received into the armed service of the United States to garrison forts, positions, stations, and other places, and to man vessels of all sorts." This was in the Union's interest, while still aligned with a moral purpose. The army was already enlisting Black soldiers along the Mississippi by the time Lincoln issued the Proclamation, and recruitment expanded afterward. Lincoln felt every man freed from slavery provided "double advantage" because he counted as two men—one subtracted from the South's labor force and one added to the Union army. He spoke repeatedly of this calculation.

The months after the Proclamation were the most successful yet for Union arms. Black laborers freed white soldiers for combat, and Black soldiers took part in combat themselves. Union armies grew. Outnumbered

Confederates had trouble replacing their losses, and hurried troops by railroad from state to state, hoping occasionally to overwhelm an isolated enemy. Increasingly capable Union generals pressed their advantages. When Grant besieged rebel forces at Vicksburg, on the Mississippi, a Confederate relief force lingered outside his lines, unable to muster the numbers to break the siege. Vicksburg surrendered on the Fourth of July. Days later Port Hudson surrendered—the final rebel stronghold on the Mississippi, which gave way after Black soldiers took part in bloody assaults. The river was now in Union hands from its source to the Gulf of Mexico.

To the north, the numbers were against Robert E. Lee when his invading army encountered the Army of the Potomac at Gettysburg. His lieutenant James Longstreet urged Lee to choose a strong defensive position and await the attack of the enemy's superior force; instead Lee attacked. His men charged so fiercely during the first three days of July that they seemed near triumph, but the blue-clad troops held higher ground with greater firepower—knocking down approaching rebels first with artillery, then with rifles, and finally with bayonets. Lee took the remnants of his army back to Virginia. During a year in command he'd maneuvered his men audaciously but failed to conserve them, which in the war of numbers was the more strategic skill. Longstreet felt Lee's style cost so many casualties that even his victories "were consuming us, and eventually would destroy us."

Lincoln was living away from the White House during these battles. The executive mansion stood by the marshy Potomac, where the air felt hardly less humid than the river, so in summertime the Lincolns stayed on the grounds of the Old Soldiers' Home—four miles from the mansion, three hundred feet uphill, and a few degrees cooler. Their house stood on a lawn, near a stone hall for military retirees, and also near the cemetery to which the retirees were bound. Sometimes the president received visitors at this breezy spot, but most days he commuted downhill for meetings at the White House, as he did on August 10, 1863. He rode a "good-sized, easy-going gray horse," according to the poet Walt Whitman, who made an entry in his notebook two days later. "I see the President almost every day, as I happen to live where he passes to or from his lodgings." He had a "dark brown face, with deep cut lines" and a "deep latent sadness in the expression." The president on horseback was accompanied by "twenty-five or thirty cavalry, with sabres drawn," while the man they guarded was "dress'd in plain black, somewhat rusty and dusty; wears a black stiff hat."

Brushing the dust of the ride off his shoulders, he went upstairs to his office. He met his cabinet that day, and considered whether to delay drafting men into the army after conscription triggered riots in New York. (Lincoln said no.) He wrote a reassuring letter to William Rosecrans, a Union general in Tennessee with whom he'd had a disagreement. ("I am not watching you with an evil eye.") He met visitors who crowded the anteroom to overflowing; some even waited on the stairs. People wanted jobs; businessmen wanted contracts; mothers wanted sons released from prison.

An aide brought in a card that bore the name of Frederick Douglass. Lincoln, sprawled on a low chair with his feet in front of him, looked up and said to send him in.

Douglass was the most famous person who visited that day, having been a celebrity for two decades. Admirers arranged to take his photograph; detractors caricatured him in cartoons. Thousands attended his speeches, and rock-throwing mobs occasionally drove him offstage. Abolitionists sent him to speak in Europe while slave states banned his books. He was regularly mentioned in newspapers and was a special favorite of conservative editors, who smeared white antislavery leaders by saying they were following this Black man's agenda. Some politicians thought it was devastating just to say his name: during the Illinois senatorial debates of 1858, Stephen Douglas connected Lincoln's beliefs to "Fred Douglass" no fewer than twenty times. His place in the national imagination was remarkable considering that he lived far from any power center, led no group or institution, and held no office. His sole source of influence was his words. For nearly sixteen years he'd edited his newspaper in Rochester under various titles, and the current one, *Douglass' Monthly*, reflected his fame as a speaker, intellectual, and memoirist. He'd grown up enslaved in Maryland under the name Frederick Bailey, then changed it after his 1838 escape to make it harder for slave-catchers to find him. His story became the basis of his books and added power to his editorials. His newspaper was "an appeal from the very heart of slavery," according to an article in his defense. "It is the sufferer uttering his own appeal."

The year leading up to his visit with Lincoln ranked among the most agonizing and triumphant of his life. At the start of that period there was no Emancipation Proclamation, and the government was ignoring his calls to employ Black troops. He collected accounts of enslaved people who risked their lives to give intelligence to the army—even when the army did not free them. The Black man was patriotic despite "every possible discouragement." In this attitude "the Negro is wise," because "whether our rulers know it or not, wish it or not, they are striking a blow for the destruction of slavery." He hoped the rulers would catch on, but he found the president backward. Lincoln was still interested in colonization, inviting a group of free Black leaders to hear his ideas and telling them the presence of Black people had brought on the war. Reading a transcript of this meeting, Douglass replied in his paper: "Every man who has an ounce of brain in his head" knew Lincoln was wrong, that "the mere presence of the colored race never could have provoked this horrid and desolating rebellion. . . . No, Mr. President, it is not the innocent horse that makes the horse thief."

When Lincoln published his Proclamation, Douglass responded as if Lincoln were a dithering homeowner who finally decided to spray water on his burning house: "Common sense, the necessities of the war, to say nothing of the dictation of justice and humanity have at last prevailed." He did believe the president would follow through: "Abraham Lincoln will take no step backward." The opposite would happen. Emancipation would spread beyond the Proclamation's limits. Days before it took effect he gave an exultant speech in a Rochester church: "Slavery once abolished in the Rebel States, will give the death wound to slavery in the border states. When Arkansas is a free State Missouri cannot be a slave State." The Proclamation was a revolutionary instrument disguised as a military document. The date of its enactment would be the greatest day in history, "a day for poetry and song."

While Lincoln saw a double advantage for the Union in employing Black troops, Douglass saw a double advantage for the troops, who would destroy slavery and demand equal rights. "Colored men going into the army and navy of the United States must expect annoyance, but let no man hold back on this account. We shall be fighting a double battle, against slavery in the South and against prejudice and proscription in the North." His words caught the attention of George Stearns, a white abolitionist recruiting a Black regiment of free Northern men, the Fifty-Fourth Massachusetts. Stearns asked for help, and Douglass produced an article headlined MEN OF COLOR, TO ARMS! He became a recruiter himself, telling potential soldiers, "You will receive the same wages, the same rations, the same equipments, the same protection, the same treatment, and the same bounty, secured to the white soldiers." He threw his reputation behind this promise, saying that after "twenty years of devotion to our common cause" he could be trusted. "The iron gate of our prison stands half open." Two of his sons enlisted, and one of them, Lewis Douglass, became a sergeant—a noncommissioned officer. The commissioned officers above Lewis—lieutenants, captains, majors—were white. They were led by Colonel Robert Shaw, a white veteran of Antietam. Shaw was qualified and courageous, but it was jarring to learn that the War Department hadn't commissioned any Black officers. Their lack of experience was no explanation: Well-connected white men had become officers and even generals with scant military backgrounds. Douglass was forced to explain treatment that was less equal than he promised.

ON JULY 4, 1863, THE DAY GRANT ACCEPTED THE SURRENDER OF Vicksburg, Douglass was in Philadelphia, attending a review of "several hundred stalwart negroes" who were in training for "the Black Brigade of Pennsylvania." Two days later he spoke at a recruiting event in Philadelphia's National Hall, "filled to overflowing" with a mixed-race crowd as a band played "John Brown's Soul Is Marching On." But discrimination undermined his recruiting. Not only did the War Department fail to commission Black officers; it failed to provide the equal pay he'd promised. White private soldiers were paid thirteen dollars per month while Black soldiers received seven, the rate for ordinary Black laborers. If troops refused to serve on those terms they would be cast as disloyal. Many chose to serve while refusing any pay; one sergeant called the injustice the "Lincoln despotism."

Confederate president Jefferson Davis answered the Emancipation Proclamation with a proclamation of his own, saying "that all negro slaves captured in arms" should be turned over to "their respective states" who would deal with them according to state law, returning them to slavery or killing them. Black troops wanted Lincoln to announce a policy of retaliation, executing a Confederate prisoner for any Black soldier killed. A newspaper in Vermont warned that "Negroes here who have enlisted are getting alarmed at the silence of the government in this respect."

It had been presumed that Black soldiers would be kept away from the greatest danger of capture; the Proclamation said they would "garrison forts, positions, stations, and other places," and didn't mention front-line combat. But combat could hardly be avoided in a war so vast and brutal, and some men wanted to prove themselves. When the Fifty-Fourth Massachusetts deployed to the islands around Charleston, Colonel Shaw asked for his regiment to have the honor of leading an attack. On July 18 they assaulted Fort Wagner, a strongpoint on Morris Island that commanded the entrance to the harbor. The fort was as well guarded by the marshy landscape as by its guns; the blue-uniformed soldiers could approach only by running one thousand yards along a sandy beach under enemy fire. Rebel cannons fired grapeshot and canister—clusters of projectiles that turned artillery into giant shotguns—which "swept us down like chaff," said Sergeant Lewis Douglass in a letter to his father, but "still our men went on and on." The troops climbed the fort's wall and briefly planted their flag, but were forced to retreat; hundreds were killed or wounded, and the dead included Colonel Shaw. Lewis reported that "the splendid 54th is cut to pieces." His sword sheath was shot off as he stood on Fort Wagner's parapet, and he ended the letter: "If I die tonight I will not die a coward. Good bye." Fears emerged that the rebels were executing prisoners. The *New York Tribune* said the Fifty-Fourth had shown their "devotion to the cause of a country which has never yet recognized their rights."

The same article on July 31 listed groups of Black men believed to have been massacred elsewhere—teamsters in Tennessee, much of a regiment in Louisiana, and every Black prisoner at Vicksburg. Douglass may have had this newspaper in hand on August 1, because he listed each of these incidents in a letter announcing his dissent from the administration. He wrote the head recruiter, George Stearns, to say he couldn't continue. "Colored men have much overrated the enlightenment, justice and generosity of our rulers at Washington. In my humble way I have contributed somewhat to that false estimate." Even he, who had wanted Black men to prove their manhood, wondered if his son and others were cannon fodder. His newspaper asked what had happened to the promise of safer duty garrisoning forts. "Was that a trick?" Were Black men being exposed to *more* danger than their white comrades? This was unfair—thousands of white men died in equally senseless charges—but there was enough discrimination to give him reason for despair.

Unwilling to lose his prize recruiter, Stearns met him in Philadelphia and said the administration was beginning to address his concerns. Lincoln had finally issued an order of retaliation against Confederate prisoners. When Douglass asked why it had taken so long, Stearns suggested that he take his case to Washington—which was a provocative idea for a man of Douglass's background. He'd never seen the capital despite his decades of political activity. A problem of geography had stopped him: He needed to pass through Maryland, where he'd escaped from slavery, and he felt unsafe there even after friends bought his free status. "Whenever I got as far south as Philadelphia, I felt that I was rubbing against my prison wall, and could not go any further." But Stearns gave him a letter that would be helpful if anyone questioned him, which said he was "to transact business connected with the Recruiting Service of the *United States Colored Volunteers.*" He passed through without incident on the Baltimore and Ohio line, crossing long stone trestles that must have made him feel he was flying over Maryland's valleys. Then the cars clattered into the District of Columbia depot, where he emerged two blocks from the Capitol. Its brand-new white dome wasn't quite complete: workers had not yet placed the Statue of Freedom on top.

Stepping out of the terminal onto New Jersey Avenue, he began a visit that tested his faith in the democratic process. He once had scorned that process; upon his escape in 1838 he became an acolyte of William Lloyd Garrison, the Boston publisher of the *Liberator*, who didn't vote and favored breaking up the Union because slavery so corrupted the Constitution: "No union with slaveholders" was a Garrison slogan. As late as 1847 he shared a stage with Garrison in New York City and declared, "I have no love for America, as such; I have no patriotism; I have no country." How could he support a country where both church and Constitution "are in favor of supporting and perpetuating this monstrous system of injustice and blood?"

But Douglass changed his views after he started an antislavery newspaper in Rochester. There, in New York's Finger Lakes region, he met other activists and grew interested in other causes: in 1848 he attended a convention at Seneca Falls, where women demanded their right to vote. In New York a Black man already *could* vote (so long as he owned $250 in property, a barrier that didn't apply to white men). He decided that "to abstain from voting was to refuse to exercise a legitimate and powerful means for abolishing slavery." There was no reason to abandon the Union when free states could outvote slave states. The Constitution "was in its letter and spirit an antislavery instrument," which never spoke slavery's name and looked to its end. The principles of the Declaration were "saving principles." During an Independence Day speech in 1852 he still separated himself from the country, talking to his listeners of "the birthday of *your* national independence"; but he later spoke of the nation as "we," observing in 1862 that Black as well as white men had fought in the armies of the Revolution: "We are only continuing the tremendous struggle, which your fathers, and my fathers began eighty-six years ago." He pragmatically supported the rise of the Republican party, even though its platform stopped short of abolition.

Republicans didn't fully return his loyalty. In 1860 he campaigned for a New York State ballot measure to erase the $250 property requirement for Black voters, but it failed even as Lincoln won the state. Nonetheless he understood the national results as an overthrow of the slave power; and his much-delayed reward for so many frustrations was the Proclamation, an achievement that he understood better than much of the country did. For a long time after January 1, Copperheads argued against abolition, but Douglass knew the argument was over. Or rather, *that* argument was over. Others remained, about the place of an entire liberated race in American society, and he had come to Washington as one of the first people to press those arguments.

REPUBLICAN SENATOR SAMUEL POMEROY AGREED TO SERVE AS Douglass's guide, and took him past the White House to the next building down Pennsylvania Avenue, the four-story structure that housed the War Department. Pomeroy wanted him to meet Edwin Stanton. They made it through the crowds in the secretary's anteroom and found Stanton, an imposing man with a massive beard, standing at his chest-high writing desk staring through his glasses. He was a terrifying presence, known to shout at visitors and even tear up the papers they brought him. His manners expressed his power: His fellow cabinet member Gideon Welles felt Stanton loved to "dominate over his fellow man," and even "took pleasure in being ungracious and rough toward those who were under his control." It was fortunate that Douglass had come in the company of Senator Pomeroy, a member of the Radical Republican faction whom Stanton cultivated. Stanton stopped the flow of visitors past his desk and conversed with Douglass for thirty minutes.

"His manner was cold and business like throughout but earnest," said Douglass afterward. He offered Stanton an education about the Black men his department was recruiting. It was a mistake, Douglass said, to regard a Black man as "an angel or a demon." He was subject to human strengths and frailties, and human incentives. "The Government in raising colored troops should conform to these essential facts. The [secretary] instantly inquired in what respect the present conditions of colored enlistments conflicted with the views I had expressed. I answered 'In the unequal pay accorded to colored soldiers and in the fact that no incentive was given to the ambition of colored soldiers.'" No man could be promoted to an officer's rank for meritorious service. Douglass was making his case in terms that Lincoln himself would have understood; he said equality was in the national interest because it would encourage Black men to fight.

Stanton agreed. He claimed to favor a bill for equal pay that Congress had failed to pass, though it wasn't clear that any change in law was necessary. On another matter Stanton was more satisfying: He favored the appointment of Black officers and proposed to commission Frederick Douglass himself. A general had been sent to organize Black regiments among the newly freed men along the Mississippi; Douglass should join him and break the color barrier.

Pomeroy next took Douglass to the White House, where Douglass sent in his card. He expected a long wait; "the stairway was crowded with applicants" and "they were white," while "I was the only dark spot among them." But within two minutes a man emerged and respectfully invited in "Mr. Douglass." He walked in to see Abraham Lincoln, who had never met him despite all the times that their critics had linked their names. The president was sprawled in his chair, his legs so long that his feet were "in different parts of the room." Then he rose and warmly extended a hand. The activist was impressed. "I have never seen a more transparent countenance. There was not the slightest shadow of embarrassment after the first moment," he said in a letter immediately afterward.

Lincoln put him at ease. "Mr. Douglass, I know you; I have read about you, and Mr. Seward has told me about you." He had even *read* Douglass. As Douglass recounted, "I had made a little speech, somewhere in New York, and it had got into the papers, and among the things I had said was this: That if I were called upon to state what I regarded as the most sad and most disheartening feature in our present political and military situation, it would not be the various disasters experienced by our armies and our navies, on flood and field, but it would be the tardy, hesitating, vacillating policy of the President of the United States." Lincoln managed to invoke Douglass's harsh words in a way that didn't derail the meeting; he simply answered the accusation. "The President said to me, 'Mr. Douglass, I have been charged with being tardy and the like'; and he went on, and partly admitted that he might seem slow; but he said, 'I am charged with vacillating; but, Mr. Douglass, I do not think the charge can be sustained; I think it cannot be shown that when I have once taken a position, I have ever retreated from it.'"

Douglass took this as Lincoln's most important remark. "Whoever else might abandon his anti slavery policy President Lincoln would stand firm to his."

The president then spoke of politics that caused him to act slowly. He considered the employment of Black soldiers an "experiment" that would bring great advantages to Black people, but he faced resistance on every detail that might imply their equality with white men. "He said that he had difficulty getting colored men into the United States uniform; that when the purpose was fixed to employ them as soldiers, several different uniforms were proposed for them, and that it was something gained when it was finally determined to clothe them like other soldiers."

Why had Lincoln waited more than half a year to issue an order of retaliation for attacks on Black soldiers? "Had he sooner issued that proclamation such was the state of public popular prejudice that an outcry would have been raised against the measure. It would be said 'Ah! We thought it would come to this. White men were to be killed for negroes.' His general view was that the battles in which negroes had distinguished themselves for bravery and general good conduct was the necessary preparation of the public mind for his proclamation." The president said something similar about unequal pay: white prejudice demanded unfairness in this early stage, but that would be corrected in time. Douglass concluded the president's approach was "reasonable." By 1864 Congress provided equal pay.

Long afterward Douglass reflected on their personal connection. "I account partially for his kindness to me because of the similarity with which I had fought my way up, we both starting at the lowest round of the ladder." Yet he didn't entirely trust the administration. Told of Stanton's proposal to make him an officer, Lincoln said he'd sign any commission Stanton sent him. He later signed a letter to assure Douglass safe passage in the South. Douglass returned to Rochester and prepared to leave, going so far as to shut down his newspaper. But a commission never arrived in the mail, and Douglass didn't want to travel south on faith without receiving the paper. Lincoln eventually did commission other Black officers, but for whatever reason Douglass never joined the army.

He resumed lending his name to the Union cause. Sometimes his speeches mentioned his meeting with the president, which was itself an advertisement for equality. He said Lincoln was "wise, great, and eloquent," but above all "honest"—about political reality. He wasn't in charge. "We are not to be saved by the captain at this time, but by the crew. We are not to be saved by Abraham Lincoln, but by the power behind the throne, greater than the throne itself. You and I and all of us have this matter in hand." They were fighting for something "incomparably better than the old Union," a new Union "in which there shall be no North, no South, no East, no West, no black, no white, but a solidarity of the nation, making every slave free, and every free man a voter."

Achieving this would require a change in the views of the crew, and after the meeting Lincoln intensified his effort to shape public opinion. He received an invitation to address a mass meeting of "unconditional Union men" back home in Springfield. "I can not leave here now," Lincoln replied, but he wrote a letter for a friend to read aloud: "You are one of the best public readers. I have but one suggestion. Read it very slowly." He seized this chance to be heard in the state capital where Democrats had repudiated his work; and on the day of the meeting Lincoln's friend shouted out the letter that was aimed at his critics. "You desire peace," he said, "and you blame me that we do not have it. But how can we attain it?" They could crush the rebellion; give up the Union; or compromise. But compromise was impossible and Lincoln wouldn't surrender the Union. That left crushing the rebellion. There was nothing for Union men to disagree about.

Lincoln named the real problem. "To be plain, you are dissatisfied with me about the negro. Quite likely there is a difference of opinion between you and myself upon that subject. I certainly wish that all men could be free, while I suppose you do not." This didn't matter, Lincoln said. The Emancipation Proclamation was helping to save the Union. "Some of the commanders of our armies in the field who have given us our most important successes, believe the emancipation policy, and the use of colored troops, constitute the heaviest blow yet dealt to the rebellion."

Weeks later Lincoln would speak at the dedication of a battlefield cemetery at Gettysburg, touching on similar themes from a much higher altitude. The 272 words of the Gettysburg Address were polished for the ages, while his 1,677 words to his critics in Springfield were raw, spoken for the moment, dwelling on race, politics, and power. "You say you will not fight to free negroes. Some of them seem willing to fight for you; but, no matter. Fight you, then, exclusively to save the Union." Whatever Black men did as soldiers left less work for white men. "Does it appear otherwise to you? But negroes, like other people, act upon motives. Why should they do any thing for us, if we will do nothing for them? If they stake their lives for us, they must be prompted by the strongest motive—even the promise of freedom. And the promise being made, must be kept."

In his meeting with Douglass he'd depended on candor: admitting he was not yet doing all that justice required. Now he was candid with white voters, reminding them that the Mississippi River was in Union hands. "The Father of Waters again goes unvexed to the sea," he said. This colorful phrase became one of Lincoln's most famous lines, an irresistible description of one of the great strategic victories of the war. But Lincoln was not merely marking a victory. He was saying that victory had come because of a move toward racial equality. Troops from every part of the country had been involved, Lincoln said—including some from "the Sunny South," who were of "more colors than one." He was telling skeptics that a measure of equality served their interests.

Frances Clayton, who served in a Union uniform, as did Mary Ellen Wise, 1847–?.

Chapter 15

SOLDIER: MARY ELLEN WISE

September 1864

CALLERS AT THE WHITE HOUSE SOMETIMES INCLUDED COMmon soldiers. Their visits to the commander in chief might be outside the chain of command, but Lincoln knew the culture of equality too well to deny them. "Anything that kept the people themselves away from him he disapproved," his secretary said. So on December 23, 1863, he saw an army corporal who seemingly had gone on leave and failed to return on time. Fearing that "he may be arrested, convicted, and punished as a deserter," he traveled to Washington in civilian clothes, trusting that the president would understand. Lincoln wrote the man an order "to report forthwith to his regiment for duty," and pardoned him provided that he honorably completed his enlistment. Weeks later a private appeared at the White House fearing a similar charge of desertion, and Lincoln wrote him a similar note. Both letters mixed generosity with pragmatism: in each case he overlooked the regulations, and also sent a soldier back to the fight.

He needed every soldier he could get. The number of Union dead was climbing into the hundreds of thousands, and victory was not in sight. In the spring of 1864 he changed commanders once again, summoning Ulysses S. Grant eastward to take charge of all Union armies. When Grant came by to receive his promotion, Lincoln explained political reality: he'd intervened repeatedly in military affairs because "the pressure from the people at the North and Congress" was "always" on him to win. He needed Grant to "take the responsibility and act." Grant understood and ordered a southward advance on Lee's army in Virginia. But Lee's battlefield losses finally forced him to conserve the men who remained; they dug protective trenches and shot down many attackers before retreating to their next line of defense. The murderous pattern repeated into the summer. Grant neared Richmond but didn't reach it. Newspapers printed long lists of soldiers killed and wounded. The dead had to be replaced through the draft, which was unpopular. And it was an election year.

The service of Black soldiers had reduced opposition to the Emancipation Proclamation, but slavery's future remained unknown. The Republican-led Senate approved abolishing slavery with the Thirteenth Amendment to the Constitution, but it stalled in the House. The fall election would decide its fate. Frederick Douglass, who normally wrote and spoke loudly at election time, fell strategically silent; he said his Republican allies "do not wish to expose themselves to the charge of being the 'N—r' party. The Negro is the deformed child, which is put out of the room when company comes."

Lincoln privately wrote a prediction in August: "It seems exceedingly probable that this Administration will not be re-elected." His defeat would put the Union at risk, because it would be taken as a vote against the war.

He grew so desperate to find manpower and votes that he listened when an army officer brought him a plan to enlist the enemy's own soldiers. Henry Huidekoper, a former Harvard classmate of Robert Todd

Lincoln, had lost an arm at Gettysburg, and Lincoln felt for him. Still determined to serve, Huidekoper proposed to recruit Union soldiers from among Confederate prisoners of war in a camp at Rock Island, Illinois. Rebels would change sides in exchange for their freedom. What made this politically appealing was that the new soldiers would be counted as if they had been drafted from Huidekoper's home state of Pennsylvania, reducing Pennsylvania's draft quota and pleasing Pennsylvania voters. Grant disapproved and Stanton called it improper, but Lincoln pushed the plan for weeks until 1,800 former Confederates traded gray uniforms for blue. To reduce their chances of defecting they were sent to guard against Indians in the West.

Lincoln was just starting to get Stanton on board with this scheme when the political environment began improving. Democrats held their convention in late August and nominated two Georges: McClellan for president and Pendleton for vice president. The victor of Antietam was popular among veterans, while Pendleton had his reputation as a defender of constitutional rights. But McClellan was a War Democrat and Pendleton a Peace Democrat, and their party endorsed a peace platform. Democrats had exposed their own divides; and their call for peace negotiations began to seem ill-timed in light of news from the battlefield. Jefferson Davis, who didn't seem to understand the war of numbers, replaced the general defending the approaches to Atlanta, who'd been slowly giving ground before a superior force and striking when he found advantage. The new commander, John Bell Hood, believed in headlong charges even after he lost the use of an arm in one battle and had a leg amputated after another. Pointing the way forward with his one good hand, Hood wasted thousands of his men in fruitless attacks and also lost the city on September 2.

On September 6 Lincoln showed a range of emotions, according to one of his visitors, a pastor who found him in his office "alone, sitting at a table covered with documents which he had been studying." By his side was a basket of peaches. He'd been eating them as he read, biting them like apples "without any visible accessories of knife and plate." He chatted with the pastor about the Democratic convention, talking "with his head leaning forward in his characteristic way, as if he would thrust his face into yours." McClellan hadn't said if he accepted his party's platform, and Lincoln joked he never would, since his great strength was "indecision."

His mood changed when a secretary stuck his head in to the office. A woman in the anteroom was seeking clemency for her son. He was accused of desertion and "inducing others to desert," and in this case the president could find no reason to pardon him.

Lincoln declined to see the mother. "Tell her that I shall do nothing about it."

The secretary replied, "She is terribly distressed. Can't I say, sir, that you are still considering it?"

"Well, if you choose; but I shall not interfere."

The pastor felt Lincoln was "almost unmanned by the report of a woman weeping at the door."

During this unsettled day another woman arrived. She said she'd been a soldier, had been wounded in action, and wanted to collect her back pay.

SHE GAVE HER NAME AS MARY ELLEN WISE, AND SAID SHE'D DISguised her name, gender, and age to join the Thirty-Fourth Indiana Volunteers. Her story was exceptionally hard to document, but before this meeting she'd been written up in several newspapers, including by reporters who found her in uniform in war zones.

Newspapers highlighted her as an example of the phenomenon of women who served. Donning uniforms as their husbands, brothers, and fathers did, they enlisted to follow friends and relations, escape trouble at home, or serve a cause larger than themselves. Their numbers were impossible to estimate because they served under aliases and because of the obliviousness of men around them. The idea of a woman cutting her hair, wearing pants, and participating in the ultimate male activity of killing was so foreign to the culture that some men didn't know it when they saw it. One male soldier's comrade was jokingly dubbed "Our Woman" by the troops, but he didn't realize she *was* a woman until later. Other men were more perceptive, but looked the other way. Authorities around Washington suspected 150 women found in uniform over time had "colluded" with the surgeons who gave them cursory examinations as they enlisted. Some women were aides to officers. It's hard to imagine how women lived in tents and bathed in streams near thousands of men without being discovered, but people bathed very infrequently. In Kentucky, a female soldier who went by the pseudonym "Frank" told a reporter she had "discovered a great many females in the army" and helped to bury three of them.

In May 1863, Ellie B. Reno was discovered after almost a year in the army, and wrote to Lincoln begging for permission "to remain in that Noble cause which I have sworn to defend." She was "willing to do any thing to aid and assist the Government" and said she would die for the cause. "I write this to ask you as a Child would ask a Father if I can remain in your Service, being as I have left my own Father and adopted you instead." There's no record that Lincoln replied; he was busy trying to get Black men into the army. But he did see Mary Ellen Wise. She said she was from Jefferson Township in Huntington County, Indiana, and would be turning eighteen in February 1865—meaning she was born in 1847. No document shows such a person from Huntington County, Indiana, though census records do show a Mary Wise who was born in 1847 and lived just outside the county. If that was the Mary Wise who visited the president, then she was a farmer's daughter. Her parents had seven children, five of them girls.

As she told the story to the newspapers, her brother enlisted at the start of the war and fourteen-year-old Mary Ellen followed "in consequence of a home made unpleasant by a step-mother." She added that "she loved the Union and was anxious to fight for it." Joining the Thirty-Fourth Indiana Volunteers, a regiment of about seven hundred, she was in "six battles and many skirmishes, has carried her musket and punished hard tack like a veteran," referring to a dry biscuit that soldiers carried on the march. She was at the battle of Shiloh and later at Stones River, in Tennessee, where she received a musket ball in her side. She was sent "from there by hospital boat to Louisville, where she went into a hospital and had her sex discovered the first time the wound was dressed." She endured "weary months of pain" until she could be sent home in the spring of 1863. It was in Louisville that she first made the papers: an article on May 21 described an unnamed female soldier with a story essentially like Mary Ellen's—she fought at Shiloh and Stones River, was wounded, came to Louisville, and was starting home. Numerous later articles included her name.

The newspapermen who met her found her so credible that they apparently didn't look for proof of her story. They would have been surprised if they had. Records for her regiment didn't show William Wise or James Wise, the pseudonyms she claimed to have used. It was still plausible that she attached herself to the Thirty-Fourth, which had three soldiers named Wise and recruits from around Huntington. But the rest of her story didn't match the history of her unit; she reported participating in different battles than her regiment did.

The simplest explanation for the discrepancies is that she invented her story. But there were other explanations; for example, that something was garbled in translation, an older newspaperman not listening well to a young woman. She could have left the Thirty-Fourth and drifted to another regiment: women who were discovered and turned out of a unit sometimes joined another. A different Indiana regiment, the Thirty-Seventh, had a record that resembled the claims she made for her service. But all that's independently confirmed is that she turned up in the South.

Later, she traveled to the South in uniform a second time. This is known because she was arrested in the spring of 1864. On a train to Nashville, she was recognized by a soldier who knew her from the Louisville hospital, and "the Military Conductor" took into custody this member of the Thirty-Fourth Indiana: "She was dressed in full uniform, and displayed the badge which indicates the rank of an orderly sergeant." It wasn't clear how she had obtained her sergeant's stripes. "The Conductor carried her to Nashville, and reported her to the Provost Marshal for disposal."

In Nashville a newspaperman met her and reported, "She likes to be a soldier first-rate." He found her admirable. "This girl, erratic as her course may have been, has patriotism enough to put to shame the deeds of some of our so-called Union men. Browned with sun and wind, with short hair worn boy's fashion, and in uniform, there is nothing to betray her sex except the head." This was one of two articles that commented on her brown skin, raising the possibility that the woman who passed as a man may also have been passing as white.

Immediately after the Nashville interview she boarded a train toward Indiana. But she didn't stay long. By midsummer 1864 she was in Washington, according to another newspaper. "Mary E. Wise, a female private of the 34th Indiana Volunteers, presented herself at the Paymaster General's office this morning and drew her pay for two years military service," said the report on August 12. The paper reported that she had been wounded not once or twice, as prior accounts had said, but three times. Also, "Mary is by no means bad looking."

This article was definite in saying she'd been paid for her service. A later article was equally definite in saying that she had *not* been paid. Or maybe she'd received only part of her pay: "There is a female here appealing for five months' back pay due her as a soldier in the army. Her name is Mary E. Wise." Her list of battles lengthened: now she'd been at Chickamauga in northern Georgia and Lookout Mountain in Tennessee. Other parts of her story matched what she'd said in the past. She still didn't get along with her stepmother, who "refused her shelter" when she returned to Indiana. This was why she had traveled to the capital. "Here her troubles have only increased," said the correspondent. "She cannot get her pay," because she didn't have papers showing a proper discharge. She was "without friends or means, wholly dependent upon the bounty of the Sanitary Commission," the organization that ran hospitals for veterans.

"In her difficulties she has, repeatedly, endeavored to refer her case to the President," the article said, but "not having influential friends to back her, she has been disappointed in all her efforts to see him."

SINCE THEN SHE'D MADE AN INFLUENTIAL FRIEND. SHE VISITED Lincoln with Charles Case, a former Republican congressman from Indiana. Lincoln knew Case, who was in office in 1860, when Indiana Republicans supported Lincoln. Leaving Congress in 1861, he recruited Indiana soldiers and performed well enough that Lincoln took note of his work in a letter. Case later received a commission as a colonel commanding a regiment in Tennessee. Lincoln even appointed him as an army paymaster, and in 1864 the Senate confirmed him. Though it's unclear how much work Case did as a paymaster, it's possible that his position brought him in contact with the woman from his former congressional district. He was just the man to vouch for her to the president, wobbly though her story may have been.

Lincoln supported people when his political friends spoke up for them. The previous year a New Jersey woman had asked him to discharge a son from the army after another son was killed at Gettysburg. Lincoln neither accepted her tale nor ordered a search of army records. Instead he wrote a letter saying he would allow the discharge "if Hon. Daniel S. Gregory will say in writing on this sheet, that he personally knows" the mother and "that he fully believes this statement." D. S. Gregory affirmed her story and her son was discharged.

When Charles Case walked in the door on September 6, the president looked up from his papers and peaches to see an ally from a state he needed to win again. Case also was one of the Radical Republicans, whom Lincoln wanted to appease. Some Radicals, still feeling Lincoln was moving too slowly against slavery, were flirting with a third-party presidential candidate—John C. Frémont, their favorite since his attempt at emancipation in 1861. If Frémont was on the ballot he would fatally split the antislavery vote.

When the meeting was over Case spoke to the *Washington Chronicle*, which gave the story this headline: A TECHNICAL POINT DISPOSED OF BY THE PRESIDENT—A LADY SOLDIER. Case described her as "a modest young girl, apparently about twenty years of age," who was ushered in the room "bearing a letter from the Paymaster General's office." She was "born of poor, but honest parents," and at the beginning of the war her parents "both died." That was why she joined her brother in the Thirty-Fourth Indiana. "Procuring a disguise, she succeeded in being accepted as a private soldier, and through two long years of arduous services, during which the regiment engaged in several severe battles, among which was that of Stone river, she prevented the discovery of her sex, though she never failed to do her duty as a soldier."

When she came to Washington a paymaster said "there was nothing in the regulations that would permit him to pay a United States soldier of the female sex." Lincoln was "deeply interested," and reached for a piece of paper. According to Case, who surely had Lincoln's blessing to publicize the story, Lincoln "wrote a note to the Paymaster General, saying that, as she had faithfully served as a soldier for two years, and received the pay as such for the greater part of the time, he could see no good reason why she was not entitled to the remainder, and therefore directed the payment of the balance, concluding with the assurance that, if hereafter it would be found to be contrary to the regulations, he himself would be responsible for the amount." A soldier was entitled to thirteen dollars per month, so Lincoln was directing a payment of sixty-five dollars, and potentially putting himself on the hook for it.

The article concluded: "The young lady retired, well pleased with her interview, and started for home in Indiana the next day, having fully accomplished the object of her visit."

Thanks to Case, Lincoln had a news story that was reprinted in multiple papers, reinforcing his image as a man of the people; he'd looked after a poor girl from the state where he'd been a poor boy. Not only that: he publicly approved of a woman who violated traditional gender norms. He knew that many women had pushed conventional boundaries to make political statements against slavery—organizing meetings, cheering Jessie Benton Frémont, writing articles and books. Harriet Beecher Stowe had visited him in the White House, and he had sent to the Library of Congress for *A Key to Uncle Tom's Cabin*, her book of documents compiled while researching slavery for her novel. Women could not vote for him in

1864, but given their activism it didn't hurt him to gesture in their direction.

Many years earlier he'd mentioned the idea of women in military service. Announcing his bid for reelection to the Illinois legislature in 1836, he published an article including this passage:

> *I go for all sharing the privileges of the government, who assist in bearing its burthens. Consequently I go for admitting all whites to the right of suffrage, who pay taxes or bear arms, (by no means excluding females.)*

He not only endorsed voting rights for some women, but also seemed to contemplate a world in which women might bear arms. Because he said "pay taxes *or* bear arms," one might infer that he simply meant to include the occasional woman who owned taxable property. But Lincoln was a precise writer who tried to say what he meant and foreclose what he didn't. When a female soldier reached his office twenty-eight years later it didn't bother him. At least by her own inconsistent account, she had done her part in the war of numbers, joining all the other kinds of people who had put on the uniform. That was the deciding factor for him.

With Lincoln's letter in hand, Mary Ellen Wise now could walk next door to the War Department to collect. But the newspaper was wrong about what she did next. Instead of starting home, she continued living with a soldier's wife at one of the area hospitals run by the Sanitary Commission. She also met a Sergeant Forehand, a member of the Veteran Reserve Corps. He'd been wounded in battle and received a disability discharge, but returned to service—the veteran reserve was called the Invalid Corps, maimed and hobbling troops who manned fortifications around Washington to ease the manpower shortage. After a brief romance the young couple married at the hospital in October, in a ceremony performed by the institution's chaplain as "quite a number of their soldier-friends" looked on.

A newspaper story cast it as a romantic ending ("Uncle Sam thereby losing a brave soldier, and the sergeant finding a good wife") but four months later she made the papers again in an article headlined A DANGEROUS WIFE. Police arrested her "on the complaint of her husband, who charged that she had followed him several days armed with a pistol and threatening to take his life." This was February 1865; she was "about 18 or 20 years old, and is considerably tanned by the sun during her service in an Indiana regiment." Sergeant Forehand didn't want to prosecute "but only wanted to be safe," so a judge ordered her "to leave the city in the first train, and she took her departure in the 6 p.m. train." Sergeant Lloyd D. Forehand returned to his home state of New Hampshire and successfully sued there for divorce, accusing his absent wife of infidelity. Late in life, according to a family tradition, he claimed his ex-wife had been a Confederate spy. There was no more evidence of that than there was for any other claim about her.

For Lincoln's purposes it didn't matter who she was. He won the November election. Democrats never resolved the conflict between their war and peace wings. Lincoln persuaded Frémont to drop the third-party bid, partly by making a sacrifice: he dismissed a member of his cabinet, Montgomery Blair, of the Blair family that the Frémonts now despised. With fewer candidates to divide the vote he increased his totals from 1860, receiving a majority of the popular vote and a landslide in the electoral vote.

In Illinois, the Democratic legislature elected in 1862 in protest against the war and the Proclamation was voted out in favor of a Republican legislature that supported both. The new legislature soon dismantled the Illinois Black Laws. The Lincoln-aligned *Illinois State Journal* celebrated the repeal of these "odious and barbarous" laws that had "so long polluted our Statute Books and disgraced the state"; residents including Lincoln's barber William Florville were freed from their restrictions by early 1865. John T. Stuart, Lincoln's onetime law partner who'd turned against him, was voted out of Congress in favor of a Lincoln ally. And in Washington that winter, the president renewed his effort to persuade the House to approve the constitutional amendment banning slavery.

Beyond his policies, the public had come to know the president through many reported encounters like that with Mary Ellen Wise—stories that portrayed him as generous, sensible, human, wise. A man who related to ordinary people. Who could be trusted to look after their interests. And who knew his one priority: supporting people who supported the war.

Campbell, 1811–1889, during his time on the Supreme Court.

Chapter 16

JUSTICE: JOHN A. CAMPBELL

April 4, 1865

SHORTLY BEFORE LINCOLN'S SECOND INAUGURATION HIS BEST friend, Joshua Speed, visited him at the White House. It was near the end of the day, and Lincoln told him to take a newspaper and sit while he disposed of callers.

Speed noticed two women "in humble attire" sitting by the fireplace. They were waiting their turn while Lincoln met people, some leaving satisfied and others not. Finally only the women remained, and Lincoln turned to them "with rather a peevish and fretful air," and said, "Well, ladies, what can I do for you?"

Both spoke at once. One was the wife, and the other the mother, of two men imprisoned for resisting the draft in western Pennsylvania. They wanted—

"Stop," Lincoln said. "Don't say any more. Give me your petition."

The older woman said they had no petition for the men to be released. They could neither write one themselves nor pay for one to be written, so "I thought it best to come and see you."

Lincoln said he understood and rang a bell, sending for Charles A.

Dana, the assistant secretary of war, who affirmed that numerous men were jailed in western Pennsylvania on the same charge. Lincoln didn't want to do a special favor for these two. But the war was nearly over, so he decided to release them all. "I believe I will turn out the *flock*," he said, and drew up an order for Dana.

The younger woman approached as if to kneel in gratitude but Lincoln said, "Don't kneel to me. Thank God and go."

When they were gone, the president told Speed it was "the only thing I have done today which has given me any pleasure."

The inauguration came March 4. Roger Taney, author of the Dred Scott decision, was dead. The new chief justice administered the oath: Salmon P. Chase, the onetime antislavery lawyer and treasury secretary, appointed by Lincoln. The white Capitol dome behind them was now complete. A military escort stood by: regiments of wounded men from the Invalid Corps, and four companies of Black troops. The weather was clear, although after recent rains the thousands who watched the ceremony were standing "in mud almost knee-deep."

Frederick Douglass stood in that crowd, having returned to the capital for the event, and afterward decided to become the first Black man to attend an inaugural reception. It was at the White House that evening. Arriving at the mansion in the company of a prominent Black woman, Douglass said, he was "seized by two policemen and forbidden to enter. I said to them they were mistaken entirely in what they were doing, that if Mr. Lincoln knew I was at the door he would order my admission, and I bolted in by them." Two other policemen caught up and began "conducting me out the window on a plank," which was being used as an exit. Douglass persuaded a passing guest to tell the president. Seconds later word came back, and he was escorted with his companion into the crowd in the East Room, "a sea of elegance and beauty." Lincoln seized his hand. He said he'd noticed Douglass at the inaugural ceremony, and asked what he thought of his speech. Douglass answered, "Mr. Lincoln, it was a sacred effort."

The inaugural address played on themes Lincoln had been pondering for some time. In 1864 he'd written of the war as God's punishment for slavery: "If God now wills the removal of a great wrong, and wills also that we of the North as well as you of the South, shall pay fairly for our complicity in that wrong, impartial history will find therein new cause to attest and revere the justice and goodness of God." His phrasing acknowledged the North's role in slavery—and even reflected times when free citizens stood by passively, as he had during his long-remembered steamboat journey with the fiddler in chains. This idea made it into the inaugural address: He suggested God had given "this terrible war" to punish "both North and South." But he also identified Southern slavery, specifically, as the "peculiar and powerful interest" that was "the cause of the war." If the war should drain all the wealth piled up by that interest, and continue "until every drop of blood drawn with the lash shall be paid by another drawn with the sword," then "the judgments of the Lord are true and righteous altogether."

In Virginia, Lee's army still held the approaches to Richmond and the nearby railway junction at Petersburg. His outnumbered, hungry, and often shoeless troops had defended their trenches all winter, resisting every Union advance. Grant was directing the months-long siege from a cabin in his headquarters camp, at a place on the James River known as City Point, and on March 20 he invited Lincoln to visit: "I would like very much to see you and I think the rest would do you good." Grant didn't add, but Lincoln would have understood, that he might arrive in time to witness the final assault on Richmond. The president accepted, and arrived on a steamer called the *River Queen*, bringing the first lady and Tad, who turned twelve during the journey. Robert Lincoln, now twenty-one, was already at headquarters serving as an assistant adjutant, or administrator. He'd missed most of the war at the insistence of his mother, who refused to lose another son, and to the embarrassment of his father, who had asked so many others to send their sons to war. Grant helped the president solve the problem by agreeing to place Robert on his staff.

The Lincolns' trip was less restful than Grant hoped. Senior officers' wives were staying at headquarters, and when the women attended a review of the troops, Mary felt a general's young wife received more attention than she. She raged about this and other perceived slights for days, berating her husband in front of other people and refusing to see Grant's wife, Julia. A witness noted the look on the president's face, "an expression of pain and sadness that cut one to the heart."

He nonetheless toured the area and saw prisoners herded to the rear. He happily turned himself into a relay messenger, receiving information from Grant, who was moving about the battlefield, and rewriting it for a telegrapher to send to Washington. When Mary returned to the White House after a few days, the president stayed. Now he did enjoy placid moments, as he told Grant in a note.

> *Yours showing Sheridan's success of to-day is just received, & highly appreciated. Having no great deal to do here, I am still sending the substance of your despatches to the Secretary of War.*
>
> *A. LINCOLN*

On Sunday morning, April 2, the Union troops broke through Lee's lines, taking many prisoners, and the way seemed almost clear to the capital. That night the blue-uniformed soldiers heard explosions, a sign their enemies were blowing up whatever munitions they couldn't move out of

Richmond; and morning revealed the Confederate trenches were abandoned.

At eight o'clock on April 3, the telegrapher in chief sent the news to Washington. Lincoln said Grant was looking to "cut off the retreating army," and that he was starting forward himself. This drew a warning from Stanton at the War Department ("Allow me respectfully to ask you to consider whether you ought to expose the nation to the consequence of any disaster to yourself in the pursuit of a treacherous and dangerous enemy") but Lincoln waved off his concern ("I will take care of myself"). He not only went to Petersburg but brought Tad. They returned to City Point that night, and Lincoln decided to visit Richmond the next day.

Admiral David Dixon Porter, the bearded commander of naval forces, escorted him up the James, which led thirty miles to Richmond through what had been enemy territory. They went on Porter's flagship, the *Malvern*, with other gunboats. They passed a barrier of rocks that the navy had just removed, then passed a Confederate minefield that had just been cleared. They passed the black hulks of Confederate ironclad warships, which the crews had sunk before abandoning them. Then Porter's gunboats began to run aground. The James was a tidal river, and it was low tide. When Porter's flagship ran aground he transferred with the president to his personal barge, a flat-bottomed small craft. Lincoln seemed amused as his guard grew smaller and smaller. He said he was reminded of a man who asked to be made an ambassador, and when Lincoln declined he asked for a lesser post. Lincoln said no again, so the man asked to be a customs official. "When he found he could not get that, he asked me for an old pair of trousers. But it is well to be humble."

They disembarked at a steamboat landing. Porter didn't know the city, so he couldn't know they faced a walk of more than two miles to the new army headquarters in the center of town. They'd gone only a few steps when they encountered several Black men, who recognized Lincoln. Porter had a tendency to dramatize the stories he told, but it may well have been, as he later said, that a man who regarded Lincoln as his liberator knelt at the president's feet. Lincoln told the man he shouldn't do that.

The crowd grew as the president walked. Quiet streets came alive with people, while others came to the upper windows of the buildings. Lincoln had trouble moving, and Porter began to worry: while the freedpeople would never harm the president he couldn't say who else was in town. He ordered twelve sailors from the barge to take up rifles with bayonets to clear the way. People continued reaching out to touch the president or talk with him. "It was a warm day," Porter said. "The atmosphere was suffocating, but Mr. Lincoln could be seen plainly by every man, woman and child, towering head and shoulders above that crowd." His face was covered in perspiration. He stopped once and said a few words to the men and women whose freedom he had decreed. He said they were as free as air. Then he tried to move, but people "could not be made to understand that they were detaining the President," Porter said; "they looked upon him as belonging to them."

At the newly established Union army headquarters, the soldiers took note of "an immense crowd of the people" down the street, and gradually realized it was the president's vast bodyguard, with Lincoln, Porter, and the sailors in the center.

His escorts left him at headquarters—the White House of the Confederacy, the former home and office of Jefferson Davis. Lincoln stepped inside, greeting soldiers and asking the housekeeper for a tour. He walked through rooms with gilded mirrors, patterned wallpaper, and elegant furniture; a rumor that Davis had sold his belongings before the evacuation was untrue. The president walked into Davis's office and sat behind the desk.

One of the army officers informed him that a Confederate official would like to see him. Lincoln said to bring the man.

THE CONFEDERATE WAS JOHN A. CAMPBELL, THE ASSISTANT SECRETARY of war. He was tall and imposing, with a wisp of gray beard, observant eyes and a nearly bald head. He was in his midfifties, and his manner suggested the majesty of the law: he'd once been a justice on the United States Supreme Court. He came across as cold, analytical, and remote, a rational man most comfortable considering the technicalities of a statute, but his life over the past few years showed where his reasoning had led him. He'd given up his lifetime seat on the court despite his doubts about the wisdom of secession, saying he felt a duty to his state of Alabama. Now he felt duty called him to end the war, so he wanted to talk with Abraham Lincoln.

Justice Campbell had a history with Lincoln. In 1861, while winding down his court duties, he'd tried one last peace effort, mediating between South Carolina and the Lincoln administration in hopes of preventing an attack on Fort Sumter. Nearly four years later he dealt directly with Lincoln in a task he understood to be equally hopeless. At the request of President Davis, he joined a three-man Confederate commission proposing to negotiate peace in February 1865. Meeting Lincoln and Seward aboard the *River Queen* off the coast of Virginia, they discussed a wild Confederate proposal to declare an armistice and send a joint Union-Confederate army to attack Mexico. France had invaded and installed its own ruler; Americans could unite to evict the French, and by the time this pleasant distraction was finished the North and South might decide not to resume their own war. This intrigued Seward, who was as attracted to elaborate schemes as to writing elaborate sentences; but Campbell knew it was insane. Lincoln had no interest. The way to peace was for Confederates to recognize federal authority and disarm.

Campbell passed back through the Union lines to his home in Richmond and was in the city when word spread of Lee's collapse on April 2. President Davis, notified through a whispered conversation while attending church, gathered his papers and his family to join the evacuation. He left the presidential mansion in the care of the housekeeper and boarded an evening train westward for Danville, Virginia, and prolonged resistance. Members of his cabinet caught the train, among them Justice Campbell's boss, Secretary of War John Breckinridge, a younger man with a full head of dark hair. He'd been the youngest vice president in United States history at thirty-six, and when still not quite forty was the presidential candidate of Southern Democrats against Lincoln in 1860. Afterward he tossed away his future prospects to join the rebellion even though his native Kentucky did not; he personified the refusal to accept the results of a free and fair election. As Breckinridge prepared to leave the War Department, Campbell told him he intended to stay and offered to represent the government in peace talks, but Breckinridge departed without giving instructions. Other War Department functionaries filed out of the office until Campbell was alone at his desk.

At midnight he walked home past empty public buildings. The last trains were gone and the city was quiet except for sounds of departing troops. He heard wagons clattering over a bridge to the south side of the James. At three o'clock a blast shook the windowpanes in his house as the Confederate navy blew up its ammunition stores. He went walking in the predawn streets, and something caught his eye: "There were lights in the Shocco tobacco warehouse resembling lamps at the distance, but in a little time there was a blaze of light and flame." Retreating soldiers had torched it. Flames reached the roof, spread to nearby flour mills, and consumed a line of stores on Carey Street. The river reflected flames as the bridges burned. The Richmond he'd known was vanishing. Looters smashed shop windows; convicts escaped the penitentiary. Refugees from burning houses gathered in the park around the statehouse. He didn't go to the office that morning—what would he do there?—and wandered home as Union troops marched into the city. Some soldiers stacked arms and helped to douse the fires.

Campbell went out that afternoon to check on the families of officials who'd fled. Nobody was bothering them. Nobody came for Campbell either, so on Tuesday morning, April 4, he started for the army headquarters to turn himself in. He gained an audience with a general and discovered he knew the man, a former US attorney who'd argued cases before the Supreme Court while Justice Campbell was on it. The general, glad to discover someone from his past, wrote an order of protection for Campbell's family and "spoke with some freedom of the course of affairs." He thought federal authorities would appoint a military governor who would rule Virginia with "forbearance." He also mentioned that Lincoln was outside town. Campbell asked to see the president, and the general said he'd try to arrange it.

Campbell expected to be summoned again to Lincoln's steamboat, but in the afternoon a federal officer knocked at his door and said the president was at Davis's house. When Campbell arrived Lincoln rose to greet him. "His manner indicated that he expected some special, and perhaps authorized, communication to him from the Confederate government," Campbell said. "I had no commission to see him." But Lincoln decided they might as well sit in a small side parlor. Lincoln called over the commander of military forces in Richmond, General Godfrey Weitzel—a German immigrant, just twenty-nine, who had risen rapidly in rank partly because of distinguished service and partly because so many other generals had been killed, wounded, or forced to retire.

Campbell acknowledged that "the war was over, and all that remained to be done was to compose the country." He asked for understanding: "I urged, that although there had been passion, petulance and animosity in the secession movements, that there were also serious differences of opinion as to constitutional obligations and responsibilities, upon which there was a ground for opposing opinions. That these had not been settled by the authorities of the country and perhaps could not be otherwise settled than by a war." He said Virginia had been slow to secede, and had only gone over to rebellion after the first shots were fired. He informed Lincoln that many in Richmond had been discussing terms of peace, though none agreed how to proceed.

Lincoln asked who was talking of peace. Campbell gave names, and it emerged what each man wanted. Lincoln wanted the rebels to lay down their arms and recognize federal authority. Campbell wanted some restoration of civil order. He also wanted Virginians to retain some control of their own affairs. Lincoln said he "wanted to have another talk," and said he'd stay in Richmond another day so that Campbell could bring some leading citizens.

Army officers objected that the president should not spend the night in the occupied city where threats might lurk, so Lincoln revised his plan. He started back to the naval flotilla, which would free itself on the rising tide, and said he'd see Campbell on the water. The next morning Campbell reported to the riverside, having found nobody in Richmond willing to accompany him but a single lawyer. Union troops guided the two men to the *Malvern*, where Campbell became the only senior Confederate ever to discuss Reconstruction directly with Lincoln.

Rebel states had gone to war to preserve their version of slavery, a mixture of feudalism and capitalism, an oligarchy based on race. The war had destroyed it. Federal troops had marched down the roads of the states' rights men, burned their crops, torched Atlanta, torn up railroads, killed and maimed their soldiers, and freed their laborers and organized them in arms against their former masters. Reconstruction was what came afterward, the restoration of loyal authority. Its terms had been debated in Washington for years. A new Unionist government had ratified a free-state constitution for Louisiana, but the future of most states was unknown. Congress had passed a uniform plan for Reconstruction but Lincoln hadn't signed it, feeling that different states should be handled differently. Strictly speaking, Campbell wasn't addressing long-term questions; he was just trying to get the community through its current chaos. But the subjects were connected; what they did now might influence what happened later.

HE WAS AN ODD PERSON TO SPEAK FOR THE REBEL CAUSE, BECAUSE he didn't consider himself strongly committed. In particular he didn't approve of slavery as it was practiced. After the war this claim was made by so many people it was hard to imagine why they had fought a war for slavery, but this is how Campbell seemed genuinely to have thought about it. He felt it was inhumane to break up families for sale, and in 1847 he proposed a law to prevent this in his state of Alabama. If slavery was a patriarchy, as its proponents claimed, then the patriarchs had a duty to care for those beneath them—so slaveholders should neither use their captives as collateral for loans nor let them be auctioned off to pay debts. Slaveholders didn't embrace this idea, which would infringe on their property rights and which many could hardly afford because they supported their lifestyles on credit. In short Campbell wanted to reform a system that could never be reformed. But he seemed not to reach the logical conclusion that it had to be destroyed, and he never imagined the federal government had anything to say about it. He was on the Supreme Court in 1857 when Chief Justice Taney wrote the Dred Scott decision. Campbell not only joined the 7–2 majority but wrote his own separate opinion, using his own reasoning to reach the same result.

Upon Lincoln's election in 1860, Campbell said the South had no *reason* to secede (Lincoln's election was "not sufficient cause") but had the *right* to secede. He went home to Alabama and lived quietly for more than a year. But when asked into the Confederate government as assistant secretary of war, he accepted. He did this in the fall of 1862, after the Emancipation Proclamation, which offended him. "The President," he said, "resorted to an extreme and extra constitutional measure. If carried into execution it changed the constitution, and the social organization of all of the States to which it had been applied." But by 1865 his reverence for the law worked on him to accept slavery's end. The Proclamation "has already become operative and vested rights," giving liberty to millions who could not be expected to give it back.

In the meeting in a cabin on the *Malvern*, Lincoln again sat with General Weitzel while Campbell settled in with the Richmond lawyer. Lincoln handed Campbell a memo he'd written.

> *As to peace, I have said before, and now repeat, that three things are indispensable.*
>
> 1. *The restoration of the national authority throughout all the States.*
> 2. *No receding by the Executive of the United States on the slavery question. . . .*
> 3. *No cessation of hostilities short of an end of the war, and the disbanding of all force hostile to the government.*

Campbell discussed these terms with the president, and settled on a way to sell them to proslavery men. The "Executive" would never change his opposition to slavery, as Lincoln's paper said, but once they returned to their duties as citizens of the United States the rebels were free to challenge him through the political process. Congress had by then passed the Thirteenth Amendment outlawing slavery, but it had yet to be ratified by three-fourths of the states as required. The white South could argue for its views like anyone else.

The two developed a way to bring the terms into effect. In Campbell's memory the notion came from Lincoln; General Weitzel felt it came from Campbell. In either case Lincoln approved: the Virginia legislature should reconvene to take the state out of the rebellion. Lincoln said "the very legislature which has been sitting in Richmond" would end the war: the state would instruct General Lee to stand down along with the surviving Virginia troops. What remained of the rebel army wouldn't amount to much. If the Virginians did this Lincoln would spare them the confiscation of their property, though he wouldn't restore their property in human beings.

The meeting broke up, each of the parties going their separate ways.

Lincoln received another visitor before the *Malvern* departed. Duff Green—Lincoln's friend who'd tried to persuade him to compromise before the war—appeared on the riverbank. Though he'd left Washington for Richmond at the start of hostilities, Green had stayed in touch, writing a letter to Lincoln in 1864, and Lincoln said to let his old friend on board. To his surprise, the white-bearded old propagandist was there to tell him off; he raged at the president for coming to Richmond to gloat and said he had blood on his hands. Green had always prized his independence, which federal troops were taking away. Lincoln lost his patience for once and angrily ordered his friend off the boat.

The president went ahead with his peace plan, and wrote instructions for General Weitzel:

> *It has been intimated to me that the gentlemen who have acted as the Legislature of Virginia, in support of the rebellion, may now now* [sic] *desire to assemble at Richmond, and take measures to withdraw the Virginia troops, and other support from resistance to the General government. If they attempt it, give them permission.*

Weitzel returned to headquarters and showed Lincoln's letter to his chief of staff, who didn't like it. "This is a political mistake," he warned. "Don't you lose that letter," because without proof that he'd been ordered to let the legislature meet, Weitzel was likely to be relieved of duty. The youthful general had no choice but to go ahead, causing a call for the meeting of the legislature to be published in a Richmond newspaper.

Justice Campbell moved about Richmond, rounding up legislators to enact the plan, and inadvertently showed what was problematic about it. In a memo on April 7, he said the purpose of the legislative session was not strictly to end Virginia's part in the war but to discuss "the establishment of a government of Virginia," which would "administer the laws in connection with the authorities of the United States." Instead of a final closeout of business, they were meeting to resume their ancient role. Virginia politicos agreed to call for the legislature to return to Richmond in late April.

Lincoln returned to Washington and disclosed his plan to Stanton, who was dismayed. Stanton, like the Radical Republicans in Congress, wanted to raze the old state structures; rebel governments were null and void. Radicals intended to rebuild Southern states as democracies, and Stanton didn't think the old legislature should be allowed to meet for any purpose.

Lincoln did nothing in response to Stanton's complaint—he had made an agreement—but on April 9 the situation changed. Lee's army, down to 28,000 ragged men, couldn't flee quickly enough to stay ahead of more than 100,000 federal troops who cut off their escape. At Appomattox Court House, Lee met Grant to surrender as Robert Todd Lincoln looked on. The Virginians lost their last leverage. "There was no longer any use for the legislature," Weitzel said.

On April 11 the president stood in a window of the White House and spoke to a crowd about Reconstruction. He dwelled on the recently established government of Louisiana. Its constitution, voted on by some twelve thousand men who'd sworn allegiance to the United States, ended slavery and left open the possibility of Black voting rights, though the new white-led government had not extended those rights by law. Lincoln said he would prefer that at least some Black citizens should vote, but he accepted the loyal government. He was feeling his way forward as he had for years, taking what progress he could and saving more for later. He was following the standard he described in the Lincoln-Douglas debates, when he said "free society" would be "never perfectly attained" but could be "approximated," adding to "the happiness and value of life to all people, of all colors, everywhere."

But he needed *some* progress. The old Virginia legislature wasn't likely to give it to him, and he decided on April 12 not to let them assemble. He wrote instructions to General Weitzel to block the gathering, and contended he was not breaking his agreement because of the way he had worded his peace terms. Justice Campbell may have assumed that Lincoln recognized the authority of the Virginia legislature, but "I have done no such thing," Lincoln said. The former Supreme Court justice had not paid close attention to the Illinois lawyer's phrasing. "I spoke of them not as a Legislature, but as 'the gentlemen who have acted as the Legislature of Virginia in support of the rebellion.' I did this on purpose to exclude the assumption that I was recognizing them as a rightful body. I dealt with them as men having power *de facto* to do a specific thing, to wit, 'to withdraw the Virginia troops.'"

Campbell's mission had failed, and he was bitter long afterward, though not at Lincoln. He assumed, as many white Southerners did, that Lincoln understood his point of view, and would have accepted Reconstruction with as little social change as possible. He felt that other men had thwarted Lincoln's intent. As the war ended, the federal government appointed a Virginia Unionist to run the state, then later reestablished military rule, and finally allowed a referendum on a new state constitution that enfranchised Black voters. Black lawmakers joined the legislature. Campbell regarded the Reconstruction governments as "the most dishonest, despicable and debased governments . . . that ever existed on this continent. I am not prepared to admit that President Lincoln would have cooperated with the politicians or the party who brought such calamities on the country. My opinion is that his purposes were to deal frankly and faithfully in accordance with the declarations made by him at Richmond."

He was partly right. Lincoln did understand his point of view, having spent much of his life around slaveholders. But he also was determined to rebuild society on a more equal basis. It was Campbell who didn't understand how little he could accomplish for the ruins of the slave republic. In his visit to Richmond, Lincoln acted largely as he had four years earlier with Duff Green: listening carefully and producing a document that seemed like it might yield what his interlocutor wanted, a step back in time. But in each case he chose his words so carefully that he left room to step forward. In discarding the old Virginia legislature, one of his last public acts, Lincoln sided with his escorts on the Richmond streets, the hundreds who surrounded him as they led him toward their destination.

Mary Todd Lincoln, 1818–1882,
around the time she became First Lady.

Chapter 17

FIRST LADY: MARY TODD LINCOLN

April 14, 1865

ON GOOD FRIDAY, GENERAL ROBERT ANDERSON RETURNED TO the ruins of Fort Sumter in Charleston, South Carolina. Four years earlier to the day, he and his garrison had evacuated the fort after enduring the rebel bombardment that started the war. Now he raised the United States flag on the little island in the harbor, where it floated over masonry walls smashed beyond recognition by years of Union artillery fire.

That same day, April 14, Lincoln convened a meeting of his cabinet in Washington. They had a guest: Ulysses S. Grant had come up from Virginia after accepting Lee's surrender. Only one large rebel force remained east of the Mississippi, and Grant said he was "hourly expecting word" of its capitulation.

Lincoln predicted the news would come soon, because he'd had a dream the previous night. It was a recurring dream he'd had "preceding nearly every great and important event of the War." Generally the news had been favorable after the dream, "and the dream itself was always the same."

Secretary of the Navy Welles asked "what this remarkable dream could be."

"It relates to your element," said Lincoln, meaning the water. Lincoln was "in some singular, indescribable vessel" and "moving with great rapidity toward an indefinite shore."

He listed several battles that had followed this dream, starting with Fort Sumter and continuing through Gettysburg and beyond. Grant observed that some of the battles on his list were not Union victories and one was not even important. Lincoln said nevertheless that he'd had the dream on those occasions; and then, having admitted that the dream was not such a reliable prophecy after all, he went on talking as if it was. "I had this strange dream again last night, and we shall, judging from the past, have great news very soon."

The men discussed the administration of the conquered states. They considered rules for resuming commerce through blockaded Southern ports and debated inconclusively who should govern Virginia. And then they adjourned. Lincoln planned a carriage ride with his wife that afternoon.

It was around three o'clock when he went down the hall to find Mary, who asked if they should invite anyone to accompany them. "No," Lincoln said, "I prefer to ride by ourselves today." So they went down the grand stairs and climbed into the carriage, and the driver flicked the reins.

It was a rare quiet moment for them. He'd had less and less time for her during the war. Now they rode together, he lean and haggard, his long legs sprawled in front of him in the carriage, and her body vanishing under a billowy dress. Her face had grown rounder over the years, though her eyes were sharp and watchful.

She'd grown up not far from his birthplace in Kentucky, though their early years were very different. Her father, Robert Todd, was a merchant in Lexington, with a brick house and garden near the center of town, where enslaved servants brought the meals and the family received visits from his friend Henry Clay. She attended elite schools, one of them a girls' boarding school where she read English literature, learned French, and studied dance. But like her future husband, she'd been very young when her mother died. Mary endured a toxic relationship with a young stepmother before she escaped to Springfield, to live with Elizabeth and Ninian Edwards, her sister and brother-in-law; but she never did escape the insecurity she'd felt during what she called her "desolate" youth.

When first in Springfield she was the center of the parties at the Edwards home. One of her many suitors said, "She is the very creature of excitement you know and never enjoys herself more than when in society and surrounded by a company of merry friends." A family friend described Mary as "a woman of quick intellect and strong passions, decided in her friendships and intense in her dislikes." William Herndon thought she "was a girl of much grace" who "moved easily" and "was a fine conversationalist and sometimes terribly sarcastic." She had "a quick insight into human nature and used it to her advantage," which was one of many double-edged remarks he made about her. She could perceive a person's weak spot and strike it.

Lincoln was attracted to her intelligence and sophistication, though something made him doubt. They seemed ready to marry at the start of 1841 when he instead broke up with her. But he agonized over his decision, fell into depression, and described himself in "hell." And she responded in a manner that was both brave and shrewd. She wrote him a letter releasing him from their engagement but declining to release herself, saying she loved him and would hold open the question of their future. By making herself vulnerable in that way, she opened herself to further wounds that he could not bear to inflict. He wrote Joshua Speed more than a year after the breakup, saying it "still kills my soul" that she was unhappy, and "I can not but reproach myself, for even wishing to be happy while she is otherwise." They resumed seeing each other and married.

Their shared ambition bonded them: People quoted her saying that he would be president someday. But marriage wasn't easy for her. She had to manage their growing family while living in a house smaller than those she had known. Her husband was often absent, campaigning or attending trials, and could also be absent at home—lost in thought, in a book, in his depression. When they did talk he often said something that enraged her, which was easy for anyone to do; she was always ready to perceive an insult. She hated William Herndon, who as her husband's friend and law partner was a rival for his attention. But she just as often deployed her passionate dislikes in her husband's defense. She believed herself the sharper judge of character and was quick to warn him when some political friend was out for himself. Lincoln, feeling that people were naturally out for themselves, shrugged it off.

She loved politics, another thing that bonded them, but unlike her husband wasn't allowed to practice it or even to vote. She couldn't develop her skills as he could. The more experienced he became, the less he needed her sharp-tongued advice. But when at last she reached the White House, she made a good impression at first. During the presidential transition she traveled to New York to upgrade her wardrobe, and the newspapers commented approvingly. At the inaugural reception she danced with Senator Stephen Douglas, and a newspaper said they looked good together, "nearly the same height and proportions"—both having rounded as they reached middle age. She seemed to adapt to the capital more easily than "her taller half."

It was common for elite Washington wives to serve as conduits from job seekers to the powerful men they knew, and she plunged into this work without any concern for feminine delicacy. Hardly had she moved into the White House when she wrote Seward seeking to have a man appointed consul to Hawaii. She campaigned for another to become commissioner of public buildings despite her husband's opposition. If patronage was power, some power would accrue to her. She attracted more publicity than previous first ladies; Jessie Frémont had captivated journalists in the 1856 campaign, and Mary stepped into the role Jessie had created. Newspapers compared her "statesmanlike tastes" to Britain's Queen Elizabeth I, and said she was "evidently intended by nature to mix somewhat in politics." But publicity was perilous. Her excessive spending reflected her unstable emotions, and reporters noticed when she redecorated the White House, ignoring her husband's lifelong effort to avoid any hint of aristocracy. An Indiana paper described custom-made carpets, red satin curtains, gilded cornices, and new furniture, all when "it takes two or three bushels of corn to buy a pound of coffee in many portions of the West." The writer renamed the White House the "White Mansion" and recalled when Lincoln campaigned in 1840 for William Henry Harrison, the Log Cabin Candidate. Lincoln surely remembered mocking Martin Van Buren's White House curtains.

Mary entertained sophisticated male friends at the White House, forming a salon where she was the center of attention; but one of the men sold an embarrassing scoop to the newspapers. She feuded with Lincoln's allies (saying after a trip she took that "*not* encountering" Thurlow Weed was "the *most agreeable* feature of the excursion"). When Willie died the nation sympathized with a mother's loss, but she grieved so long and so publicly that she irritated even her supporters; everybody was grieving for somebody. She attended séances. She tried to communicate with Willie and reported talking with his spirit. And she lashed out at people publicly, as she had at City Point.

Coexisting with her demanded that Lincoln hone his empathy, patience, and perspective. He ignored her transgressions while focusing on what seemed more important. If she made a cutting remark in front of other people he let it pass. Often he disengaged; did he *really* not notice how much she was spending on dresses and trips to New York? Occasionally he went his own way to face his melancholy. She couldn't bear to walk in Willie's room after he died. He sat in it regularly alone.

The skills he needed at home resembled some he needed for work. He responded to George McClellan's crises roughly as he did hers, offering soothing words and setting aside whatever the general might have done wrong. It's hard to say if difficult men trained him to handle his marriage, or if his marriage trained him to handle difficult men. But it's conceivable that if he'd had a happier union he would have been less prepared to serve the Union. He had, in any case, kept both together.

As the carriage rolled through the city, Mary said she was almost startled by his cheerfulness.

"And well I may feel so, Mary," he said. "I consider this day the war has come to a close." Then he said more: "We must *both* be more cheerful in the future—between the war and the loss of our darling Willie—we have both, been very miserable."

This was surely the message he'd been planning to deliver on their carriage ride alone. He was telling her to take this moment to rein herself in, to reset the emotions that she had allowed to run wild. He hadn't given up trying to improve their life together, and by saying "both" he assumed some responsibility. He'd given his mental health and his marriage insufficient time. Now time was opening up. He still had nearly four years to serve as president, and she nearly four as first lady. They had a chance to be happy.

Then the carriage ride was over. They went upstairs and dressed to go to the theater.

JOHN WILKES BOOTH SHOT LINCOLN THAT NIGHT WITH A PISTOL to the back of his head. Mary was sitting beside him in the presidential box at Ford's Theatre. An army major attending the play with them rose to confront the assassin, who stabbed him with a knife and leaped down to the stage. A few shouted words—he told the audience in Latin, "Thus always to tyrants!"—and Booth was gone. Twelve days later, federal troops found and killed him in Virginia.

Booth was a Confederate sympathizer who'd been plotting against Lincoln for months and assigned other killings to his collaborators. A would-be assassin stabbed Seward, who was recuperating in bed from a carriage accident. But a soldier and two sons of the secretary of state wrestled the attacker off his victim and Seward survived. A third man assigned to kill Vice President Andrew Johnson stopped at a bar on his way and never arrived.

Johnson became president upon Lincoln's death. He'd been added to the ticket in 1864 as a loyal Tennessean, a symbol of Union, and his view of society seemed unimportant until Lincoln's assassination. Johnson had grown up poor, and hated slaveholding aristocrats whose power and wealth perverted all notions of equality among white men; but having humbled the aristocracy he couldn't bring himself to support equality for Black men. He soon battled Congress over Reconstruction. The fight culminated in his impeachment, though the Senate acquitted him and he finished his term. In 1868 Ulysses S. Grant won the presidency and upheld Reconstruction; mixed-race governments won elections, backed by federal troops. Frederick Douglass started a newspaper to defend the progress that had been made, though within a few years white supremacists staged violent takeovers of some states and began curtailing voting rights.

Mary Todd Lincoln was cast adrift. Because her status depended entirely on her husband, his death robbed her of her position as first lady and even of the rooms where she slept. She left the White House with Tad, relocating to Chicago, where they were oppressed by the debts she'd run up; the presidential salary that she might have used to pay them was gone. She tried to sell the gowns she'd worn as first lady, but the sale brought little money even as she was accused of trading on her martyred husband's name. When Democrats took up her cause, accusing Republicans of stinginess toward a grieving widow, Mary fanned the publicity and even battled Thurlow Weed, who publicly questioned her ethics. She later lobbied her late husband's allies in Congress to vote her a lifetime pension. Appealing to an influential friend for help, she referred repeatedly to her dead spouse and said, "I am almost helpless. There are days when I cannot walk straight." She was not a smooth political operator but relentlessly pursued her interests. Though some lawmakers openly questioned her character in debate, Congress approved $3,000 per year, many times greater than the pensions for soldiers or their widows and enough for a comfortable existence.

Tad died in 1871 at eighteen, the fourth time Mary had endured a life cut short, leaving Robert as her sole surviving family member. He had thought her insane for years, and as her behavior grew more erratic he had her committed to an asylum in 1875. Again she showed political skill, organizing a successful public campaign for her emancipation. Released to her sister's home in Springfield, she was free to resume her life and also to visit her husband's tomb, which had been built in the way she wanted. Illinois leaders originally planned to entomb Lincoln on a special block of land in the center of Springfield, but she insisted that he would have preferred the rolling grounds of Oak Ridge Cemetery at the edge of town. The state reluctantly put his body there, but prepared to build a monument to him at the downtown location. She threatened to relocate his body to Washington unless they instead built the monument over his tomb in the cemetery. They did as she said.

For the remainder of her days and long beyond, people speculated on what might have happened if events on April 14 had been slightly different. If the policeman assigned to guard Lincoln had stayed at his post instead of moving for a better view of the play, he might have stopped the assassin. If Ulysses and Julia Grant had not declined Lincoln's invitation to come to the theater, Grant might have brought competent bodyguards. Mary didn't think anything would have mattered. "If he had remained, at the W[hite] H[ouse] on that night of darkness, when the fiends prevailed, he would have been horribly *cut to pieces*," she wrote. "Those fiends, had too long contemplated, this inhuman murder, to have allowed, *him*, to escape."

Her husband might have agreed. During the war his nativist friend Joseph Gillespie traveled from Illinois to Washington and found Lincoln walking alone on Pennsylvania Avenue. When Gillespie expressed concern for his security, Lincoln replied that "no precautions he could take would be availing if they were determined to kill him." He said that adding security would be like plugging one gap in a fence "when the fence was down all along."

In a larger sense Lincoln couldn't bring himself to worry about his death. He'd often said people's lives were directed by some force larger than themselves. That force might or might not be God, depending on when he considered the question; he embraced no specific religious creed. He once confessed that in "early life" he believed in "the Doctrine of Necessity," an idea that "the human mind is impelled to action . . . by some power over which the mind itself has no control." He stopped talking about this idea, fearing it would alienate voters, but kept thinking it. He wrote something similar in 1862, when he said God could end the war "by his mere quiet power, on the minds of the now contestants." Mary said he "had no hope—and no faith in the usual acceptation of that word." She quoted him saying a rhyme: "What is to be will be / and no cares of ours can arrest the decree." He was a fatalist. Calamities must come, as they had for him as a boy.

His fatalism extended to the electorate of his republic—not that the people would do wrong, but that they would exercise their sovereign power no matter what anyone did. He told Gillespie that the voice of the people was the voice of God. He was referencing an old Latin phrase—*vox populi vox dei.* Politicians liked this saying because the electorate was inscrutable; voters themselves could not always articulate reasons for their choices, yet democratic leaders had to respect their judgments. (A later president, Theodore Roosevelt, said more skeptically that the voice of the people might be the voice of God, but no more than 51 percent of the time.) It's impossible to know Lincoln's exact spiritual belief. But if we set aside the mystical elements of his ideas, we're left with an earthly insight that he also expressed, and that helps to explain his life and politics. People *were* shaped by a force larger than themselves, and that force was their environment—or as he put it, their circumstances.

As he told Gillespie, "our beneficent institutions" did not come from the inherent genius of the American people; they had grown out of fortunate circumstances at the time of the nation's birth. Less fortunate circumstances led to slavery, and he considered them so powerful he didn't even blame the slaveholders who were born into that system and perpetuated it. A summary of one of his speeches put it this way:

> *He first declared that the Southern slaveholders were neither better, nor worse than we of the North, and that we of the North were no better than they. If we were situated as they are, we should act and feel as they do; and if they were situated as we are, they should act and feel as we do; and we never ought to lose sight of this fact in discussing the subject.*

Slaveholders were not bad people, simply people in a bad system, which they naturally acted out of self-interest to defend. His quarrel was not with them but with their circumstances. He said his own actions were governed by circumstances. In recounting his decision to issue the Emancipation Proclamation he said, "I claim not to have controlled events, but confess plainly that events have controlled me." In every step toward liberation he took into account both the need to win the war and the need to maintain democratic support. *Vox populi vox dei.*

But it was too modest to say he merely responded to necessity. It was better to say that he understood the power of circumstances and tried to advance his goals within them. He knew the people he wanted to lead and met them as they were. He spoke of things that mattered to them, nudging just enough people just as far as they were willing to go. Eventually the antislavery movement changed the circumstances, winning a presidential election in a way that no party ever had, then winning a second election that came in the form of civil war. At the war's end he was killed by a man who believed that *he* was changing history, but Lincoln had made his impression.

After his death the states ratified the Thirteenth Amendment banning slavery. The Fourteenth and Fifteenth followed, assuring equal protection of the laws and equal voting rights. The amendments were applied unevenly at first and even less as time went on. In numerous cases, Supreme Court justices concluded that the words in those amendments did not mean what they meant. But the words remained in the Constitution, to be redeemed in decades to come. They became part of the circumstances for later struggles, an influence on generations not yet born.

Sources and Acknowledgments

My first ambition for this book was to tell Lincoln's life story through his meetings with a diverse set of people. I thought it would illuminate both Lincoln and his country, and my publisher, Ann Godoff, embraced the idea in a phone call. "We are the sum of our interactions," she said, then astutely guided my efforts to sum up Lincoln.

While writing I also was covering the 2020 election, the attempt to overturn its result, and the attack on the Capitol on January 6, 2021. One man carried a Confederate flag through the building, which the original Confederates never managed. The same period featured protests over racial justice, demands to remove Confederate statues, and countereffforts to limit discussions of race and slavery in schools. The history I was writing *was* the news. Gradually I understood that Lincoln's meetings said something urgent: by engaging with people who differed and building coalitions in a crisis, he demonstrated a survival skill for self-government.

This focus led my research to unexpected places. So many words have been written about Lincoln that it's perilous to claim anything is new—how could you possibly be sure?—so I'll say only that much was new to *me.* Some of the sixteen meetings in this book seemed almost never to have been studied, while others were mentioned in books but overshadowed by other events. Even the famous interactions emerged in a different light for me when seen in the context of the others. In general I found less material about Lincoln's encounters with less-reputable people, which tended to be the meetings I found most interesting. Taken together, the meetings greatly clarified my understanding of the reasons behind Lincoln's rise, his approach to slavery, and his management of people. I've tried to preserve that clarity through this book's brevity.

Much of my research came early in the pandemic, when libraries were closed. Fortunately resources were available. The Library of Congress maintains digital images of the Lincoln Papers and other collections. Keepers of archives and historic sites scanned documents to send me; they include the Speed home at Farmington, the Madison County Archival Library, the Abraham Lincoln Presidential Library, the Sangamon County Historical Society, Lincoln's New Salem State Historic Site, the Illinois State Archive, the Illinois Supreme Court Historic Preservation Commission, the Springfield Historical Society, and the Association of Foreign Intelligence Officers. Gordon Yellowman of the Cheyenne and Arapaho Tribes passed on Cheyenne oral traditions. The University of Illinois hosts one of several valuable digital newspaper archives, while HathiTrust digitizes books from research libraries.

After restrictions eased, Michelle Krowl at the Library of Congress showed me drafts of Lincoln's first inaugural address, the pages water-stained from past storage in a carpet bag. The Old State Capitol in Springfield was closed for restoration, but Justin Blandford gave me a hard hat and led the way to the legislative chamber where Lincoln delivered the House Divided speech. Lincoln's house was nearby, as was a reconstruction of the village of New Salem. In Washington, my journalism has brought me to the old House chamber, the White House, and the Lincoln Cottage at the Old Soldiers' Home.

My wife, Carolee, has been my greatest supporter—offering wise feedback and advice about research while also enduring weekends and evenings spent writing. Our children, Ava, Ana, and Molly, were nearby and sometimes affected my thinking, much of which I did while driving them around. My parents, Judith and Roland Inskeep, introduced me to Lincoln, while my brothers, Bruce and Jim, have been supportive since we played with Lincoln Logs in Indiana. Friends read and commented on chapters: Nishant Dahiya, Noel King, Scott Detrow, and my agent, Gail Ross. Other supportive friends asked how this book was going and politely endured the answer. Casey Denis, Gail Brussel, and others at Penguin Press have been generous to me for years.

The notes and bibliography itemize my debts to generations of scholars and Lincoln obsessives whose work across centuries made mine possible. My shelves have filled with Lincoln books—memoirs, diaries, studies of places Lincoln lived, oral histories, psychological analyses, and books by people who gathered so much information that the covers barely contain it. William Herndon interviewed or corresponded with hundreds of people who knew Lincoln; the resulting notes and letters fill an 864-page book, edited by Douglas L. Wilson and Rodney O. Davis. *Lincoln Day by Day*, by Earl S. Miers and C. Percy Powell, is a 1,164-page chronology of every verified event in Lincoln's life. Ida Tarbell, the muckraking journalist of the late nineteenth and early twentieth centuries, wrote a four-volume biography—and Carl Sandburg wrote six volumes. Even larger is

The Collected Works of Abraham Lincoln—eight volumes edited by Roy P. Basler compiling every word that Lincoln is verified to have written or said in a speech—a basic source for all modern biographies. Writing history is a relay, which is also true of history itself. We build, if we can, on the legacies that are left us.

Notes

Where a document is available from several sources, I cite the most accessible. For Lincoln's writings and speeches, that's usually the *Collected Works of Abraham Lincoln,* abbreviated CW. Letters to Lincoln come from many sources, but I often cite the Abraham Lincoln Papers at the Library of Congress, which also holds the Herndon-Weik Collection and other relevant collections, and is abbreviated here as LOC.

INTRODUCTION

xiii **"a saint of humanity":** "Tolstoy Calls Lincoln the Greatest," a *New York World* article reprinted in the *Pittsburgh Post,* February 14, 1909, 33.

xiii **"accidental instrument":** "Reply to Oliver P. Morton at Indianapolis, Indiana," February 11, 1861, CW, vol. 4, 193.

xiv **"I shall adopt":** To Horace Greeley, August 22, 1862, CW, vol. 5, 389.

xiv **"an idiot":** To Mary Ellen McClellan, August 16, 1861, in George B. McClellan, *McClellan's Own Story* (New York: Webster, 1887), 86.

xiv **"passion for making himself":** All quotes except about the Emancipation Proclamation are from "The President and His Speeches," *Douglass' Monthly,* September 1862, in Philip S. Foner, ed., *The Life and Writings of Frederick Douglass,* vol. 3 (New York: International, 1952), 267–68.

xiv **this "obvious" course:** "Emancipation Proclaimed," *Douglass' Monthly,* October 1862, in Foner, ed., *Life and Writings,* vol. 3, 274.

xiv **"If for this":** "To Joshua F. Speed," August 24, 1855, CW, vol. 2, 320.

xv **"Has Douglas the *exclusive right*":** "Seventh and Last Debate with Stephen A. Douglas at Alton, Illinois," October 15, 1858, CW, vol. 3, 298.

xv **friend's upturned hat:** Charles Friend to Herndon, August 20, 1889, in Douglas L. Wilson and Rodney O. Davis, eds., *Herndon's Informants: Letters, Interviews, and Statements about Abraham Lincoln* (Urbana: University of Illinois Press, 1998), 676.

xv **"Beneath a smooth surface of candor":** Leonard Swett to Herndon, January 17, 1866, in Wilson and Davis, eds., *Herndon's Informants*, 168.

xvi **"Let this be strictly confidential":** "To Owen Lovejoy," March 8, 1858, CW, vol. 2, 436.

xvi **thirteen-year-old memorandum:** Judge David Davis delivered the document on protective tariffs to Simon Cameron, who later mailed it back. "Fragments of a Tariff Discussion," 1847 [?], CW, vol. 1, 407.

xvi **"good for nothing at all":** "Last Public Address," April 11, 1865, CW, vol. 8, 403.

xvi **"What I forbear":** "To Horace Greeley," August 22, 1862, CW, vol. 5, 388.

xvi **acted entirely out of self-interest:** Guelzo, "Abraham Lincoln and the Doctrine of Necessity," 63.

xvii **"look to their self-interest":** "Address on Colonization to a Deputation of Negroes," August 14, 1862, CW, vol. 5, 374.

xvii **used the word *interest* far more often:** Author's count in Lincoln's *Collected Works*: *interest*, 518 times, sometimes referring to interest on a loan or in a subject, but usually to public, private, or self-interest; *liberty*, 184 times; *freedom*, 160 times; *moral*, 137. *Motive* appears 41 times.

xvii **invoking self-interest twice:** "To James C. Conkling," August 26, 1863, CW, vol. 6, 409.

xvii **"moral sense and self-interest":** "Speech at Springfield, Illinois," June 26, 1857, CW, vol. 2, 409.

CHAPTER 1: PROTAGONIST: ABRAHAM LINCOLN

2 **"in this sad world":** "To Fanny McCullough," December 23, 1862, CW, vol. 6, 16.

2 **"Education defective":** "Brief Autobiography," June [15?], 1858, CW, 2, 459.

2 **"never speaking or asking questions":** Sarah Bush Lincoln to Herndon, September 8, 1865, in Wilson and Davis, eds., *Herndon's Informants*, 107.

2 **"perceptions were sharpened":** Mentor Graham to Herndon, c. 1865–66, in Wilson and Davis, eds., *Herndon's Informants*, 450.

2 **his mind was "a great storehouse":** Robert L. Wilson to Herndon, February 10, 1866, in Wilson and Davis, eds., *Herndon's Informants*, 204.

2 **repeat the sermon:** David Turnham to Herndon, September 15, 1865, in Wilson and Davis, eds., *Herndon's Informants*, 122.

2 **On other occasions:** Grigsby to Herndon, September 12, 1865, in Wilson and Davis, eds., *Herndon's Informants*, 114.

3 **lizard that crawled:** Benjamin Thomas, *Lincoln's New Salem* (Springfield, IL: Abraham Lincoln Association, 1934), 43.

3 **any other damn Dutchman:** H. S. Huidekoper, *Personal Notes and Reminiscences of Lincoln* (Philadelphia: Bicking, 1896), 9.

3 **he told of an Irishman:** This seems the best interpretation of Charles Friend's garbled recounting to Herndon, August 20, 1889, in Wilson and Davis, eds., *Herndon's Informants*, 676.

3 **"running rigs":** Dennis Hanks to Herndon, September 8, 1865, in Wilson and Davis, eds., *Herndon's Informants*, 105.

3 **"to tease, banter, or ridicule":** Wilson and Davis, eds., *Herndon's Informants*, 105.

3 **would-be robbers:** Autobiography Written for John L. Scripps, June 1860, CW, vol. 4, 62.

3 **believed she was born out of wedlock:** So he told his friend William Herndon. William Herndon, *Herndon's Life of Lincoln* (1942; reprint. New York: Da Capo, 1983), 3.

4 **gristmill stood on stilts:** Its location and appearance are documented in a map by onetime New Salem resident R. J. Onstot, in the collection of Lincoln's New Salem Historic Site.

4 **"when one turned over":** William Greene to Herndon, May 30, 1865, in Wilson and Davis, eds., *Herndon's Informants*, 17.

4 **subscribe to the *Louisville Journal*:** William Dean Howells, *Life of Abraham Lincoln* (Springfield, IL: Abraham Lincoln Association, 1938), 32.

4 **stuffing a man in a barrel:** T. G. Onstot, *Pioneers of Menard and Mason Counties* (Peoria: J. W. Franks, 1902), 83.

5 **seven families:** Thomas, *Lincoln's New Salem*, 13.

5 **cast a ballot for Jack Armstrong:** Clary's Grove poll book, August 1, 1831, Illinois State Archive, PAL.

5 **Armstrong became first sergeant:** Lincoln's muster roll for the company includes the name of "John Armstrong, 1 Serg." "Muster Roll of Lincoln's Company," May 27, 1832, CW, vol. 1, 11.

6 **part-time federal position:** "Autobiography Written for John L. Scripps," c. June 1860, CW, vol. 4, 65.

6 **surveyed the farm:** "Certificate of Survey for Russell Godbey," January 14, 1834, CW, vol. 1, 20.

6 **"I voted for him":** Godbey interview with Herndon, 1865–66, in Wilson and Davis, eds., *Herndon's Informants*, 450.

6 **"insolvent debtors":** "Notice to Illinois Legislature of a Bill Supplemental to an Act Entitled 'An Act for the Relief of Insolvent Debtors . . . ,'" December 12, 1835, CW, vol. 1, 41.

7 **one hundred well-connected guests:** Mary Todd to Mercy Ann Levering, December 1840, exact date uncertain. Justin G. Turner and Linda Levitt Turner, *Mary Todd Lincoln: Her Life and Letters* (New York: Knopf, 1972), 20.

7 **"I was born":** "Communication to the People of Sangamo County," March 9, 1832, CW, vol. 1, 8.

7 **"natural equality":** "Exposition," *United States Telegraph*, July 12, 1828, 3.

8 **"Log-Cabin Party":** Gail Collins, *William Henry Harrison* (New York: Henry Holt, 2012), 95.

8 **more than twenty times:** Author's count, *Old Soldier*, 1840.

8 **payment of $3,875.35:** "Democratic Curtains," *Old Soldier*, September 10, 1840, 4.

8 **a log cabin on wheels:** "The Inauguration," *Daily Madisonian*, March 6, 1841, 3.

8 **"a political marriage":** Draft of portion of Herndon's *Life of Lincoln*, manuscript/mixed material, Herndon-Weik Collection, Group IV, 3, 11.

8 **"Lincoln lost":** Draft of portion of Herndon's *Life of Lincoln*, manuscript/mixed material, Herndon-Weik Collection, Group IV, 3, 12–13.

8 **"I am, as I have always been":** Conversation related by William Herndon, draft manuscript, Herndon-Weik Collection, Library of Congress, 25b–c.

9 **a room in Springfield's Globe Tavern:** Some sources say "rooms," although Lincoln referred to "our room" in a letter to Joshua Speed, May 18, 1843, CW, vol. 1, 324.

9 **"I have been put down here":** "To Martin S. Morris," March 26, 1843, CW, vol. 1, 320.

9 **"strange, friendless, uneducated penniless boy":** "To Martin S. Morris."

9 **"greater man":** "Speech to the Springfield Scott Club," August 14, 1852, CW, vol. 2, 136.

9 **"Did you know":** "Speech in House of Representatives on the Presidential Question," July 27, 1848, CW, vol. 1, 509.

9 **"She is my equal":** "Speech at Springfield, Illinois," June 26, 1857, CW, vol. 2, 405.

10 **girl in Ninian Edwards's home:** Richard E. Hart, "Springfield's African Americans as a Part of the Lincoln Community," *Journal of the Abraham Lincoln Association* 20 (Winter 1999), 43–44.

10 **nine feather beds:** John Speed personal estate inventory, 1840, Farmington archives.

10 **wasn't sure of his manners:** Mildred Ann Bullitt to Thomas Bullitt, January 2, 1861, Farmington archives.

11 **the cast-iron stove:** John Speed estate inventory, 1840, Farmington archives.

11 **inheritance of fifty-seven people:** John Speed estate inventory.

11 **"They were chained six and six":** "To Mary Speed," September 27, 1841, CW, vol. 1, 260.

11 **Six thousand people:** T. D. Clark, "The Slave Trade between Kentucky and the Cotton Kingdom," *Mississippi Valley Historical Review* 21 (December 1934), 333.

12 **"every time I touch the Ohio":** "To Joshua F. Speed," August 24, 1855, CW, vol. 2, 320.

12 **"injustice and bad policy":** "Protest in Illinois Legislature on Slavery," March 3, 1837, CW, vol. 1, 75.

CHAPTER 2: PROVOCATEUR: JOSHUA GIDDINGS

16 **"If the whig abolitionists":** "To Williamson Durley," October 3, 1845, CW, vol. 1, 347.

16 **"principal subject":** "Speech at Lacon, Illinois," July 18, 1846, CW, vol. 1, 382.

16 **"never denied":** "Handbill Replying to Charges of Infidelity," July 31, 1846, CW, vol. 1, 382.

16 **"many men who possess":** *Lacon Gazette,* October 30, 1847, excerpted in Paul Findley, *A. Lincoln: The Crucible of Congress* (Fairfield, CA: James Stevenson, 2004), 61.

16 **Duff Green's Row:** So it was called in newspapers including "Mrs. Whitewell," *Washington Union,* October 12, 1847, 3.

17 **An inventor had just persuaded Congress:** The contemporary newspaper stories that attest to this little-known event include "Lighting the Capitol," *Farmers' Cabinet,* August 12, 1847, 2.

17 **"solar gas":** "Crotchet's Solar Gas at the Capitol," *Weekly Union,* December 4, 1847, 7.

17 **tank in the basement:** A drawing of Crutchett's is part of US Patent No. 3, 573.

17 **solar gas chandelier:** "Crotchet's Solar Gas at the Capitol."

17 **"we could read the smallest print":** "The Solar Gas Lights," *Carolina Watchman,* December 2, 1847, 1.

17 **"half-insane mumbling":** "Speech in United States House of Representatives: The War with Mexico," January 12, 1848, CW, vol. 1, 440.

17 **"All the house":** "To Mary Todd Lincoln," April 16, 1848, CW, vol. 1, 465.

18 **schooner called the *Pearl*:** Contemporary accounts of the escape include "The Runaway Slaves," *New York Herald,* April 19, 1848, 2; a concise modern summary can be found in Mary Beth Corrigan, "1848: The Pearl," *Washington History* 32 (Fall 2020), 26.

18 **"would have fallen":** "The Runaway Slaves."

18 **He visited the boat's crew:** George W. Julian, *The Life of Joshua R. Giddings* (Chicago: A. C. McClurg, 1892), 242.

18 **defiantly finished his business:** Statement by Giddings, April 20, 1848, Appendix to the *Congressional Globe,* April 25, 1848, 30th Congress, House of Representatives, 1st Session, 519n.

19 **"Our Northern friends":** Julian, *Life of Giddings,* 52.

19 **"liberty of speech":** "Mr. Adams," *Liberator*, February 18, 1837, 2.

19 **The House voted to censure:** Julian, *Life of Giddings*, 125.

19 **"troubled waters":** "Speech of Mr. Wick," April 25, 1848, Appendix to the *Congressional Globe*, 30th Congress, House of Representatives, 1st Session, 666.

19 **"indisputable right":** "Speech of Mr. J.R. Giddings," 519.

19 **"It cannot be so":** "Speech of Mr. J.R. Giddings," 520.

19 **Lincoln was present:** He voted on an amendment that day. *Journal of the House of Representatives*, April 25, 1848, 721.

20 **"The Free Soil platform":** Walter Buell, *Joshua R. Giddings: A Sketch* (Cleveland: William W. Williams, 1882), 176–77.

20 **"This question of the *extension*":** "Speech at Worcester, Massachusetts," September 12, 1848, CW, vol. 2, 2.

20 **"the time will soon arrive":** Frederick W. Seward, ed., *Seward at Washington, as Senator and Secretary of State: A Memoir of His Life, With Selections From His Letters, 1846–1861* (New York: Derby and Miller, 1891), 79.

21 **"Mr. Lincoln called on me":** Giddings journal, January 8, 1849, Giddings Papers, MSS 53.

21 **"absolute social ostracism":** Buell, *Joshua R. Giddings*, 179.

21 **"noble looking":** Allen C. Clark, "Colonel William Winston Seaton and His Mayoralty," *Records of the Columbia Historical Society* 29–30 (1928), 3.

22 **built where the mayor wanted:** Polk reportedly favored the grassy area between Twelfth and Fourteenth Streets on what is now the National Mall; Seaton favored a location farther east, where the Smithsonian Castle now stands. "Smithsonian Institute," *New York Tribune*, September 10, 1846, 1.

22 **"the model schools":** Clark, "Colonel William Winston Seaton," 69–70.

22 **"gradual solution":** Josephine Seaton, *William Winston Seaton of the National Intelligencer: A Biographical Sketch* (Boston: Osgood, 1871), 264.

22 **"the whole framework and foundation":** Seaton, *William Winston Seaton*, 266.

22 **"Every free white male citizen":** "Remarks and Resolution: Introduced in United States House of Representatives Concerning Abolition of Slavery in the District of Columbia," January 10, 1849, CW, vol. 2, 21.

23 **"I believed it as good a bill":** Giddings journal, January 11, 1849, Giddings Papers, MSS 53.

23 **"did not undeceive":** So Lincoln confessed that evening to Giddings, who wrote in his journal: "The Mayor thought I should be opposed to it and Mr. Lincoln thinking that such an idea may be useful did not undeceive him." Giddings journal, January 9, 1849, Giddings Papers, MSS 53.

23 **"about fifteen of the leading citizens":** "Remarks and Resolution," January 10, 1849, CW, vol. 2, 22.

23 **"Who are they":** *Congressional Globe,* January 10, 1849, 212.

23 **"Great confusion throughout the House":** *Sangamo Journal,* January 11, 1849, 3.

23 **"I was abandoned":** Findley, *A. Lincoln: Crucible of Congress,* 139.

23 **contagion of antislavery talk:** He is quoted expressing this fear in 1820. Seaton, *William Winston Seaton,* 145.

24 **triggered a mass meeting:** "A Small Voice from the South," *Richmond Enquirer,* January 23, 1849, 4.

24 **"Congress has no power":** "A Voice from the South."

24 **"Address of the Southern Delegates":** It was printed under that title in the *Charleston Courier,* February 1, 1849, 2.

24 **"The wealth of all":** "Speech on the Reception of Abolition Petitions," February 1837, in John C. Calhoun, *Speeches of John C. Calhoun* (New York: Harper & Brothers, 1843), 225–26.

CHAPTER 3: PARTISAN: JUDGE DOUGLAS

27 **Mary vetoed:** John T. Stuart to Herndon, [1865–66], in Wilson and Davis, eds., *Herndon's Informants,* 480.

27 **Her father had just died of cholera:** Turner and Turner, *Mary Todd Lincoln,* 40.

27 **"I suppose you had not learned":** "To John D. Johnston," February 23, 1850, CW, vol. 2, 76–77.

27 **recorded the names:** "Family Record Written by Abraham Lincoln," [1851?], CW, vol. 2, 94–95.

28 **125 cases over more than a decade:** Matthew Pinsker, "After 1850: Reassessing the Impact of the Fugitive Slave Law," in Damian Pargas, ed., *Fugitive Slaves and Spaces of Freedom in North America* (Tallahassee: University Press of Florida, 2018), 94.

28 **"used to annoy me":** Herndon, *Life of Lincoln,* 332.

29 **hurt Northern workingmen:** Roy Morris Jr., *The Long Pursuit* (New York: HarperCollins, 2008), 38.

29 **"frank and personal friend":** George Fort Milton, *The Eve of Conflict* (Boston: Houghton Mifflin, 1934), 23.

29 **"sit on a red piano stool":** Milton, *Eve of Conflict,* 23.

30 **he left the property in his wife's name:** A sympathetic account of this transaction is in Milton, *Eve of Conflict,* 34–35. A more critical examination is in Caine Jordan, Emerson Mount, and Kai Perry Parker, "'A Disgrace to All Slave-Holders': The University of Chicago's Founding Ties to Slavery and the Path to Reparations," *Journal of African American History* 103 (Winter–Spring 2018), 163–78.

30 **"his remarkable energy and boldness":** "Our United States Senators," in the *Quincy Daily Herald,* June 5, 1854, 2.

31 **"I shall be assailed":** William Gardner, *Life of Stephen A. Douglas* (Boston: Roxburgh, 1905), 67.

32 **"meetings opposed to the Nebraska bill":** "The Anti-slavery Excitement," *Semi-Weekly Standard*, March 29, 1854, 3.

32 **an article headlined EQUAL RIGHTS:** *Eastern Times*, July 6, 1854, 2.

32 **Douglas himself, addressing:** "Senator Douglas's Speech to the People in New York," *Daily Union*, June 8, 1854, 3.

32 **hecklers shouted him down:** "The Great 'Vindication' Meeting," *Chicago Tribune*, September 2, 1854, 1.

33 **a man taking a walk:** John Boehner to the author, "John Boehner on the 'Noisemakers' of the Republican Party," NPR, April 12, 2021.

33 **"The masses":** "To Joshua F. Speed," August 24, 1855, CW, vol. 2, 322.

33 **"nosing for weeks in the State Library":** *Illinois Register*, quoted in Milton, *Eve of Conflict*, 180.

33 **"loudly called for":** "Speech at Winchester, Illinois," August 26, 1854, CW, vol. 2, 227.

33 **"Democratic Mass Meeting":** *Weekly Pantagraph*, September 27, 1854, 1.

33 **"most cordially as old friends":** Angle, Paul M., ed. *Abraham Lincoln, by Some Men Who Knew Him* (Chicago: Americana House, 1950), 42.

33 **Douglas had called the Missouri Compromise "sacred":** "Speech at Bloomington, Illinois," September 26, 1854, CW, vol. 2, 236.

34 **"between ten and twelve hundred persons":** *Missouri Republican*, October 6, 1854, 2.

34 **"Before I proceed":** *Missouri Republican*, October 6, 1854, 2.

34 **Lincoln stood by the stairs:** David Herbert Donald, *Lincoln* (New York: Simon & Schuster, 1995), 174.

34 **"awkward in his posture":** Gustave Koerner, *Memoirs of Gustave Koerner, 1809–1896*, ed. Thomas J. McCormack (Cedar Rapids, IA: Torch Press, 1909), vol. 2, 61.

35 **"What social or political right":** "Speech at Springfield, Illinois," October 4, 1854, CW, vol. 2, 245.

35 **first time on record:** The author's search of Lincoln's Collected Works finds no such reference prior to that date.

35 **"cheer after cheer":** "Springfield, Illinois," *Vermont Watchman and State Journal*, October 27, 1854, 1.

35 **"all was still, and deep attention":** "The Nebraska Discussion at Springfield," *Weekly Iowa State Gazette*, October 18, 1854, 1.

35 **"effortless volume":** Milton, *Eve of Conflict*, 3.

35 **"bold in his assertions":** Koerner, *Memoirs*, vol. 2, 59–60.

36 **"Self government is right":** "Speech at Peoria, Illinois," October 16, 1854, CW, vol. 2, 266.

37 **the most sophisticated of Lincoln's life:** Eric Foner notes it was also his longest speech of his life, some 17,000 words. Foner, *The Fiery Trial*, 65.

37 **"It has come round":** "To Thomas J. Henderson," November 27, 1854, CW, vol. 2, 288.

37 **"Never take your whole fee":** "Fragment: Notes for a Law Lecture," [July 1, 1850?], CW, vol. 2, 82.

37 **"You don't know all":** Jayne to Herndon, in Wilson and Davis, eds., *Herndon's Informants*, 266.

38 **resigning the seat:** "To Noah W. Matheny," November 25, 1854, CW, vol. 2, 287.

38 **great reluctance:** Koerner, *Memoirs*, vol. 2, 616.

38 **"the friends of Shields are not without hope":** Washburne to Lincoln, December 12, 1854, Abraham Lincoln Papers, Series 1, General Correspondence, 1833–1916, LOC.

38 **three o'clock in the afternoon:** "Senatorial Election," *Illinois State Journal*, February 9, 1855, 2.

38 **"our little gay circle":** She used that phrase in a letter to Josiah G. Holland, December 4, 1865. She identified "Douglas, Trumbull, Baker, Hardin, Shields" as members of the circle in a letter to Mary Jane Welles, December 6, 1865. Both letters in Turner and Turner, *Mary Todd Lincoln*, 293, 295.

39 **People cheered in the chamber:** "Senatorial Election," *Illinois State Journal*, February 9, 1855, 2.

39 **Illinois had "rebuked" Douglas:** "Senatorial Election."

39 **"The flag flies beautifully":** Untitled item, *Illinois State Journal*, February 9, 1855, 2.

39 **Lincoln never should have yielded:** Lincoln to Washburne, February 9, 1855, CW, vol. 2, 305.

39 **she largely broke off contact:** Donald, *Lincoln*, 184.

CHAPTER 4: EXTREMIST: OWEN LOVEJOY

41 ***"I'm not an abolitionist!":*** *Joliet Signal*, April 28, 1863, 1.

42 **"If all earthly power":** "Speech at Peoria, Illinois," October 16, 1854, CW, vol. 2, 255.

42 **"there are not surplus shipping":** "Speech at Peoria, Illinois."

43 **"Is it not . . . a total destruction":** "Speech at Peoria, Illinois," 266.

43 **he emigrated from Maine:** Joseph C. Lovejoy and Owen Lovejoy, *Memoir of the Rev. Elijah P. Lovejoy* (New York: John S. Taylor, 1838), 27.

43 **"blood as red":** Paul Simon, *Freedom's Champion: Elijah Lovejoy* (Carbondale: Southern Illinois University Press, 1994), 29.

43 **tied him to a tree:** Simon, *Freedom's Champion*, 47–48.

43 **Elijah criticized their vigilante justice:** Norman Harris, *History of Negro Servitude in Illinois* (Chicago: A. C. McClurg, 1904), 76.

44 **threw it in the river:** Harris, *History of Negro Servitude*, 77.

44 **shot and killed Elijah:** Harris, *History of Negro Servitude*, 94.

44 **knelt by his brother's body:** David Heagle, *The Great Anti-slavery Agitator* (Princeton: Streeter, 1886), 19.

44 **"the first American martyr":** Lovejoy and Lovejoy, *Memoir of Elijah P. Lovejoy*, 12.

44 **Princeton his base:** Heagle, *Great Anti-slavery Agitator*, 6.

44 **"I am going to preach":** Heagle, *Great Anti-slavery Agitator*, 21.

44 **struck by eggs and clods of dirt:** Heagle, *Great Anti-slavery Agitator*, 21–22.

44 **Owen went to trial and was acquitted:** Harris, *History of Negro Servitude*, 111.

45 **"We ought to obey God rather than men":** Heagle, *Great Anti-slavery Agitator*, 27–28.

45 **"the most potent influence":** "Christian Anti-slavery Convention," *Ottawa Free Trader*, June 1, 1850, 2.

45 **presidential elector:** "The Electoral Candidates," *Ottawa Free Trader*, November 1, 1844, 2.

45 **Lovejoy ran for Congress:** "Official Canvass of Will County," *Joliet Signal*, August 15, 1848, 2. Also Jane Ann Moore and William F. Moore, *Owen Lovejoy and the Coalition for Equality* (Urbana: University of Illinois Press, 2020), 58.

45 **It was called:** Moore and Moore, *Owen Lovejoy*, 80.

46 **Lovejoy personally invited Lincoln:** So said Lincoln in his 1858 debates with Douglas. "Mr. Lincoln's Reply" in "First Debate with Stephen A. Douglas at Ottawa, Illinois," August 21, 1858, CW, vol. 3, 13.

46 **advised Lincoln to leave town:** Herndon, *Life of Lincoln*, 299.

46 **"the space was ample," twenty-six delegates:** Ezra Prince, ed., *Transactions of the McLean County Historical Society*, vol. 3 (Bloomington, IL: Pantagraph, 1900), 16, 45.

46 **"the leading spirits on the floor":** Prince, ed., *Transactions*, vol. 3, 44.

46 **"freedom is national":** Prince, ed., *Transactions*, vol. 3, 45.

46 **"brother of him who fell at Alton":** "A Great Triumph," *National Era*, January 11, 1855, 1.

46 **spoke for an hour and forty-five minutes:** "House of Representatives," *Illinois State Journal*, February 7, 1855, 2.

46 **"I cannot and will not obey":** "Progress of Opinion in Illinois," *Pittsburgh Gazette*, March 15, 1855, 1.

47 **"This Government cannot last":** "Address before the Young Men's Lyceum of Springfield, Illinois," January 27, 1838, CW, vol. 1, 111.

47 **"Stand with anybody":** "Speech at Peoria, Illinois," October 16, 1854, CW, vol. 2, 273.

47 **"While I have pen":** "To Ichabod Codding," November 27, 1854, CW, vol. 2, 288.

48 **"As to Lovejoy":** Jesse O. Norton to Lincoln, December 12, 1854, Abraham Lincoln Papers, Series 1, General Correspondence, 1833–1916, LOC.

48 **"My brother, who is elected":** Thomas B. Talcott to Lincoln, December 14, 1854, Abraham Lincoln Papers, Series 1, General Correspondence, 1833–1916, LOC.

48 **"has hopes for Lovejoy":** Leonard Swett to Lincoln, December 22, 1855, Abraham Lincoln Papers, Series 1, General Correspondence, 1833–1916, LOC.

48 **promoted him to Lovejoy:** Washburne to Lincoln, December 26, 1854, Abraham Lincoln Papers, Series 1, General Correspondence, 1833–1916, LOC.

48 **Owen voted for Lincoln:** *Illinois State Journal*, February 9, 1855, 2.

48 **"abolitionist of the Lovejoy stamp":** He was Thomas Talcott. *Illinois State Journal*, February 9, 1855, 2.

48 **"My dear Sir":** "To Owen Lovejoy," August 11, 1855, CW, vol. 2, 316.

49 **"I think I am a whig":** "To Joshua F. Speed," August 24, 1855, CW, vol. 2, 323.

49 **several editors were late:** So said Paul Selby, in Prince, ed., *Transactions*, vol. 3, 36.

49 **the editor of the *Illinois State Journal* failed:** "Convention of Anti-Nebraska Editors," *Illinois State Journal*, February 25, 1856, 2.

49 **the most electable choice:** Prince, ed., *Transactions,* vol. 3, 39.

49 **"The verandahs, halls and doorways":** "The Anti-Nebraska Convention," *Democratic Press*, May 30, 1856, in Prince, ed., *Transactions*, vol. 3, 168.

49 **"athletic personality":** Edward Magdol, *Owen Lovejoy: Abolitionist in Congress* (New Brunswick: Rutgers University Press), 143.

50 **"didn't expect to make a speech then":** "Speech at Bloomington, Illinois," May 28, 1856, CW, vol. 2, 340–41.

50 **"as near the center":** *Salem Weekly Advocate,* September 8, 1858, 2.

50 **Two railroads passed through Bloomington:** A Bloomington newspaper, drawing on its archives, described the opening in Bill Kemp, "Railroads' Arrival in 1853 Momentous Event in City History," *Pantagraph*, May 17, 2008.

50 **WAR IN KANSAS:** "War in Kansas," *Chicago Tribune*, May 20, 1856, 2.

50 **"Some eyewitnesses":** *Rock Island Argus*, May 24, 1856, 2.

51 **"Most intense excitement prevails":** "Telegraphic News," *Daily Gate City*, June 2, 1856, 2.

51 **three main speeches:** Other sources refer to additional speeches during the day, but these seem to be the principal ones. "The Bloomington Convention," *Democratic Press*, May 31, 1856, in Prince, ed., *Transactions*, vol. 3, 174.

51 **"time to light the fires of the revolution":** "National Republican Convention," *National Anti-slavery Standard*, March 1, 1856, 2.

51 **"Mr. Lovejoy stated":** "The Bloomington Convention," 174.

51 **Lovejoy had been saying:** Moore and Moore, *Owen Lovejoy,* 108.

51 **"agreeably disappointed":** Moore and Moore, *Owen Lovejoy,* 108.

51 **"amid deafening applause":** "Speech of Bloomington, Illinois," May 29, 1856, CW, vol. 2, 341.

51 **"I attempted":** Herndon, *Life of Lincoln,* 384.

52 **"I shall not mar":** "The Bloomington Convention," 174.

52 **"ready to fuse":** "Speech of Bloomington, Illinois," May 29, 1856, CW, vol. 2, 341.

52 **"the large hall was still densely packed":** "The Bloomington Convention," 175.

52 **"Mr. Lincoln must write it":** "The Bloomington Convention," 174.

52 **"newly baptized and freshly born":** "The Bloomington Convention," 174.

53 **"Men of all shades":** "From Illinois," *New York Tribune,* June 12, 1856, 6.

53 **nominated Lovejoy for Congress:** He was nominated July 2. "Third Congressional District," *Moline Workman,* July 9, 1856, 1.

53 **"the notorious abolition disunionist":** "Parson Lovejoy," *Rock Island Argus,* July 8, 1856, 2. The same paper quotes the *Chicago Tribune* about "unfounded charges."

53 **"it turned me blind":** "To Henry C. Whitney," July 9, 1856, CW, vol. 2, 347.

53 **"They came singly and in crowds":** "The Ratification Meeting at Princeton," *Minnesota Weekly Times,* July 19, 1856, 2.

53 **"The prairies are on fire":** "Political Items," *New York Tribune,* October 13, 1856, 4.

54 **"He was my most generous friend":** "To John H. Bryant," May 30, 1864, CW, vol. 7, 366.

CHAPTER 5: NATIVIST: JOSEPH GILLESPIE

58 **"extrajudicial opinions":** "The Joint Standing Committee," *Hartford Courant,* June 11, 1857, 2.

58 **"enemies to the constitution":** "Speech of Judge Douglas," *Illinois State Register,* June 15, 1857, 2.

58 **"offer no resistance":** "Speech at Springfield, Illinois," June 26, 1857, CW, vol. 2, 400–408.

59 **a "spirited" meeting:** "The Republicans of Illinois," *New York Tribune,* June 21, 1858, 4.

59 **"wholly inappropriate":** Leonard Swett to Herndon, January 17, 1866, in Wilson and Davis, eds., *Herndon's Informants,* 162–63.

59 **He filled eight pages:** "1858 Campaign Strategy," [July 1858?], CW, vol. 2, 476.

60 **"air line route":** Advertisement, *Alton Daily Courier,* September 13, 1858, 4.

60 **natural gas chandeliers:** "Alton Steam and Gas Pipe Works," *Alton Weekly Telegraph,* October 21, 1858, 4.

60 **Two daily newspapers:** Newspaper databases contain a myriad of Alton newspaper titles through the years, of which the *Telegraph* and *Courier* were the principal ones through the 1850s.

60 **facing the public square:** W. R. Brink, *History of Madison County, Illinois* (Edwardsville, IL: W. R. Brink, 1882), 340.

60 **known Lincoln:** Gillespie to Herndon, January 31, 1866, in Wilson and Davis, eds., *Herndon's Informants*, 186.

61 **"this gymnastic performance":** "Conspiracy of the Federal Members of the Legislature," *Ottawa Free Trader*, December 18, 1840, 2.

61 **Gillespie was one of the brethren:** Along with another lawmaker named Gridley. Gillespie to Herndon, January 31, 1866, in Wilson and Davis, eds., *Herndon's Informants*, 188.

61 **"had an astonishing memory":** Gillespie to Herndon, January 31, 1866, in Wilson and Davis, eds., *Herndon's Informants*, 187.

61 **They shared information:** Their conversations are referenced in Lincoln's letter to David A. Smith, December 3, 1847, CW, vol. 1, 416.

61 **he asked Gillespie:** "To Joseph Gillespie," May 19, 1849, CW, vol. 2, 50.

61 **"I know, and acknowledge":** "To Joseph Gillespie," December 1, 1854, CW, vol. 2, 290.

61 **voting for Lincoln:** Gillespie cast an apparently symbolic vote for Cyrus Edwards, a member of the Edwards clan, on the first ballot, but later switched to Lincoln before moving to Lyman Trumbull on the final ballot as Lincoln instructed. *Illinois State Journal*, February 9, 1855, 2.

61 **"not very aspiring":** Gillespie to Herndon, January 31, 1866, in Wilson and Davis, eds., *Herndon's Informants*, 181.

61 **"the interference":** John Hancock Lee, *The Origin and Progress of the American Party in Politics* (Philadelphia: Elliott and Gihon, 1855), vii.

61 **Another book said:** Anonymous, *The Wide-Awake Gift: A Know-Nothing Token for 1855, by One of 'Em* (New York: J.C. Derby, 1855), 252.

62 **"Native American doctrine":** "Letter from Upper Alton," *Alton Weekly Telegraph*, October 19, 1854, 2.

62 **"Know Nothing style" . . . "Wide-Awake hats":** "Hat and Cap Store," *Alton Weekly Telegraph*, December 28, 1854, 3.

62 **Some called themselves "Wide Awakes":** Humphrey Desmond, *The Know-Nothing Party: A Sketch* (Washington: New Century Press, 1904), 77. A contemporary example of this term's use is the title of the 1855 book by Anonymous, *The Wide-Awake Gift: A Know-Nothing Token for 1855*.

62 **"grossly misrepresented":** Lee, *Origin and Progress of the American Party in Politics*, v–vi.

62 **"fusion of Whigs":** "Election News," *Salem Weekly Advocate*, November 28, 1854, 2.

62 **When attacked by Democrats:** One example, in which a Democrat speaking from the same platform as Gillespie denounced the secret societies, is detailed in "Political Correspondence," *Alton Weekly Courier*, November 2, 1854, 2.

62 **"purely American sentiment and feeling":** He was appointed a delegate to a national Know-Nothing council. "The Know Nothing State Council," *Ottawa Free Trader*, July 21, 1855, 2.

62 **His parents married in Ireland's:** Brink, *History of Madison County*, 87.

63 **"the corrupting influences":** "The Know Nothing State Council."

63 **"I should prefer emigrating":** "To Joshua F. Speed," August 24, 1855, CW, vol. 2, 323.

63 **"mostly my old political":** "To Owen Lovejoy," August 11, 1855, CW, vol. 2, 316.

63 **"Until we can get the elements":** "To Owen Lovejoy."

64 **"union" against slavery:** "Col Archer Declines," *Freeport Daily Journal*, May 26, 1856, 2. A full account of this sleight of hand can be found in Reinhard H. Luthin, "Abraham Lincoln Becomes a Republican," *Political Science Quarterly* 69 (September 1944), 420–38.

64 **Gillespie helped to organize:** Luthin, "Abraham Lincoln Becomes a Republican," 431.

64 **"against political proscription":** "From Illinois," *New York Tribune*, June 12, 1856, 6.

64 **Lincoln kept an old newspaper clipping:** CW, vol. 2, 482n.

64 **Addressing a crowd:** Koerner, *Memoirs*, vol. 2, 59.

64 **"He advocates, boldly and clearly":** "Speech of Stephen A. Douglas," *Illinois State Journal*, July 21, 1858, 4.

64 **wouldn't take advantage:** "The Ball Opened at Chicago," *Illinois State Journal*, July 13, 1858, 3.

65 **"I did not say":** "Speech at Chicago, Illinois," July 10, 1858, CW, vol. 2, 491.

65 **"it is industriously circulated":** David Davis to Lincoln, August 3, 1858, Abraham Lincoln Papers, Series 1, General Correspondence, 1833–1916, LOC.

65 **"Lincoln has evidently learned":** "Mr. Douglas's Speech," in "First Debate with Stephen A. Douglas at Ottawa, Illinois," CW, vol. 3, 10.

66 **"We must struggle":** "1858 Campaign Strategy," CW, vol. 2, 480.

66 **considered Alton "all-important":** "The State Senate," *Illinois State Journal*, August 28, 1858, 2.

66 **"making very confident calculation":** "To Joseph Gillespie," July 16, 1858, CW, vol. 2, 503.

66 **"will carry off at least one half":** To Abraham Lincoln, July 18, 1858, Abraham Lincoln Papers, Series 1, General Correspondence, 1833–1916, manuscript/mixed material, LOC.

66 **"We must not lose that district":** "To Joseph Gillespie," July 25, 1858, CW, vol. 2, 523.

66 **"was instituted to secure":** "Speech at Edwardsville, Illinois," September 11, 1858, CW, vol. 3, 92.

67 **Their long buggy ride:** Gillespie to Herndon, January 31, 1866, in Wilson and Davis, eds., *Herndon's Informants*, 1818. There is no record of Lincoln giving a speech at

Greenville around September 12, 1858, though he said in a letter that he expected to be there around September 11. "To Jediah F. Alexander," August 2, 1858, CW, vol. 2, 532.

67 **the colorful "anecdotes":** Gillespie to Herndon, December 8, 1866, in Wilson and Davis, eds., *Herndon's Informants*, 508.

67 **Lincoln said he "loved" Gillespie:** Charles B. Zane interview with Herndon, undated, in Wilson and Davis, eds., *Herndon's Informants*, 705.

67 **"looked with disfavor":** Gillespie to Herndon, December 8, 1866, in Wilson and Davis, eds., *Herndon's Informants*, 508.

67 **holding a joint convention:** "Proceedings of the People's Mass Convention," *Alton Daily Courier*, September 20, 1858, 2.

68 **the People's Ticket:** "Douglas in Madison County," *Alton Daily Courier*, October 7, 1858, 2.

68 **Lincoln felt so "anxious":** "To Joseph Gillespie," September 16, 1858, CW, vol. 8, 416.

68 **"Upper Alton Americans":** "Democratic Meeting in Upper Alton," *Alton Weekly Telegraph*, October 21, 1858, 4.

68 **caught the same steamboat:** "Last Joint Debate," *Alton Daily Courier*, October 16, 1858, reported that Lincoln and Douglas "reached the city before daylight" on October 15. "Seventh and Last Debate," *Chicago Press and Tribune*, October 18, 1858, gives the time as five o'clock in the morning. Reprinted in Edwin Erle Sparks, ed., *The Lincoln-Douglas Debates of 1858* (Springfield: Illinois State Historical Library, 1908), 500, 508.

68 **behemoth 250 feet long:** It was called the *City of Louisiana*. "Seventh and Last Debate," *Chicago Press and Tribune*, October 18, 1858, in Sparks, ed., *Lincoln-Douglas Debates*, 509. Details of its construction in "Keokuk Packet Line," *Quincy Herald*, March 27, 1858, 2; "Steamers Leaving To-Day," *Cincinnati Daily Commercial*, April 10, 1858, 4; "River Intelligence," *Louisville Daily Democrat*, September 21, 1858, 4.

68 **"furnished and fitted up":** "The Steamer *City of Louisiana*," *Quincy Herald*, March 24, 1858, 2.

68 **each had time:** "Lincoln Triumphant!," *Alton Weekly Courier*, October 21, 1858, 1.

68 **overcast with a threat of rain:** "Last Joint Debate," *Alton Daily Courier*, October 16, 1858, in Sparks, ed., *Lincoln-Douglas Debates*, 500.

68 **both received callers:** Sparks, ed., *Lincoln-Douglas Debates*, 500.

68 **he was in Alton that day:** So said the next day's paper. "Persona," *Alton Daily Courier*, October 16, 1858, 3.

69 **"Let us go up and see Mary":** Koerner, *Memoirs*, vol. 2, 66–67.

69 **a wound from a soldier's bayonet:** Koerner, *Memoirs*, vol. 1, 228.

69 **He settled with:** Koerner, *Memoirs*, vol. 1, 292–3.

69 **reading *Uncle Tom's Cabin*:** Koerner, *Memoirs*, vol. 1, 586.

70 **A ceremonial cannon boomed:** "The Trip to Alton," *St. Louis Evening News*, October 16, 1858, in Sparks, ed., *Lincoln-Douglas Debates*, 508.

70 **Springfield Cadets poured:** "Last Joint Debate," *Alton Daily Courier*, October 16, 1858, in Sparks, ed., *Lincoln-Douglas Debates*, 500.

70 **found Douglas looking "bloated":** Koerner, *Memoirs*, vol. 2, 67.

70 **his left hand:** "Judge Douglas," *Memphis Daily Appeal*, October 23, 1858, 1.

70 **"Judge Douglas's voice":** "The Canvass in Illinois," *New York Post*, October 20, 1858, in Sparks, ed., *The Lincoln-Douglas Debates*, 499.

70 **"This government *can* endure forever":** All Douglas and Lincoln quotes from "Seventh and Last Debate with Stephen A. Douglas at Alton, Illinois," October 15, 1858, CW, vol. 3, 283–325.

71 **"Although sun-burnt":** Koerner, *Memoirs*, vol. 2, 67.

71 **receiving applause for "several minutes":** "Lincoln and Douglas at Alton," *Quincy Whig and Republican*, October 19, 1858, 2.

73 **167 for Lincoln:** "The Seventh and Last Great Debate," *Peoria Transcript*, October 18, 1858, in Sparks, ed., *The Lincoln-Douglas Debates*, 506.

73 **"met about fifteen Celts":** "To Norman B. Judd," October 20, 1858, CW, vol. 3, 330.

73 **they would have held:** Bruce Collins, "The Lincoln-Douglas Contest of 1858 and Illinois' Electorate," *Journal of American Studies* 20 (December 1986), 409.

CHAPTER 6: FIXER: THURLOW WEED

77 **"The facts with which":** "Address at Cooper Institute," February 27, 1860, CW, vol. 3, 522.

78 **"menaces of destruction":** "Address at Cooper Institute," 550.

78 **"He makes his bid":** "Another Anti-slavery Lecturer among Us," *New York Herald*, February 27, 1860, 4.

78 **"uproarious applause":** "Speech of the Hon. Abraham Lincoln," *New York Herald*, February 28, 1860, 2–3.

78 **"I am glad to know":** "Notes for Speech at Hartford, Connecticut," March 5, 1860, CW, vol. 4, 7–8.

78 **They appropriated a name:** As noted in chapter five, the term dates back at least to the mid-1850s, used by nativist groups long before it was adopted by Lincoln supporters.

79 **Joseph Gillespie was presiding:** William Baringer, *Lincoln's Rise to Power* (Boston: Little, Brown, 1937), 184.

79 **"the Rail Candidate for President":** Donald, *Lincoln*, 375.

79 **"stepped in to witness":** Untitled news item, *Bedford Enquirer*, June 8, 1860, 2.

79 **Lincoln and his allies:** Donald, *Lincoln*, 377.

79 **"I have sometimes doubted":** Swett to Herndon, January 17, 1866, in Wilson and Davis, eds., *Herndon's Informants*, 167.

79 **"He never asked my advice":** Davis interview with Herndon, September 19, 1866, in Wilson and Davis, eds., *Herndon's Informants*, 346–48.

79 **When he sat for a portrait:** *Hon. Thurlow Weed.* [Between 1855 and 1865.] Photograph. Brady-Handy photograph collection, LOC.

80 **Seward suggested, revealingly:** Seward to Weed, December 30, 1865, in Thurlow W. Barnes, *Memoir of Thurlow Weed* (Boston: Houghton Mifflin, 1884), 128.

80 **The candidates he recruited:** Frederick W. Seward, ed., *William H. Seward: An Autobiography, from 1801–1834; with a Memoir of His Life, and Selections from his Letters, 1831–1846* (New York: Derby and Miller, 1891), 79–80.

80 **accommodating strong personalities:** David Herbert Donald analyzes this side of Seward's character in *"We Are Lincoln Men: Abraham Lincoln and His Friends"* (New York: Simon & Schuster, 2003), 150–53.

81 **thousands of dollars:** Glyndon G. Van Deusen, *Thurlow Weed: Wizard of the Lobby* (Boston: Little, Brown, 1947), 101.

81 **told Weed to assemble:** Glyndon G. Van Deusen, *William Henry Seward* (New York: Oxford, 1967), 53.

81 **suit for his inauguration:** Van Deusen, *Thurlow Weed*, 102.

81 **persuade her to come:** Van Deusen, *William Henry Seward*, 52.

81 **but expressed concern:** Van Deusen, *Thurlow Weed*, 102.

81 **"irrepressible conflict":** Van Deusen, *William Henry Seward*, 193.

82 **"During the more than thirty years":** "From the World," *Albany Evening Journal*, August 27, 1860, 2.

83 **They were "Irrepressibles,":** Murat Halstead, *Fire the Salute!* (1860; reprint. Kingsport, Tenn.: Kingsport Press, 1960), 3.

83 **"The number of private bottles":** Halstead, *Fire the Salute!*, 4.

83 **They arrived in Chicago:** Halstead, *Fire the Salute!, 4.*

83 **"I want a nominee for Vice":** Weed to Seward, April 17, 1860, William Henry Seward Papers, University of Rochester.

83 **"Some of us":** Theodore Little to Weed, April 30, 1860, William Henry Seward Papers.

84 **"A free republican government":** Seward speech, March 3, 1858, *Congressional Globe*, 35th Congress, 1st Session, 944.

84 **could accept Douglas's popular sovereignty:** Van Deusen, *William Henry Seward,* 189–90.

84 **"normal condition of all the territory":** "National Republican Convention," *Chicago Tribune*, May 18, 1860, 4.

84 **"It was reported":** Halstead, *Fire the Salute!*, 34.

85 **Davis and Swett asked:** Leonard Swett, "Life and Services of David Davis," *Annual Report of the Illinois State Bar Association* (1887), 79.

85 **"They entertain no particle of doubt":** Halstead, *Fire the Salute!*, 30.

85 **enormous funds:** Donald, *Lincoln*, 248.

85 **"some wag pinned one of them":** Halstead, *Fire the Salute!*, 7.

86 **"cannot claim for him":** "The Chicago Nominations," *Douglass' Monthly*, June 1860, 276.

86 **"It was believed":** "How It Was Done," *Chicago Press and Tribune*, May 25, 1860, 2.

86 **THE WINNING MAN:** *Chicago Tribune*, May 15, 1860, 2.

86 **"there were thousands cheering":** Halstead, *Fire the Salute!*, 45.

87 **"annoyed and dejected":** Harriet Weed, ed., *Autobiography of Thurlow Weed* (Boston: Houghton Mifflin, 1884), 602.

87 **"I informed them very frankly":** Weed, ed., *Autobiography*, 602.

87 **"do my duty":** Weed, ed., *Autobiography*, 602.

87 **Davis and Swett considered this:** They had offered to bring him to Lincoln. Harriet Weed, ed., *Autobiography*, 601. Afterward Lincoln wrote to Swett, "You heard Weed converse with me." "To Leonard Swett," May 30, 1860, CW, vol. 4, 57.

87 **"Greeley was malignant":** Weed to Seward, May 20, 1860, William Henry Seward Papers.

88 **would not yet have received the offer:** Governor John Wood had mailed a letter, postmarked the previous day from Qunсy, Illinois, offering the use of his reception room. May 23, 1860, Illinois State Archives.

88 **"secret intrigues":** "Thurlow Weed in Springfield," *Illinois State Register*, May 25, 1860, 2.

88 **"That's a lie":** "How the Boobies Lie," *Chicago Tribune*, May 28, 1860, 2.

88 **Lincoln was already thinking of this:** "To William H. Seward," December 8, 1860, CW, vol. 4, 148.

88 **debtors' prison:** Van Deusen, *Thurlow Weed*, 5.

88 **"When he was eight":** Barnes, *Memoir of Thurlow Weed*, 2.

88 **"I found Mr. Lincoln sagacious":** Weed, ed., *Autobiography*, 603.

89 **"This conversation lasted":** Weed, ed., *Autobiography*, 603.

89 **"showed no signs":** "To Lyman Trumbull," June 5, 1860, CW, vol. 4, 71.

89 **a man of good character:** Van Deusen, *Thurlow Weed*, 256.

89 **"As to the matter":** "To Thurlow Weed," February 4, 1861, CW, vol. 4, 185.

CHAPTER 7: CONSPIRACY THEORIST: DUFF GREEN

93 **"It has been my purpose":** "Remarks at a Republican Rally, Springfield, Illinois," August 8, 1860, CW, vol. 4, 91.

94 **"What is it I could say":** "To George T. M. Davis," October 27, 1860, CW, vol. 4, 132–33.

94 **"Who is afraid":** "Seward's Speech at St. Paul," *Detroit Free Press*, September 21, 1860, 1.

94 **"Monster Excursion Trains":** "Grand Rally of the People," *Chicago Tribune*, October 3, 1860, 1.

94 **twenty thousand people:** "Magnificent Wide Awake Displays," *Cass County Republican*, October 11, 1860, 2.

94 **"This country is in more danger":** Morris, *Long Pursuit*, 190.

95 **"such a cheer":** *New York Tribune*, November 10, 1860, excerpted in Herbert Mitgang, *Lincoln: A Press Portrait* (New York: Fordham University Press, 2000), 203–4.

95 **"almost alone":** Mitgang, *Lincoln*.

95 **He went home to Mary:** Welles, *Diary of Gideon Welles*.

95 **"I then felt":** Gideon Welles, *Diary of Gideon Welles Secretary of the Navy under Lincoln and Johnson*, 3 vols. (Boston: Houghton Mifflin, 1911), vol. 1, 82.

95 **"He never overlooked":** Herndon, *Life of Lincoln*, 376.

95 **"start a running conversation":** Henry Villard, *Lincoln on the Eve of '61* (New York: Knopf, 1941), 14.

95 **"live disunionist":** Villard, *Lincoln on the Eve of '61*, 41.

95 **"Every newspaper he opened":** Villard, *Lincoln on the Eve of '61*, 23.

96 **"Is it desired":** "To John A. Gilmer," December 15, 1860, CW, vol. 4, 151–52.

96 **"a united Commonwealth":** "Independence Day," *Charleston Courier*, December 21, 1860, 2.

96 **persuade the United States:** "Postal Accommodations," *Charleston Courier*, December 21, 1860, 2.

96 **FOREIGN NEWS:** *Illinois State Journal*, December 22, 1860, 2.

96 **"absolve themselves":** "The Republican Party Stands by the Constitution," *Illinois State Journal*, December 25, 1860, 2.

96 **"No state can":** "To Thurlow Weed," December 17, 1860, CW, vol. 4, 154.

97 **"hoping that I could":** Duff Green, *Facts and Suggestions, Biographical, Historical, Financial and Political* (New York: Richardson, 1866), 226.

97 **eventual relation by marriage:** W. Stephen Belko, *The Invincible Duff Green: Whig of the West* (Columbia: University of Missouri Press, 2006), 24.

97 **"based on equality":** "Imprisonment for Debt," *United States Telegraph*, February 2, 1828, 4.

97 **"that every man is entitled":** "From the Dublin Weekly Register July 26," *United States Telegraph*, November 8, 1828, 2.

97 **Green opposed special treatment:** "Congressional," *United States Telegraph*, June 18, 1828, 2.

97 **"this system of refined cruelty":** "Imprisonment for Debt," *United States Telegraph*, February 2, 1828, 4.

97 **"The *fundamental principle*":** "Address of the Jackson State Convention to the People of Maryland," *United States Telegraph*, July 29, 1828, 2.

98 **"His independence was responsible":** Belko, *Invincible Duff Green*, 28.

98 **"that man is selfish":** Green, *Facts and Suggestions*, 22.

98 **knocked him into a gutter:** Fletcher M. Green, "Duff Green, Militant Journalist of the Old School," *American Historical Review* 52 (January 1947), 252.

98 **repeated his original insults:** Green's letter is reprinted in "Fracas at Washington," *Newbern Sentinel*, January 7, 1833, 2.

98 **relaxed his opposition to his creditor:** A sympathetic account of this episode can be found in Belko, *Invincible Duff Green*, 277–79.

99 **reported back to the foreign minister:** The imagined reports were going back to Prince Metternich, supposedly. *Baltimore Pilot*, January 25, 1841, 4.

99 **"Slavery has always existed":** Quoted in Green, "Duff Green, Militant Journalist of the Old School," 257.

99 **promote slavery in schools:** Green, "Duff Green, Militant Journalist of the Old School," 257.

99 **"The immigration from Europe":** "Foreign Influence," *American Statesman*, December 25, 1856, 2.

99 **asked his fellow Whig:** As in a letter to Green, May 18, 1849, CW, vol. 2, 49–50.

100 **"To the People":** Green, *Facts and Suggestions*, 218.

100 **"and reserved my influence":** Green, *Facts and Suggestions*, 225.

101 **"urged me to go to Springfield":** Green, *Facts and Suggestions*, 226.

101 **escaped the notice:** The author's search of the *Illinois Journal* and *Illinois Register* found no mention of Green in the relevant time period, nor did searches of multiple databases find any mention until after the New Year, when Green returned to Washington and news services there reported his visit.

101 **"remember me to your amiable lady":** Duff Green to Lincoln, January 7, 1861, Abraham Lincoln Papers, Series 1, General Correspondence, 1833–1916, LOC.

101 **"speaks of Mr. Lincoln":** "Interview of Duff Green with Mr. Lincoln on the Crisis," *New York Herald*, January 6, 1861, 1.

102 **"that secession is revolution or rebellion":** "Letter from Gov. Wycliffe," *Illinois State Journal*, December 27, 1860, 2.

103 **"absolute control":** "Interview of Duff Green with Mr. Lincoln on the Crisis."

104 **"Duff Green is out here":** "To Lyman Trumbull," December 28, 1860, CW, vol. 4, 163.

104 **"despairing of any action":** "Interview of Duff Green with Mr. Lincoln on the Crisis."

104 **"Entertain no proposition":** "To William Kellogg," December 11, 1860, CW, vol. 4, 150.

104 **"would lose us everything":** "To Thurlow Weed," December 17, 1860, CW, vol. 4, 154.

105 **"scattered to the winds":** Milton, *Eve of Conflict*, 531.

105 **"placed party first":** Milton, *Eve of Conflict*, 522.

105 **"So far as the Republican Party":** Henry Adams, *The Great Secession Winter of 1860–61* (New York: Barnes, 1958), 26.

105 **"took on the characteristics":** Drew Gilpin Faust, ed., *The Ideology of Slavery* (Baton Rouge: Louisiana State University Press, 1981), 3–4.

105 **"Southern thought must justify":** George Fitzhugh, "Southern Thought," in Faust, ed., *Ideology of Slavery*, 276–77.

106 **"pauper banditti":** Fitzhugh's book is quoted at length in "Letter from Francis P. Blair," *National Era*, October 2, 1856, 4.

106 **celebrating Fitzhugh's book:** "Sociology for the South," *Charleston Mercury*, April 21, 1855, 2.

CHAPTER 8: OUTCAST: WILLIAM FLORVILLE

109 **"from a young to an old man":** "Farewell Address at Springfield, Illinois," February 11, 1861, CW, vol. 4, 190.

110 **Lincoln knew Florville's son:** The elder Florville gave an update on the son to Lincoln in his 1863 letter. Florville to Lincoln, December 27, 1863, Abraham Lincoln Papers, Series 1, General Correspondence, 1833–1916, LOC. Birth date from 1880 census.

110 **"a Smart boy for his age":** Florville to Lincoln, December 27, 1863, Abraham Lincoln Papers, Series 1, General Correspondence, 1833–1916, LOC.

110 **"Nothing is so necessary":** Quoted in Hudson, "William Florville: Lincoln's Barber and Friend," *Negro History Bulletin* 37 (September 1974), 280.

110 **"I will always use":** "William Florville," *Illinois State Register*, May 28, 1841, 4.

110 **born on the north coast of Haiti:** "Death of William Florville," *Illinois State Journal*, April 14, 1868, 4.

110 **He was born in 1807:** "Death of William Florville."

110 **his godmother took:** John E. Washington, who spoke with descendants, says the move came after a political upheaval in 1821–22, *They Knew Lincoln* (1942; reprint. New York: Oxford, 2018), 186; researcher Mary Beth Roderick, via the Springfield Historical Society, identified a ship's passenger arrival log of a "Master Flowile" to Baltimore on June 30, 1823.

110 **apprentice to a barber:** Washington, *They Knew Lincoln*, 186.

110 **So in late 1831:** "Death of William Florville," *Illinois State Register*, April 16, 1868, 4.

111 **about two hundred people by 1860:** Richard E. Hart, "Springfield's African Americans as a Part of the Lincoln Community," *Journal of the Abraham Lincoln Association* 20 (Winter 1999), 41.

111 **He played clarinet:** Washington, *They Knew Lincoln*, 189.

111 **supported an effort:** "A School Master Wanted," *Sangamo Journal*, May 28, 1846, 3.

111 **first-ever Catholic mass:** Washington, *They Knew Lincoln*, 199.

111 **"those duties":** "Barber's Shop Removed," *Sangamo Journal*, April 2, 1841, 3.

111 **oversized mirror:** Washington, *They Knew Lincoln*, 185.

111 **"large collection of paintings":** Washington, *They Knew Lincoln*, 197.

111 **removing razors from his presence:** Joshua Speed to Herndon, 1865–66, in Wilson and Davis, eds., *Herndon's Informants*, 475.

111 **"The *Razor* is not to be trusted":** Washington, *They Knew Lincoln*, 197.

111 **put former locations up for sale:** "For Sale at a Bargain," *Sangamo Journal*, December 2, 1842, 3.

112 **shaved the man a final time:** Washington, *They Knew Lincoln*, 192.

112 **"our 'Billy the Barber'":** "To Charles R. Welles," September 27, 1852, CW, vol. 2, 159.

112 **"Notice Extraordinaire":** Quoted in Hudson, "William Florville," 280.

112 **"my faithful subjects":** Washington, *They Knew Lincoln*, 193–95.

112 **"the Heir Apparent":** Washington, *They Knew Lincoln*, 194.

112 **"Proclamation Extraordinary":** *Sangamo Journal*, January 16, 1845, 4.

113 **required to file evidence:** Elmer Gertz, "The Black Laws of Illinois," *Journal of the Illinois State Historical Society* 56 (Autumn 1963), 463.

113 **"The owner of said":** "Notice," *Illinois State Register*, January 1, 1841, 4.

113 **"among us as underlings":** "Speech at Peoria, Illinois," October 16, 1854, CW, vol. 2, 254.

113 **"never manifested any impatience":** "Fifth Debate with Stephen A. Douglas, at Galesburg, Illinois," October 7, 1858, CW, vol. 3, 222.

114 **"proposal to put":** "Richard Yates' Vote," *Illinois State Register*, October 12, 1854, 4.

114 **Democratic majority decided:** Moore and Moore, *Owen Lovejoy*, 82.

114 **local Colonization Society:** "Illinois State Colonization Society," *Illinois State Journal*, February 10, 1858, 1.

114 **meeting at Clinton's Hall:** Untitled article, *Illinois State Journal*, February 18, 1858, 3.

114 **"We have been unable to ascertain":** Untitled article, *Illinois State Journal*, February 18, 1858, 3.

115 **"There was an extravagant display":** "A Nigger Ball," *Illinois State Register*, August 22, 1860, 3.

115 **"general business man":** "A Nigger Ball."

115 **"Florville is a young man":** "Correction," *Illinois State Register*, August 23, 1860, 3.

115 **"putting on airs":** Villard, *Lincoln on the Eve of '61*, 16.

116 **"Billy, let's give them a chance":** Harold Holzer, *Lincoln President-Elect* (New York: Simon & Schuster, 2008), 85.

116 **"You will look":** CW, vol. 4, 130n.

116 **"As to the whiskers":** "To Grace Bedell," October 19, 1860, CW, vol. 4, 129.

116 **One visitor was the Republican governor:** Florville to Lincoln, December 27, 1863, Abraham Lincoln Papers, Series 1, General Correspondence, 1833–1916, LOC.

116 **"irresistible feeling of gratitude":** Florville to Lincoln, December 27, 1863, Abraham Lincoln Papers, Series 1, General Correspondence, 1833–1916, Library of Congress.

117 **"If any good reason exists":** "Annual Message to Congress," December 3, 1861, CW, vol. 5, 39.

CHAPTER 9: EDITOR: WILLIAM HENRY SEWARD

119 **"special qualifications":** "The Chicago Convention," *New York Times*, May 24, 1860, 4.

119 **subjected to "humiliations":** To Frances Seward, May 30, 1860, in Frederick W. Seward, ed., *Seward at Washington, 1846–1861* (New York: Derby, 1891), 454.

120 **"Believe me sincere":** Frederick Seward, ed., *Seward at Washington, 1846–1861*, 462.

120 **"It now really looks":** "To William H. Seward," October 12, 1860, CW, vol. 4, 126.

120 **"I will try":** To Frances Seward, December 28, 1860, in Frederick Seward, ed., *Seward at Washington, 1846–1861*, 487.

120 **"Treason is all around":** Frederick Seward, ed., *Seward at Washington, 1846–1861*, 488.

120 **dropped a pistol:** "Scenes at the Capitol Saturday," *National Republican*, January 14, 1861, 3.

120 **"meet prejudice with conciliation":** John Hay and John G. Nicolay, *Abraham Lincoln: A History* (New York: Century, 1890), vol. 3, 322.

120 **He even grew vague:** Van Deusen, *William Henry Seward*, 245.

120 **he told a Virginia friend:** Van Deusen, *William Henry Seward*, 247.

120 **"I am the only hopeful":** Van Deusen, *William Henry Seward*, 246.

121 **"If the forts":** "To Francis P. Blair, Sr.," December 21, 1860, CW, vol. 4, 157.

121 **He suggested Southern Unionists:** To Lincoln, December 28, 1860, Abraham Lincoln Papers, Series 1, General Correspondence, 1833–1916, LOC.

121 **"I shall have trouble":** "To William H. Seward," January 12, 1861, CW, vol. 4, 173.

122 **"simply insists upon holding":** "Speech from the Balcony of the Bates House in Indianapolis, Indiana," February 11, 1861, CW, vol. 4, 195.

122 **"hope to the world":** "Speech in Independence Hall, Philadelphia, Pennsylvania," February 22, 1861, CW, vol. 4, 240.

122 **"there was no conspiracy":** Ward Hill Lamon, *The Life of Abraham Lincoln* (Boston: James R. Osgood, 1872), 513.

122 **a berth too short for him:** Lamon, *Life of Abraham Lincoln*, 524.

122 **Capitol came into view:** Lamon, *Life of Abraham Lincoln*, 525.

123 **By his own account:** To Frances Seward, February 23, 1861, in Frederick Seward, ed., *Seward at Washington, 1846–1861*, 511.

123 **their breakfast together:** Among other accounts is Lamon, *Life of Abraham Lincoln*, 526.

123 **greet the future commander in chief:** Earl S. Miers and C. Percy Powell, eds., *Lincoln Day by Day* (Washington, DC: Lincoln Sesquicentennial Commission, 1960), vol. 2, 21.

123 **"one part of the business":** Frederick Seward, ed., *Seward at Washington, 1846–1861*, 511.

124 **"for the fashion of this world":** "Local News," *National Republican*, February 25, 1861, 3.

124 **"made several allusions":** "Local News."

124 **"I, my dear sir":** "To Lincoln, Sunday Evening, February 24, 1861," in Hay and Nicolay, *Lincoln*, vol. 3, 320.

124 **"the Chicago platform":** "First Inaugural Address—First Edition and Revisions," CW, March 4, 1861, vol. 4, 249.

126 **"guardian angel of the nation":** CW, vol. 4, 262n.

127 **"Whatever the inaugural gained":** Hay and Nicolay, *Lincoln*, vol. 3, 322.

127 **beneath a cloudy sky:** "The New Government," *New York Herald*, March 5, 1861, 1.

127 **"looked very agitated":** "The New Government," *New York Herald*, March 5, 1861, 1.

127 **personally supervising a battery of artillery:** Hay and Nicolay, *Lincoln*, vol. 3, 325.

127 **"We are grievously disappointed":** "The Important Inaugural," *Charleston Courier*, March 5, 1861, 2.

128 **"little better than our worst fears":** *Douglass' Monthly*, April 1861, in Foner, ed., *Life and Writings*, vol. 3, 72.

128 **"He reached the Capitol":** *Douglass' Monthly*, April 1861, in Foner, ed., *Life and Writings*, vol. 3, 71.

128 **"moderate men of both parties":** "News from the State Capital," *New York Herald*, March 5, 1861, 5.

129 **"compound Cabinet":** To Frances Seward, March 8, 1861, Frederick Seward, ed., *Seward at Washington, 1846–1861*, 518.

129 **"My Dear Sir":** To Lincoln, March 2, 1861, reproduced in Hay and Nicolay, *Lincoln*, 370.

129 **"from the man":** Hay and Nicolay, *Lincoln*, 371.

129 **"I can't afford":** Hay and Nicolay, *Lincoln*, 371.

129 **"I believe I can endure":** To Frances Seward, March 8, 1861, Frederick Seward, ed., *Seward at Washington, 1846–1861*, 518.

130 **who would summon them:** Welles recounts this in his *Diary*, vol. 1, 8.

130 **"acting at times from impulse":** Gideon Welles, *Lincoln and Seward* (New York: Sheldon, 1874), 9.

130 **"Some Thoughts":** To Lincoln, April 1, 1861, in Hay and Nicolay, *Lincoln*, vol. 3, 445.

130 **"*I* must do it":** "To William H. Seward," April 1, 1861, CW, vol. 4, 317.

131 **blurred what Republicans stood for:** T. Harry Williams, *Lincoln and the Radicals* (Madison: University of Wisconsin Press, 1941), 15.

131 **"Seward has a passion":** Welles, August 12, 1862, *Diary*, vol. 1, 79.

CHAPTER 10: EMISSARY: JESSIE BENTON FRÉMONT

135 **"failing of execution":** "Message to Congress in Special Session," July 4, 1861, CW, vol. 4, 430.

136 **"bombardment of their cities":** "To Winfield Scott," April 25, 1861, CW, vol. 4, 344.

136 **He assigned Joshua Speed:** "To Robert Anderson," May 14, 1861, CW, vol. 4, 369.

137 **"Suppose you step over at once":** To William H. Seward, July 3, 1861, CW, vol. 4, 420.

138 **"a noble-spirited woman":** To Frances Seward, January 4, 1854, in Frederick Seward, ed., *Seward at Washington, 1846–1861*, 217.

138 **"quiet earnest industrious":** Hay, August 28, 1861, in John Hay, *Inside Lincoln's White House: The Complete Civil War Diary of John Hay,* eds. Michael Burlingame and John R. Turner Ettlinger (Carbondale: Southern Illinois University Press, 1997), 24.

138 **"Do you know who I am":** Recounted in Hoffman to John C. Frémont, April 29, 1852, Mary Lee Spence, ed., *Expeditions of John Charles Frémont* (Urbana: University of Illinois Press, 1973), vol. 3, 354–59.

138 **"It is not fit":** Quoted by Jessie Frémont in Pamela Herr and Mary Lee Spence, *The Letters of Jessie Benton Frémont* (Urbana: University of Illinois Press, 1993), 267.

138 **"Everything was changed":** Jessie Benton Frémont, *Souvenirs of My Time* (Boston: Lothrop, 1887), 166.

139 **Saint Louis, unlike the rest:** Tom Chaffin, *Pathfinder: John Charles Frémont and the Course of American Empire* (New York: Farrar, Straus and Giroux, 2002), 458.

139 **"I find it impossible":** To John Frémont, July 26, 1861, in Jessie Benton Frémont and Francis Preston Frémont, *Great Events in the Life of Major General John C. Frémont, F.R.G.S. Chevalier de l'Ordre pour le Merite; etc. and Jessie Benton Frémont* (Unpublished, Bancroft Library collection, 1891), 233.

139 **"troops on paper":** To Elizabeth Blair Lee, July 27, 1861, Herr and Spence, eds., *Letters of Jessie Benton Frémont*, 255.

139 **Jessie had a wealthy cousin:** Frémont, *Souvenirs of My Time*, 167.

139 **she tied a red:** "The Fremont Rifles at St. Louis," *Chicago Tribune*, September 26, 2.

140 **"so that all could have":** "From Our Own Correspondent," *Cincinnati Daily Press*, September 20, 1861, 3.

140 **"Camp Jessie":** "Gen S. R. Curtis," *Quad City Times*, September 17, 1861, 2.

140 **"She acts as his private secretary":** The account in the *Tribune* was repeated verbatim in some papers and seems to have been the basis for paeans to Jessie in others. "Jessie Fremont," *Chicago Tribune*, August 16, 1861, 1.

140 **"Now I hope":** Some sources record this as a letter to John, but the original shows it is addressed to Jessie. To Jessie Benton Frémont, August 13, 1861, Abraham Lincoln Papers, Series 1, General Correspondence, 1833–1916, manuscript/mixed material, LOC.

141 **shortly after daybreak on August 30:** Frémont, *Great Events*, 252.

141 **reading the newspapers:** Hay and Nicolay, *Lincoln*, vol. 4, 416.

141 **"Fire must be met with water":** "How to End the War," *Douglass' Monthly*, May 1861, 451.

142 **"struck the entire Cabinet":** "Our Special Washington Despatches," *New York Herald*, September 8, 1861, 1.

142 **"joyful satisfaction":** "How It Was Received," *Chicago Tribune*, September 2, 1861, 1.

142 **"the most important document":** "General Fremont's Proclamation," *New York Despatch*, September 4, 1861, 4.

142 **"If the rebellion":** *Cincinnati Daily Press*, September 2, 1861, 2.

142 **"servile insurrection":** "To the Editors of the *Daily Press*," *Cincinnati Daily Press*, September 6, 1861, 3.

142 **"The nation cried":** "A Pulpit Response to Fremont," *Chicago Tribune*, September 4, 1861, 2.

142 **"one of the most glorious consequences":** *Congressional Globe*, August 2, 1861, 37th Congress, First Session, 414–15.

143 **the final legislation:** Williams, *Lincoln and the Radicals*, 27.

143 **"deeds of manumission":** One such deed is copied by Frémont in *Great Events*, 267.

143 **"confiscated property":** "General Frémont's Proclamation," Foner, ed., *Life and Writings*, vol. 3, 160.

143 **"The very fact":** "Fremont's Proclamation," *Joliet Signal*, September 10, 1861, 2.

143 **"ecstacies over Frémont's infamous proclamation":** "The Cincinnati Gazette," *Louisville Courier*, September 3, 1861, 2.

143 **"would, by turning loose":** "Voice of the People," *Louisville Courier*, September 7, 1861, 1.

144 **"most disastrous results":** To Lincoln, September 13, 1861, Abraham Lincoln Papers, Series 1, General Correspondence, 1833–1916, manuscript/mixed material, LOC.

144 **"The very arms we had furnished":** "To Orville H. Browning," September 22, 1861, CW, vol. 4, 533.

144 **"two points":** "To John C. Fremont," September 2, 1861, CW, vol. 4, 506.

144 **"If I were to retract":** To Lincoln, September 8, 1861, Abraham Lincoln Papers, Series 1, General Correspondence, 1833–1916, manuscript/mixed material, LOC.

144 **He didn't send:** Allan Nevins, *Frémont: Pathmarker of the West* (New York: Appleton, 1939), 316.

145 **"I left by the night train":** Excerpt from *Great Events,* Herr and Spence, eds., *Letters of Jessie Benton Frémont,* 264.

145 **The messenger returned:** Herr and Spence, eds., *Letters of Jessie Benton Frémont,* 265.

145 **"I thought it best":** Her fullest account of the meeting is in Herr and Spence, eds., *Letters of Jessie Benton Frémont,* 264–67.

145 **"All my life":** Excerpt from *Great Events,* Herr and Spence, eds., *Letters of Jessie Benton Frémont,* 265.

146 **"I never allow":** Michael Burlingame, *An American Marriage: The Untold Story of Abraham Lincoln and Mary Todd* (New York: Pegasus, 2021), 251.

146 **"the President did not speak":** Her account of the meeting is in an excerpt from *Great Events,* Herr and Spence, eds., *Letters of Jessie Benton Frémont,* 265.

147 **"embarrassed in the presence":** Donald, We Are Lincoln Men, 113.

147 **"She . . . taxed me so violently":** Hay and Nicolay, *Lincoln,* vol. 4, 415.

147 **"Who would have expected":** Excerpt from *Great Events,* Herr and Spence, eds., *Letters of Jessie Benton Frémont,* 267.

148 **"Fremont's proclamation":** "To Orville H. Browning," September 22, 1861, CW, vol. 4, 531–32.

149 **"Your answer, just received":** To John C. Fremont, September 11, 1861, CW, vol. 4, 518.

149 **Frémont first read Lincoln's order:** CW, vol. 4, 518n.

149 **"The action of Fremont":** "General Frémont's Proclamation," Foner, ed., *Life and Writings,* vol. 3, 160.

149 **"pusillanimous and pro-slavery":** "Fremont and Freedom," Foner, ed., *Life and Writings,* vol. 3, 174.

149 **"FREMONT AND FREEDOM":** Foner, ed., *Life and Writings,* vol. 3, 174.

149 **"is losing the confidence":** "To David Hunter," September 9, 1861, CW, vol. 4, 513.

150 **"I am now convinced":** Samuel R. Curtis, excerpted in Hay and Nicolay, *Lincoln,* vol. 4, 432.

150 **"The Proclamation of Gen. Fremont":** "The War and Slavery," *New York Times,* September 3, 1861, 4.

CHAPTER 11: STRATEGIST: GEORGE B. MCCLELLAN

153 **"a gentle, but firm":** "Memoranda of Military Policy Suggested by the Bull Run Defeat," July 23, 1861, CW, vol. 4, 457.

154 **waived its requirements:** Stephen W. Sears, *George B. McClellan: The Young Napoleon* (New York: Ticknor & Fields, 1988), 1.

155 **"I find myself":** To Ellen McClellan, July 27, 1861, in Stephen W. Sears, ed., *The Civil War Papers of George B. McClellan* (New York: Ticknor & Fields, 1989), 70.

155 **a paper praising Napoleon's skill:** Sears, *George B. McClellan*, 11.

155 **"frequent military marches":** "To General Officers, Division of the Potomac," August 4, 1861, Sears, ed., *Civil War Papers*, 77.

155 **"No general had ever better cause":** To Mary Ellen McClellan, July 17, 1862, in McClellan, *McClellan's Own Story*, 451.

155 **"display such overwhelming strength":** To Lincoln, August 2, 1861, McClellan, *McClellan's Own Story*, 71–72.

155 **273,000 men:** McClellan, *McClellan's Own Story*, 73.

156 **He took to calling:** McClellan, *McClellan's Own Story*, 152.

156 **"a terrible place":** To Mary Ellen McClellan, August 16, 1861, McClellan, *McClellan's Own Story*, 86–87.

156 **"the enemy have":** McClellan, *McClellan's Own Story*, 86.

156 **the general declined:** Donald, *Lincoln*, 510.

156 **went upstairs to bed:** Sears, *George B. McClellan*, 132.

157 **"If you will give":** "To George B. McClellan," February 3, 1862, CW, vol. 5, 119.

157 **"I think you had better":** "To George B. McClellan," April 6, 1862, CW, vol. 5, 182.

157 **comparing the president to the driver of a buggy:** Williams, *Lincoln and the Radicals*, 3.

157 **"We are to pursue":** "How Goes the War?," *New York Tribune*, December 6, 1861, 5.

157 **presumed to speak:** "The Satanic Abolition Element in Congress and in the Press," *New York Herald*, December 7, 1861, 6.

158 **they reminded her of Willie:** Burlingame, *American Marriage*, 80.

158 **couldn't bear the music:** Jean H. Baker, *Mary Todd Lincoln: A Biography* (New York: Norton, 1987), 216.

158 **Tad, who wore a uniform:** Huidekoper, *Personal Notes*, 12.

158 **an astonishing risk:** Chase, quoted in Hay and Nicolay, *Lincoln*, vol. 5, 236.

159 **"If I save":** To Stanton, June 28, 1862, Sears, ed., *Civil War Papers*, 305.

159 **promised to send:** "To George B. McClellan," July 4, 1862, CW, vol. 5, 305.

159 **"heroism and skill":** "To George B. McClellan," July 5, 1862, CW, vol. 5, 307.

159 **"masterpiece of strategy":** "To George B. McClellan," July 6, 1862, CW, vol. 5, 308.

159 **McClellan stepped aboard:** McClellan, *McClellan's Own Story*, 487.

159 **thanked the general:** McClellan, *McClellan's Own Story*, 487.

159 ***"I had to order"*:** To Ellen McClellan, July 17, 1862, Sears, ed., *Civil War Papers*, 362.

159 **troops warmly welcomed:** Sears, *George B. McClellan*, 226.

159 **could safely board ships and retreat:** "Memorandum of Interviews between Lincoln and Officers of the Army of the Potomac," July 8–9, 1862, CW, vol. 5, 310.

160 **"His reply may be":** To Mary Ellen McClellan, July 20, 1862, Sears, ed., *Civil War Papers*, 367.

160 **"poor, maimed, brave fellows":** To Mary Ellen McClellan, July 26, 1862, in McClellan, *McClellan's Own Story*, 455.

160 **"We will, on the contrary":** "To the Union Men of Western Virginia," May 26, 1861, Sears, ed., *Civil War Papers*, 26.

160 **"Somehow or other":** Sears, *George B. McClellan*, 5.

160 **"upon the highest principles":** To Lincoln, July 7, 1862, in McClellan, *McClellan's Own Story*, 488.

161 **favored gradual emancipation:** McClellan, *McClellan's Own Story*, 34.

161 **believed only in "idleness":** McClellan, *McClellan's Own Story*, 34.

161 **"He dwelt earnestly":** Welles, *Diary*, undated entry, vol. 1, 70.

161 **such a "momentous" step:** Welles, *Diary*, vol. 1.

161 **"weary, care-worn and troubled":** Orville H. Browning, July 15, 1862, *The Diary of Orville Hickman Browning* (Springfield: Illinois State Historical Library, 1925), vol. 1, 559–60.

162 **US Coast Survey map:** Edwin Hergesheimer, "Map Showing the Distribution of the Slave Population of the Southern States," 1861, LOC.

162 **"spoke of the importance":** Browning, July 24, 1862, *Diary*, vol. 1, 562.

163 **"that if by magic":** Browning, July 25, 1862, *Diary*, vol. 1, 563.

163 **"passive, cowardly and treacherous":** "The President and His Speeches," *Douglass' Monthly*, September 1862, in Foner, ed., *Life and Writings*, vol. 3, 268.

163 **"disastrously remiss":** "The Prayer of Twenty Millions," *New York Tribune*, dated August 19 and published August 20, 1862, quoted in CW, vol. 5, 389n.

163 **"I would save the Union":** "To Horace Greeley," August 22, 1862, CW, vol. 5, 388.

164 **"does not understand strategy":** Sears, *George B. McClellan*, 241.

164 **"flat treason":** Sears, *George B. McClellan*, 241.

165 **"a braggart and a liar":** His remark is noted in Welles, September 2, 1862, *Diary*, vol. 1, 104.

165 **"so absorbed in his scheme":** Welles, August 17, 1862, *Diary*, vol. 1, 83.

165 **"that he ought to be shot":** Welles, September 1, 1862, *Diary*, vol. 1, 102.

165 **"There is considerable uneasiness":** Welles, August 31, 1862, *Diary*, vol. 1, 99.

166 **"distressed and depressed":** Welles, September 1, 1862, *Diary*, vol. 1, 100.

166 **"I am entirely tired out":** To McClellan, August 31, 1862, in McClellan, *McClellan's Own Story*, 525.

166 **"trembling with excitement":** Welles, September 2, 1862, *Diary*, vol. 1, 104.

166 **ripped his last summer uniform:** To Mary Ellen McClellan, August 21, 1862, in McClellan, *McClellan's Own Story*, 470.

166 **"Pope is ordered":** To Mary Ellen McClellan, September 2, 1862, in Sears, ed., *Civil War Papers*, 428.

167 **"asserted that it was impossible":** McClellan, *McClellan's Own Story*, 535.

167 **yellow sash and sword:** Sears, *George B. McClellan*, 260.

167 **roared in celebration:** McClellan, *McClellan's Own Story*, 537. The general "was received by his troops with the most enthusiastic demonstrations of gratification and pleasure." Dispatch from the *Baltimore American*, in "Military Matters," *Alexandria Gazette*, September 4, 1862, 3.

167 **"said he had done":** Welles, *Diary*, September 2, 1862, vol. 1, 105.

167 **Lincoln might hang himself:** CW, vol. 5, 404n.

167 **"a national calamity":** Welles, *Diary*, September 2, 1862, vol. 1, 105.

167 **"the slows":** Welles, *Lincoln and Seward*, 13.

167 **"as promptly and well":** Welles, *Lincoln and Seward*, 13.

167 **"The will of God":** "Meditation on the Divine Will," [September 2, 1862?], CW, vol. 5, 403–4.

168 **had been "unpardonable":** Hay, September 5, 1862, in *Inside Lincoln's White House*, 38–39.

168 **"This evening some twenty or thirty thousand":** Welles, *Diary*, September 6, 1862, vol. 1, 111.

169 **"all persons held as slaves":** "Preliminary Emancipation Proclamation," September 22, 1862, CW, vol. 5, 434.

170 **"When, early in the war":** "To Albert G. Hodges," April 4, 1864, CW, vol. 7, 281–82.

170 **"wishes to outgeneral":** Welles, *Diary*, September 3, 1862, vol. 1, 107.

170 **"independent of his Cabinet":** Welles, *Lincoln and Seward*, 10.

CHAPTER 12: SOVEREIGN: LEAN BEAR

173 **He chose a five-foot gauge:** "Order Establishing Gauge of Union Pacific Railroad," January 21, 1863, CW, vol. 6, 68.

173 **1832 Supreme Court ruling:** *Worcester v. Georgia*, authored by John Marshall.

174 **"maniacs or wild beasts":** John A. Haymond, *The Infamous Dakota War Trials* (Jefferson, NC: McFarland, 2016), 48.

174 **telling the commission to make "revisions":** Haymond, *Infamous Dakota War Trials*, 90.

174 **"threaten the Administration":** Welles, December 4, 1862, *Diary*, vol. 1, 186.

175 **"proven to have participated":** "To the Senate," December 11, 1862, CW, vol. 5, 551.

175 **"the novelty of the occasion":** "Our Indian Relations," *National Intelligencer*, March 27, 1863, 6.

175 **Seward, Chase, and Welles came:** "Our Indian Relations."

175 **aged sixteen and eighteen:** "The Indian Chiefs in New York!," *Sunday Dispatch*, April 12, 1863, 2.

175 **ladies' hats:** Two people who seem to be the brides appear in ladies' hats in a photograph taken just after the meeting. Brady, "Indian Delegation," 1863, Library of Congress Prints and Photographs Division.

176 **"every person":** "Our Indian Relations," *National Intelligencer*, March 27, 1863, 6.

176 **born in 1813:** George Bird Grinnell, *The Fighting Cheyennes* (New York: Scribner, 1915), 139n.

176 **"an old brave man":** George Bird Grinnell, *By Cheyenne Campfires* (New Haven: Yale University, 1926), 54.

176 **"Go slowly":** Grinnell, *By Cheyenne Campfires, 54.*

176 **brought his son to war:** He is shown at war against the Pawnee with his son, in Grinnell, *By Cheyenne Campfires*, 55.

177 **$50,000 per year:** Treaty terms are described in "Report to the President of the Indian Peace Commission," in *Annual Report of the Commissioner of Indian Affairs, for the Year 1868*, (Washington, DC: Government Printing Office, 1868), 32.

177 **"Indian nations against the commission":** Report to the President of the Indian Peace Commission."

177 **signed as a witness:** Treaty with Arapaho and Cheyenne, February 18, 1861. Native American Law Center collection.

178 **"Avo-na-co":** Treaty with Arapaho and Cheyenne.

178 **cut overland to Fort Leavenworth:** "News of the Week," *Harrisburg Patriot*, March 26, 1863, 8.

178 **"gentle and amiable faces":** "Our Indian Relations."

178 **"Say to them":** "Grand Council of Indians," *National Republican*, March 27, 1863, 3.

178 **"weak and nervous":** "Grand Council of Indians."

178 **was an omen:** Oral tradition related to the author by Gordon Yellowman, Director, Culture and Language Program, Cheyenne and Arapaho Tribes, December 2022.

179 **"with perfect freedom":** "Grand Council of Indians."

179 **"a natural orator":** "Our Indian Relations."

179 **"the chiefs who had come":** "Grand Council of Indians."

179 **"The President is the Great Chief":** "Grand Council of Indians."

179 **"Many white people":** "Grand Council of Indians."

179 **"He asked the president":** "The President and the Wild Indians," *Evening Star*, March 27, 1863, 3.

180 **"We pale-faced people":** The full Lincoln speech is in "Speech to Indians," March 27, 1863, CW, vol. 6, 151.

183 **"bread, raw meat and coffee":** Stan Hoig, *The Peace Chiefs of the Cheyennes*, (Norman: University of Oklahoma Press, 1980), 73.

183 **"the antics of the monkeys":** All quotes in this paragraph from Hoig, *Peace Chiefs of the Cheyennes.*

183 **molested the first Indians they found:** "Report to the President of the Indian Peace Commission," in *Annual Report of the Commissioner of Indian Affairs*, 34.

183 **"A number of us mounted":** Grinnell, *Fighting Cheyennes*, 138–40.

184 **killing him along with his son:** Weeks, *Farewell, My Nation* (Wheeling, WV: Harlan Davidson, 1990), 115.

184 **"Over $300,000 worth":** "The Indian War," *New York Times*, September 1, 1864, 5.

184 **"the savage tide":** "The Indian Outbreak," *New York Times*, September 8, 1864, 2.

184 **"to kill Indians":** "Report to the President of the Indian Peace Commission," 35.

184 **God sanctioned the massacre:** Weeks, *Farewell, My Nation*, 116.

185 **"useless and expensive":** "Report to the President of the Indian Peace Commission," 35.

CHAPTER 13: DISSIDENT: GEORGE H. PENDLETON

187 **Those attending included:** "Democratic Anti-war Meeting," *Illinois State Journal*, January 7, 1863, 2.

187 **"a crusade":** "Democratic Anti-war Meeting."

188 **Taney ordered a court appearance:** A detailed account of the case is in William H. Rehnquist, *All the Laws but One: Civil Liberties in Wartime* (New York: Knopf, 2001), 26–39.

188 **"are all the laws":** "Message to Congress," July 4, 1861, CW, vol. 4, 430.

188 **"Each public officer":** "Speech at Springfield, Illinois," July 26, 1857, CW, vol. 2, 402.

189 **"No free people":** G. M. D. Bloss, *Life and Speeches of George H. Pendleton* (Cincinnati: Miami Printing, 1868), 43–44.

189 **served as Hamilton's second:** Bloss, *Life and Speeches*, 6.

189 **called as a witness:** "The Washington Tragedy," *Cincinnati Daily Press*, April 21, 1859, 3.

189 **"Peace is the first step":** George H. Pendleton, *Speech on the Enlistment of Negro Soldiers* (Washington, DC: House of Representatives, 1863), 7.

189 **"The Union and the Government:** Serenade in Washington, December 19, 1860, in Bloss, *Life and Speeches*, 30.

190 **Pendleton became more obstructive:** Mach, *Gentleman George*, 79.

190 **"they will meet":** Pendleton, *Speech on the Enlistment of Negro Soldiers*, 4.

191 **"The habit of declaring sympathies":** In Benjamin Perley Poore, *Life and Public Services of General Ambrose Burnside* (Providence: J. A. and R. A. Reid, 1882), 206–7.

191 **"denounced General Burnside's order":** "From Columbus," *Wisconsin State Journal*, May 2, 1863, 1.

191 **canopy and a giant American flag:** James L. Vallandigham, *Life of Clement L. Vallandigham* (Baltimore: Turnbull, 1872), 265.

191 **"an injurious, cruel":** *Chicago Times*, as reproduced in "Vallandigham the Traitor," *Chicago Tribune*, May 7, 1863, 2.

191 **he "spat" on General Order 38:** Vallandigham, *Life*, 266.

191 **"wicked Abolition war":** Vallandigham, *Life*, 267.

192 **"The hissing Copperhead":** "The News," *Chicago Tribune*, May 2, 1861, 1.

192 **fired a pistol:** "From Cincinnati," *Chicago Tribune*, May 6, 1863, 1.

192 **burned the office:** "From Cincinnati."

192 **"I am here":** Hay and Nicolay, *Lincoln*, vol. 7, 332.

192 **ordering the opposition *Chicago Times*:** General Order 84, in Poore, *Life and Public Services*, 210.

192 **"a constant source":** Hay and Nicolay, *Lincoln*, vol. 7, 338.

192 **"It was an error":** Welles, May 19, 1863, *Diary*, vol. 1, 306.

193 **"would excite far less sympathy":** Hay and Nicolay, *Lincoln*, vol. 7, 338.

193 **Pendleton went to meet him:** Thomas S. Mach, *"Gentleman George" Hunt Pendleton* (Kent, OH: Kent State University, 2007), 86.

193 **"created much feeling":** Welles, June 3, 1863, *Diary*, vol. 1, 321.

193 **"When I shall wish":** "To Ambrose E. Burnside," May 29, 1863, CW, vol. 6, 237.

193 **"a clear, flagrant":** "To Erastus Corning and Others," June 12, 1863, CW, vol. 6, 260–69.

194 **"more than regal":** CW, vol. 6, 269n.

194 **Pendleton was its chairman:** "From Washington," *Cincinnati Commercial Tribune*, June 26, 1863, 3.

194 **"My dear sir":** Chase to Lincoln, June 25, 1863, Abraham Lincoln Papers, Series 1, General Correspondence, 1833–1916, manuscript/mixed material, LOC.

194 **"nearly half an hour":** "Washington," *Vermont Chronicle*, June 30, 1863, 3.

194 **the next morning:** "From Washington," *Cincinnati Commercial Tribune*, June 26, 1863, 3.

195 **telegram from his pocket:** Welles, June 28, 1863, *Diary*, vol. 1, 348.

195 **"Save giving too much":** Welles, June 28, 1863, *Diary*, vol. 1, 347.

196 **"well provided and supported":** "To Matthew Birchard and Others," June 29, 1863, CW, vol. 6, 305–6.

196 **"Unless among":** "Address on Colonization to a Deputation of Negroes," August 14, 1862, CW, vol. 5, 374.

196 **"legal" and "deserved":** CW, vol. 6, 306n.

196 **a "fashionable" crowd:** "Democratic Union Association," *New York World*, July 6, 1863, 2.

196 **"ambassador from the Democracy":** "Speech of Hon. Geo. H. Pendleton," *Washington Evening Union*, July 9, 1863, 2.

197 **"The President says":** Welles, October 13, 1863, *Diary*, vol. 1, 469.

197 **"I stopped in":** Welles, October 13, 1863, *Diary*, vol. 1, 470.

CHAPTER 14: ACTIVIST: FREDERICK DOUGLASS

199 **"double advantage":** "Annual Message to Congress," December 8, 1863, CW, vol. 7, 50.

199 **He spoke repeatedly of this calculation:** Another occasion was recorded in "Interview with Alexander W. Randall and Joseph T. Mills," August 19, 1864, CW, vol. 7, 507.

200 **"were consuming us":** Jeffry D. Wert, *General James Longstreet* (New York: Simon & Schuster, 2015), 343.

201 **"good-sized, easy-going":** Walt Whitman, *Memoranda during the War* (1875: reprint, Bedford, Mass.: Applewood, 1990), 27–28.

201 **"I am not watching you":** "To William S. Rosecrans," August 10, 1863, CW, vol. 6, 377.

201 **this Black man's agenda:** One example is "Negro Equality," *Jasper Weekly Courier*, June 13, 1863, 1.

202 **Stephen Douglas connected:** First through Seventh Debates, CW, vol. 3, 1–325.

202 **"an appeal":** "Frederick Douglass at Home," *Douglass' Monthly*, August 1860, 314.

202 **"every possible discouragement":** "Services of Colored Men," *Douglass' Monthly*, July 1862, in Foner, ed., *Life and Writings*, vol. 3, 234–35.

202 **"Every man who has an ounce":** "The President and His Speeches," *Douglass' Monthly*, September 1862, in Foner, ed., *Life and Writings*, vol. 3, 267–68.

203 **"Common sense":** "Emancipation Proclaimed," in Foner, ed., *Life and Writings*, vol. 3, 273–74.

203 **"Slavery once abolished":** Remarks at Zion Church, December 28, 1862, in Foner, ed., *Life and Writings*, vol. 3, 311.

203 **"Colored men going into the army":** "Condition of the Country," *Douglass' Monthly*, February 1863, in Foner, ed., *Life and Writings*, vol. 3, 317.

203 **MEN OF COLOR, TO ARMS:** *Douglass' Monthly*, March 1863, in Foner, ed., *Life and Writings*, vol. 3, 318.

204 **"several hundred stalwart negroes":** "The Black Brigade," *Western Reserve Chronicle*, July 15, 1863, 1.

204 **"filled to overflowing":** "Mass Meeting of Colored People," *Philadelphia Press*, July 7, 1863, 2.

204 **Black soldiers received seven:** David W. Blight, *Frederick Douglass* (New York: Simon & Schuster, 2018), 402–3.

204 **"Lincoln despotism":** Donald Yacovone, ed., *A Voice of Thunder: A Black Soldier's Civil War* (Champaign: University of Illinois, 1998), 78.

204 **"that all negro slaves":** "Jeff. Davis' Proclamation," *Vermont Chronicle*, January 6, 1863, 3.

205 **"Negroes here who have enlisted":** "Retaliation as to Negro Soldiers," *Vermont Journal*, May 30, 1863, 1.

205 **"swept us down like chaff":** "From Charleston," *Douglass' Monthly*, August 1863, 853.

205 **"devotion to the cause":** "From Charleston."

206 **"Colored men":** "To Major G. L. Stearns," in Foner, ed., *Life and Writings*, vol. 3, 849.

206 **"Was that a trick":** "The Commander in Chief and His Black Soldiers," *Douglass' Monthly*, August 1863, 850.

206 **Stearns met him in Philadelphia:** Blight, *Frederick Douglass*, 406.

206 **"Whenever I got as far south":** Frederick Douglass, "Our Work Is Not Done," December 3–4, 1863, in Foner, ed., *Life and Writings*, vol. 3, 383.

206 **"to transact business":** From George Stearns, August 8, 1863. General correspondence, Douglass Papers, Library of Congress.

207 **"I have no love for America":** "Speech of Frederick Douglass," *New York Tribune*, May 13, 1847, 1.

207 **"to abstain from voting":** Frederick Douglass, *Life and Times of Frederick Douglass* (Boston: De Wolfe, 1892), 260–61.

207 **"saving principles":** Frederick Douglass, "What to the Slave Is Your Fourth of July?," in Foner, ed., *Life and Writings*, vol. 2, 185.

207 **"*your* national independence":** Douglass, "What to the Slave Is Your Fourth of July?," in Foner, ed., *Life and Writings*, vol. 2, 182.

207 **"We are only continuing":** "The Slaveholders' Rebellion," *Douglass' Monthly*, August 1862, 689.

208 **failed even as Lincoln won:** Blight, *Frederick Douglass*, 325.

208 **"dominate over his fellow man":** Welles undated memoir, *Diary*, vol. 1, 67–68.

209 **"His manner was cold":** Frederick Douglass to George L. Stearns, August 12, 1863, in Brooks D. Simpson, ed., *The Civil War: The Third Year Told by Those Who Lived It* (New York: Library of America, 2013), 457.

209 **"the stairway":** Douglass, "Our Work Is Not Done," 384.

209 **"in different parts":** Douglass, "Our Work Is Not Done."

210 **"I have never seen":** Frederick Douglass to George L. Stearns, August 12, 1863, in Simpson, ed., *The Civil War: The Third Year Told by Those Who Lived It*, 458.

210 **"Mr. Douglass, I know you":** Douglass, "Our Work Is Not Done," 384.

210 **"I had made a little speech":** "Our Work Is Not Done."

210 **"Whoever else might":** Frederick Douglass to George L. Stearns, August 12, 1863, in Simpson, ed., *The Civil War*, 459.

210 **He considered the employment:** "Abraham Lincoln," *New York Tribune*, July 5, 1885, 3.

211 **"Had he sooner issued":** "Abraham Lincoln."

211 **Douglass concluded the president's approach:** "Our Work Is Not Done," 385.

211 **"I account partially":** "Abraham Lincoln," 3.

211 **Douglass never joined:** A critical assessment of his failure to travel south is in Blight, *Frederick Douglass*, 410–11.

211 **"wise, great, and eloquent":** "Our Work Is Not Done," 386.

212 **"unconditional Union men":** "To James C. Conkling," August 20, 1863, CW, vol. 6, 399.

212 **"I can not leave here":** "To James C. Conkling," August 27, 1863, CW, vol. 6, 414.

212 **"You desire peace":** "To James C. Conkling," August 26, 1863, CW, vol. 6, 409.

CHAPTER 15: SOLDIER: MARY ELLEN WISE

215 **"Anything that kept":** Hay to Herndon, September 5, 1866, in Wilson and Davis, eds., *Herndon's Informants*, 331.

215 **"he may be arrested":** "To Whom It May Concern," December 23, 1863, CW, vol. 7, 89.

215 **a similar note:** "To Whom It May Concern," January 18, 1864, CW, vol. 7, 137.

216 **"the pressure from the people":** Ulysses S. Grant, *Personal Memoirs of U.S. Grant* (London: Sampson Low, 1895), vol. 2, 407–8.

216 **"do not wish":** The elision of "N—r" is in the source. To Theodore Tilton, October 15, 1864, in Foner, ed., *Life and Writings*, vol. 3, 424.

216 **"It seems exceedingly probable":** "Memorandum Concerning His Probable Failure of Re-election," August 23, 1864, CW, vol. 7, 514.

217 **until 1,800 former Confederates traded:** Huidekoper, *Personal Notes*, 19.

217 **his office "alone":** J. P. Thompson in "A Talk with President Lincoln," in Charles Addison Richardson, ed., *Household Reading: Selections from the Congregationalist, 1849–1866* (Boston: Galen James, 1867), 209.

218 **since his great strength was "indecision":** "Talk with President Lincoln."

218 **"almost unmanned":** "Talk with President Lincoln."

219 **"Our Woman":** Lauren Cook Burgess, *A Uncommon Soldier: The Civil War Letters of Sarah Rosetta Wakeman* (New York: Oxford University Press, 1994), 4.

219 **"colluded" with the surgeons:** "Female Soldiers," *Buffalo Weekly Express*, June 28, 1864, 1.

219 **the pseudonym "Frank":** [Headline illegible], *Louisville Courier-Journal*, April 29, 1863, 3.

219 **"to remain in that Noble cause":** Reno to Lincoln, May 11, 1863. Abraham Lincoln Papers, Series 2, General Correspondence, 1858–1864, manuscript/mixed material, LOC.

219 **census records do show:** "A Female Soldier Boy," *Daily Union Vedette*, June 4, 1864, 2.

220 **outside the county:** It was Whitley County. Thomas Graves, U.S Census, Washington Township, July 31, 1860. Schedule 1, Line 19, 255. Retrieved via genealogybank.com.

220 **"in consequence":** "A Female Soldier Boy," *Daily Union Vedette*, June 4, 1864, 2.

220 **"six battles":** "A Female Soldier Boy," *Memphis Bulletin*, May 13, 1864, 2.

220 **"from there by hospital boat":** "A Female Soldier Boy."

220 **unnamed female soldier:** The article described a woman "who has been in service twenty-two months," roughly as Mary Ellen Wise would have been, and who said she "was in the battles of Shiloh and Stone River, and was twice wounded severely." The article also said she was on her way home. Other details didn't match Mary Ellen's story as she told it elsewhere, but there were variations in every account. "A Female Soldier," *Louisville Courier-Journal*, May 21, 1863, 3.

220 **recruits from around Huntington:** One recruit wrote home to the Huntington newspaper after the troops marched off to war. "From the 34th Regiment," *Indiana Herald*, November 27, 1861, 2.

221 **sometimes joined another:** An account of one female soldier claimed that she managed to blend in with seven different regiments over time. "Another Female Soldier," *Louisville Courier-Journal*, December 21, 1863, 1.

221 **"the Military Conductor":** This article does not name Mary Ellen Wise, but describes her as "a female soldier, who has served over two years with the 34th Indiana regiment, and participated in several battles," and the description of her arrest matches her own later account of it. After her arrest, another article written in Nashville named her. "A Female Soldier," *Louisville Courier-Journal*, April 30, 1864, 3.

221 **"She likes to be a soldier":** "A Female Soldier Boy," *Memphis Bulletin*, May 13, 1864, 2.

221 **"Mary E. Wise, a female private":** "A Female Solider Draws Her Pay for Two Years' Military Service," *Evening Star*, August 12, 1864, 2.

222 **"There is a female here":** "A Female Soldier," *New Orleans Times-Democrat*, September 12, 1864, 8.

222 **Lincoln took note:** "To Simon Cameron," September 13, 1861, CW, vol. 4, 520–21.

222 **commanding a regiment in Tennessee:** "To Edwin M. Stanton," May 23, 1864, CW, vol. 7, 358.

222 **the Senate confirmed him:** *U.S. Senate Journal*, 38th Cong., 1st sess., April 20, 1864, 498.

223 **"if Hon. Daniel S. Gregory":** "To Edwin M. Stanton," October 16, 1863, CW, vol. 6, 520.

223 **was one of the Radical Republicans:** Peggy Siegel, "Charles Case: A Radical Republican in the Irrepressible Conflict," *Indiana Magazine of History* 107 (December 2011), 327–60.

223 **A TECHNICAL POINT:** from the *Washington Chronicle*, in the *Jeffersonian*, November 10, 1864, 1.

224 **sent to the Library of Congress:** on June 16, 1862. Miers an Powell, eds., *Lincoln Day by Day*, 121.

225 **"I go for all sharing":** "To the Editor of the *Sangamo Journal*," June 13, 1836, CW, vol. 1, 48.

225 **She also met a Sergeant Forehand:** *Washington Chronicle*, in the *United States Service Magazine*, March 1865, 272.

225 **the Invalid Corps:** James Rowe Adams, "A Confederate Spy in the White House?," *Intelligencer*, Winter/Spring 2010, 32.

226 **"quite a number":** "A Confederate Spy in the White House?"

226 **"Uncle Sam thereby losing":** *Washington Chronicle*, in the *United States Service Magazine*, March 1865, 272.

226 **A DANGEROUS WIFE:** *Evening Star*, February 4, 1865, 2.

226 **successfully sued there for divorce:** Adams, "A Confederate Spy in the White House?," 34–35.

226 **claimed his ex-wife:** "A Confederate Spy in the White House?," 29–37.

226 **"odious and barbarous":** "The Twenty-Fourth General Assembly," *Illinois State Journal*, February 17, 1865, 2.

CHAPTER 16: JUSTICE: JOHN A. CAMPBELL

229 **"in humble attire":** Speed to Herndon, January 12, 1866, in Wilson and Davis, eds., *Herndon's Informants*, 157.

230 **"mud almost knee-deep":** "From Washington," *New York Times*, March 6, 1865, 1.

230 **"seized by two policemen":** "Frederick Douglass's Reminiscences," *New York Tribune*, July 5, 1885, 3.

231 **"If God now wills":** "To Albert G. Hodges," April 4, 1864, CW, vol. 7, 282.

231 **"this terrible war":** "Second Inaugural Address," March 4, 1865, CW, vol. 8, 333.

231 **"I would like very much":** CW, vol. 8, 367n.

232 **"an expression of pain":** A thorough reconstruction is in Burlingame, *American Marriage*, 251–57.

232 **"Yours showing Sheridan's":** "To Ulysses S. Grant," April 1, 1865, CW, vol. 8, 379.

233 **"cut off the retreating army":** "To Edwin M. Stanton," April 3, 1865, CW, vol. 8, 384.

232 **"Allow me respectfully":** CW, vol. 8, 384–85n.

233 **"I will take care":** "To Edwin M. Stanton," April 3, 1865, CW, vol. 8, 385.

233 **"When he found":** David Dixon Porter attributes a great deal of dialogue to Lincoln in his memoir, most of which cannot be taken as more than a loose paraphrase of what Lincoln said, if even that, because it was written some twenty years later in language that doesn't seem like Lincoln's. But the joke sounds like an authentic Lincoln story that might be remembered. *Incidents and Anecdotes of the Civil War* (New York: D. Appleton, 1886), 294–95.

234 **"It was a warm day":** Porter, *Incidents*, 299.

234 **"could not be made":** Porter, *Incidents*, 297.

234 **"an immense crowd":** "Grant," *New York Herald*, April 7, 1865, 1.

234 **had sold his belongings:** "Official Dispatch," *New York Tribune*, April 6, 1865, 5.

235 **bring the man:** "A Consultation," *New York Herald*, April 9, 1865, 5.

235 **cold, analytical, and remote:** George W. Duncan, "John Archibald Campbell," in Thomas McAdory Owen, ed., *Transactions of the Alabama Historical Society, 1904*, vol. 5, 137.

235 **This intrigued Seward:** He asked the Confederates for a full explanation of their plan even after Lincoln had rejected it. John Campbell, *Remeniscences and Documents Relating to the Civil War in the Year 1865* (Baltimore: John Murphy, 1880), 12–13.

236 **Campbell told him:** Campbell, *Recollections*, 7.

236 **He heard wagons clattering:** Campbell, *Recollections*, 4.

236 **"There were lights":** Campbell, *Recollections*, 4–5.

236 **Carey Street:** Campbell's spelling; modern maps spell it "Cary." Campbell, *Recollections*, 5.

237 **in the park:** Campbell, *Recollections*, 3.

237 **"spoke with some freedom":** Campbell, *Recollections*, 6.

237 **"His manner indicated":** Campbell recounts the conversation in *Recollections*, 7–9.

238 **"wanted to have another talk":** Campbell, *Recollections*, 8.

239 **proposed a law:** Duncan, "John Archibald Campbell," 110.

240 **"not sufficient cause":** To Daniel Chandler, November 24, 1860, in Duncan, "John Archibald Campbell," 146.

240 **"The President":** Campbell, *Recollections*, 11.

240 **"has already become":** Campbell, *Recollections*, 24.

240 **"As to peace":** "To John A. Campbell," April 5, 1865, CW, vol. 8, 386.

241 **"the very legislature":** Campbell, *Recollections*, 12.

241 **a letter to Lincoln in 1864:** Green to Lincoln, January 20, 1864, Abraham Lincoln Papers, Series 1, General Correspondence, 1833–1916, Library of Congress.

241 **Lincoln lost his patience:** Porter, *Incidents*, 306–8.

242 **"It has been intimated":** "To Godfrey Weitzel," April 6, 1865, CW, vol. 8, 389.

242 **"This is a political":** Godfrey Weitzel, *Richmond Occupied* (Richmond: Civil War Centennial Committee, 1965), 58.

242 **"the establishment of a government":** Campbell to Anderson, April 7, 1865, in Campbell, *Recollections*, 23.

243 **"There was no longer":** Weitzel, *Richmond Occupied*, 62.

243 **"I have done no such thing":** "To Godfrey Weitzel," April 12, 1865, CW, vol. 8, 406–7.

244 **Campbell regarded the Reconstruction governments:** Campbell, *Recollections*, 22.

CHAPTER 17: FIRST LADY: MARY TODD LINCOLN

247 **"preceding nearly every great":** The cabinet meeting is recounted in Welles, *Diary*, vol. 2, 280–83.

248 **"No," Lincoln said:** To Francis Bicknell Carpenter, November 15, 1865, in Turner and Turner, *Mary Todd Lincoln*, 284.

249 **English literature, learned French:** Turner and Turner, *Mary Todd Lincoln*, 8.

249 **what she called her "desolate" youth:** Turner and Turner, *Mary Todd Lincoln*, 9.

249 **"She is the very creature of excitement":** Turner and Turner, *Mary Todd Lincoln*, 12.

249 **"a woman of quick intellect":** William Jayne to Herndon, August 17, 1887, in Wilson and Davis, eds., *Herndon's Informants*, 625.

249 **"was a girl of much grace":** "Lincoln & Mary Todd," a draft for *Herndon's Life of Lincoln*, likely 1887, Herndon-Weik Collection, Library of Congress.

249 **described himself in "hell":** "To Joshua F. Speed," February 3, 1842, CW, vol. 1, 268.

249 **She wrote him a letter:** Elizabeth Edwards to Herndon, January 10, 1866, in Wilson and Davis, eds., *Herndon's Informants*, 444.

250 **"still kills my soul":** "To Joshua F. Speed," March 27, 1842, CW, vol. 1, 282.

250 **"nearly the same":** "Inaugural Ball in Washington," *New York Herald*, March 6, 1861, 8.

250 **"her taller half":** "Inaugural Ball in Washington."

251 **appointed consul to Hawaii:** March 22, 1861, in Turner and Turner, *Mary Todd Lincoln*, 81.

251 **commissioner of public buildings:** To Lamon, April 11, 1861, in Turner and Turner, *Mary Todd Lincoln*, 83.

251 **"statesmanlike tastes":** "The President's Wife," *New Hampshire Statesman*, October 19, 1861, 4.

251 **"it takes two or three":** *Daily State Sentinel*, January 8, 1862, 2.

251 **sold an embarrassing scoop:** Turner and Turner, *Mary Todd Lincoln*, 97.

251 **"*not* encountering":** To Abram Wakeman, April 13, 1865. Reproduced in Turner and Turner, *Mary Todd Lincoln*, 220.

252 **He sat in it:** Baker, *Mary Todd Lincoln*, 213.

252 **"And well I may":** To Francis Bicknell Carpetnter, November 15, 1865, in Turner and Turner, *Mary Todd Lincoln*, 285.

254 **battled Thurlow Weed:** Baker, *Mary Todd Lincoln*, 276.

254 **"I am almost helpless":** To James Orne, May 28, 1870, in Thomas F. Schwartz and Anne V. Shaughnessy, "Unpublished Mary Lincoln Letters," *Journal of the Abraham Lincoln Association* 11 (1990), 34–40.

254 **$3,000 per year:** Turner and Turner, *Mary Todd Lincoln*, 572.

254 **She threatened to relocate:** To Richard Oglesby, June 5, 1865, in Turner and Turner, *Mary Todd Lincoln*, 241.

255 **"If he had remained":** To Francis Bicknell Carpenter, November 15, 1865, in Turner and Turner, *Mary Todd Lincoln*, 285.

255 **"no precautions":** Gillespie to Herndon, January 31, 1866, in Wilson and Davis, eds., *Herndon's Informants*, 185.

255 **"early life":** "Handbill Replying to Charges of Infidelity," July 31, 1846, CW, vol. 1, 382.

255 **"by his mere quiet power":** "Meditation on the Divine Will," [September 1862?], CW, vol. 5, 404.

255 **"had no hope":** Mary Todd Lincoln interview with Herndon, September 1866, in Wilson and Davis, eds., *Herndon's Informants*, 358.

256 **"What is to be will be":** Mary Todd Lincoln interview in Wilson and Davis, eds., *Herndon's Informants*, 358.

256 **He told Gillespie:** Gillespie to Herndon, January 31, 1866, in Wilson and Davis, eds., *Herndon's Informants*, 184.

256 **"our beneficent institutions":** Gillespie to Herndon, December 8, 1866, in Wilson and Davis, eds., *Herndon's Informants*, 508.

256 **"He first declared":** Speech at Bloomington, September 12, 1854, CW, vol. 7, 230.

257 **"I claim not":** "To Albert G. Hodges," April 4, 1864, CW, vol. 7, 282.

Bibliography

ARCHIVAL COLLECTIONS

Abraham Lincoln Papers, Library of Congress
Abraham Lincoln Presidential Library and Museum, Springfield, Illinois
American State Papers, Library of Congress
Andrew Jackson Papers, Library of Congress
Brady-Handy Collection, photographs, Library of Congress
Farmington Historic Plantation archives, Louisville, Kentucky
Frémont papers, Bancroft Library, University of California, Berkeley
Herndon-Weik Collection, Library of Congress
Illinois State Archives
Indiana State Archives
Joshua Giddings Papers, Ohio History Connection
Lincoln's New Salem State Historic Site Archive, Illinois
Madison County Historical Society Archival Library, Illinois
Native American Law Center archives, University of Tulsa
Soldiers and Sailors Database, National Park Service
Thurlow Weed Papers, University of Rochester
United States Census records, via Genealogybank.com
William Henry Seward Papers, University of Rochester

BOUND COLLECTIONS OF LETTERS, SPEECHES, AND WRITINGS

Basler, Roy P., ed. *The Collected Works of Abraham Lincoln.* 8 vols. New Brunswick, NJ: Rutgers University Press, 1953.

Burgess, Lauren Cook, ed. *An Uncommon Soldier: The Civil War Letters of Sarah Rosetta Wakeman, alias Private Lyons Wakeman, 153rd Regiment, New York State Volunteers.* New York: Oxford University Press, 1996.

Calhoun, John C. *Speeches of John C. Calhoun.* New York: Harper & Brothers, 1843.

Congressional Globe: Containing Debates and Proceedings of the Second Session Forty-Second Congress, with an Appendix, Embracing the Laws Passed at That Session Classic Reprint, 2017; Washington, DC: J. C. Rives.

Foner, Philip S., ed. *The Life and Writings of Frederick Douglass.* 5 vols. New York: International, 1952.

Herr, Pamela, and Mary Lee Spence, eds. *The Letters of Jessie Benton Frémont.* Urbana: University of Illinois Press, 1993.

Mitgang, Herbert, ed. *Abraham Lincoln: A Press Portrait.* New York: Fordham University Press, 2000.

Pendleton, George H. *Speech on the Enlistment of Negro Soldiers.* Washington, DC: House of Representatives, 1863.

Sears, Stephen W., ed. *The Civil War Papers of George B. McClellan.* New York: Ticknor & Fields, 1989.

Senate Journal. 38th Cong., 1st sess., April 20, 1864, 498.

Simpson, Brooks D., ed. *The Civil War: The Third Year Told by Those Who Lived It.* New York: Library of America, 2013.

Sparks, Edwin Erle, ed. *The Lincoln-Douglas Debates of 1858.* Springfield: Illinois State Historical Library, 1908.

Stanton, Elizabeth Cady. *Eighty Years and More: Memoirs of Elizabeth Cady Stanton (1815–1897).* Prague: Madison and Adams, 2019.

Turner, Justin G., and Linda Levitt Turner. *Mary Todd Lincoln: Her Life and Letters.* New York: Knopf, 1972.

Villard, Henry. *Lincoln on the Eve of '61.* New York: Knopf, 1941.

Wilson, Douglas L., and Rodney O. Davis, eds. *Herndon's Informants: Letters, Interviews, and Statements about Abraham Lincoln.* Urbana: University of Illinois Press, 1998.

MEMOIRS, DIARIES, AND OTHER FIRSTHAND ACCOUNTS

Adams, Henry. *The Great Secession Winter of 1860–61 and Other Essays.* Edited by George Hochfield. New York: Sagamore Press, 1958.

BIBLIOGRAPHY

Angle, Paul M., ed. *Abraham Lincoln, by Some Men Who Knew Him*. Chicago: Americana House, 1950.

Anonymous. *The Wide-Awake Gift: A Know-Nothing Token for 1855*. New York: J.C. Derby, 1855.

Barnes, Thurlow W. *Memoir of Thurlow Weed*. Boston: Houghton Mifflin, 1884.

Bullard, F. Lauriston, ed. *The Diary of a Public Man*. New Brunswick: Rutgers University Press, 1946.

Browning, Orville H. *Diary of Orville Hickman Browning*. Vol. 1. Springfield: Illinois State Historical Library, 1925.

Campbell, John. *Recollections of the Evacuation of Richmond, April 2d, 1865*. Baltimore: John Murphy, 1880.

———. *Reminiscences and Documents Relating to the Civil War During the Year 1865*. Baltimore: John Murphy, 1887.

Fitzhugh, George. *Sociology for the South, or The Failure of Free Society*. Richmond: A. Morris, 1854.

Frémont, Jessie Benton. *Souvenirs of My Time*. Boston: D. Lothrop, 1887.

Frémont, Jessie Benton, and Francis Preston Frémont. *Great Events in the Life of Major General John C. Frémont, F.R.G.S. Chevalier de l'Ordre pour le Merite; etc. and of Jessie Benton Frémont*. Unpublished, Bancroft Library collection, 1891.

Gillespie, Joseph. *Recollections of Early Illinois and Her Noted Men*. Chicago: Fergus, 1880.

Grant, Ulysses S. *Personal Memoirs of U.S. Grant*. London: Sampson Low, 1895.

Green, Duff. *Facts and Suggestions, Biographical, Historical, Financial and Political*. New York: Richardson, 1866.

Halstead, Murat. *Fire the Salute!* 1860. Reprint, Kingsport, Tenn.: Kingsport Press, 1960.

Hay, John. *Inside Lincoln's White House: The Complete Civil War Diary of John Hay*. Edited by Michael Burlingame and John R. Turner Ettlinger. Carbondale: Southern Illinois University Press, 1997.

Howe, Daniel Walker. *The Political Culture of the American Whigs*. Chicago: University of Chicago Press, 1984.

Howells, William Dean. *Life of Abraham Lincoln*. Springfield, IL: Abraham Lincoln Association, 1938.

Huidekoper, H. S. *Personal Notes and Reminiscences of Lincoln*. Philadelphia: Bicking, 1896.

Inskeep, Steve. *Jacksonland: President Andrew Jackson, Cherokee Chief John Ross, and a Great American Land Grab*. New York: Penguin Press, 2015.

Keckley, Elizabeth. *Behind the Scenes, or Thirty Years a Slave, and Four Years in the White House*. New York: G. W. Carleton, 1868.

Koerner, Gustave. *Memoirs of Gustave Koerner, 1809–1896*. Edited by Thomas J. McCormack. 2 vols. Cedar Rapids, IA: Torch Press, 1909.

Livermore, Mary. *My Story of the War.* Hartford, Conn.: A. D. Worthington, 1890.

Lovejoy, Joseph C., and Owen Lovejoy. *Memoir of the Rev. Elijah P. Lovejoy.* New York: John S. Taylor, 1838.

McClellan, George B. *McClellan's Own Story.* New York: C. L. Webster, 1887.

Porter, David Dixon. *Incidents and Anecdotes of the Civil War.* New York: D. Appleton, 1886.

Richardson, Charles Addison, ed. *Household Reading: Selections from the Congregationalist, 1849–1866.* Boston: Galen James, 1867.

Seward, Frederick W., ed. *William H. Seward: An Autobiography, from 1801–1834; with a Memoir of His Life, and Selections from his Letters, 1831–1846.* (Also known as vol. 1 of his memoirs.) New York: Derby and Miller, 1891.

———. *Seward at Washington, as Senator and Secretary of State: A Memoir of His Life, With Selections From His Letters, 1846–1861.* (Also known as vol. 2 of his memoirs.) New York: Derby and Miller, 1891.

———. *Seward at Washington, as Senator and Secretary of State: A Memoir of His Life, With Selections From His Letters, 1861–1872.* (Also known as vol. 3 of his memoirs.) New York: Derby and Miller, 1891.

Troup, George M. *Governor's Message to the General Assembly of the State of Georgia, At the Opening of the Extra Session, May 23, 1825.* Milledgeville: Camak & Ragland, 1825.

Various authors. *Annual Report of the Commissioner of Indian Affairs, for the Year 1868.* Washington, DC: Government Printing Office, 1868.

Weed, Harriet, ed. *Autobiography of Thurlow Weed.* Boston: Houghton Mifflin, 1884.

Weitzel, Godfrey. *Richmond Occupied.* Richmond: Civil War Centennial Committee, 1965.

Welles, Gideon. *Diary of Gideon Welles, Secretary of the Navy under Lincoln and Johnson.* 3 vols. Boston: Houghton Mifflin, 1911.

———. *Lincoln and Seward.* New York: Sheldon, 1874.

Whitman, Walt. *Memoranda during the War.* 1875. Reprint, Bedford, Mass.: Applewood, 1990.

Whitney, Henry. *Life on the Circuit with Lincoln.* Caldwell, ID: Caxton, 1940.

CONTEMPORARY NEWSPAPERS

Most newspapers were accessed through digital databases, primarily the Chronicling America database at the Library of Congress; the Illinois Digital Newspaper Collections; newspapers.com; and genealogybank.com.

Alexandria Gazette
Alton Daily Courier
Alton Weekly Telegraph

BIBLIOGRAPHY

American Statesman
Baltimore Pilot
Bedford Enquirer
Buffalo Weekly Express
Carolina Watchman
Charleston Courier
Charleston Mercury
Chicago Tribune
Cincinnati Daily Press
Daily Gate City
Daily Madisonian
Daily Union
Daily Union Vedette
Douglass' Monthly
Eastern Times
Evening Journal
Evening Star
Farmer's Cabinet
Freeport Daily Journal
Harrisburg Patriot
Hartford Courant
Illinois Register
Indiana Herald
Jeffersonian
Joliet Signal
Liberator
Louisville Courier
Memphis Bulletin
Memphis Daily Appeal
Minnesota Weekly Times
Missouri Republican
Moline Workman
National Anti-Slavery Standard
National Era
National Intelligencer
National Republican
Newbern Sentinel
New Hampshire Statesman
New York Herald

New York Post
New York Times
New-York Tribune
New York World
Old Soldier
Ottawa Free Trader
Philadelphia Press
Pittsburgh Gazette
Quad-City Times
Quincy Daily Herald
Quincy Whig and Republican
Rock Island Argus
Salem Weekly Advocate
Sangamo Journal (later *Illinois State Journal*)
Semi-Weekly Standard
St. Louis Evening News
Sunday Dispatch
United States Service Magazine
United States' Telegraph
Vermont Chronicle
Vermont Journal
Washington Union
Weekly Iowa State Gazette
Weekly Pantagraph
Weekly Union
Western Reserve Chronicle
Wisconsin State Journal

MAPS AND DIAGRAMS

Hergesheimer, Edwin. "Map Showing the Distribution of the Slave Population of the Southern States," 1861, LOC.

Onstot, R. J. "New Salem, Home of Abraham Lincoln 1831 to 1837." Lincoln's New Salem State Historic Site collection.

BIOGRAPHIES AND OTHER HISTORIES

Arnold, Isaac. *The Life of Abraham Lincoln.* Chicago: Jansen, McClurg, 1885.

Baker, Jean H. *Mary Todd Lincoln: A Biography.* New York: Norton, 1987.

Baringer, William. *Lincoln's Rise to Power.* Boston: Little, Brown, 1937.

Belko, W. Stephen. *The Invincible Duff Green: Whig of the West.* Columbia: University of Missouri Press, 2006.

Blight, David. W. *Frederick Douglass.* New York: Simon & Schuster, 2018.

Bloss, G. M. D. *Life and Speeches of George H. Pendleton.* Cincinnati: Miami Printing, 1868.

Brink, W. R. *History of Madison County, Illinois.* Edwardsville, IL: W. R. Brink, 1882.

Brown, Dee. *The Galvanized Yankees.* New York: Open Road, 2012.

Buell, Walter. *Joshua R. Giddings: A Sketch.* Cleveland: William W. Williams, 1882.

Burlingame, Michael. *An American Marriage: The Untold Story of Abraham Lincoln and Mary Todd.* New York: Pegasus, 2021.

Chaffin, Tom. *Pathfinder: John Charles Frémont and the Course of American Empire.* New York: Farrar, Straus and Giroux, 2002.

Collins, Gail. *William Henry Harrison.* New York: Henry Holt, 2012.

Condon, William H. *Life of Major-General James Shields.* Chicago: Blakely, 1900.

Connor, Henry. *John Archibald Campbell.* Boston: Houghton Mifflin, 1920.

Desmond, Humphrey. *The Know-Nothing Party: A Sketch.* Washington: New Century Press, 1904.

Donald, David Herbert. *Lincoln.* New York: Simon & Schuster, 1995.

———. *We Are Lincoln Men: Abraham Lincoln and His Friends.* New York: Simon & Schuster, 2003.

Douglass, Frederick. *Narrative of the Life of Frederick Douglass.* Boston: Anti-slavery Office, 1849.

———. *Life and Times of Frederick Douglass.* Boston: De Wolfe, Fiske, 1892.

Faust, Drew Gilpin, ed. *The Ideology of Slavery.* Baton Rouge: Louisiana State University Press, 1981.

Findley, Paul. *A. Lincoln: The Crucible of Congress.* Fairfield, CA: James Stevenson, 2004.

Fleischner, Jennifer. *Mrs. Lincoln and Mrs. Keckley.* New York: Crown, 2004.

Foner, Eric. *The Fiery Trial: Abraham Lincoln and American Slavery.* New York: Norton, 2010.

Freeman, Joanne. *The Field of Blood: Violence in Congress and the Road to Civil War.* New York: Farrar, Straus and Giroux, 2018.

Gardner, William. *Life of Stephen A. Douglas.* Boston: Roxburgh, 1905.

Gienapp, William. *Origins of the Republican Party, 1852–1856.* New York: Oxford University Press, 1987.

Grinnell, George Bird. *By Cheyenne Campfires.* New Haven: Yale University Press, 1926.

———. *The Fighting Cheyennes.* New York: Scribner, 1915.

Hamilton, Charles, and Lloyd Ostendorf. *Lincoln in Photographs.* Norman: University of Oklahoma Press, 1963.

Harriel, Shelby. *Behind the Rifle: Women Soldiers in Civil War Mississippi*. Jackson: University Press of Mississippi, 2019.

Harris, Norman. *History of Negro Servitude in Illinois*. Chicago: A. C. McClurg, 1904.

Hay, John, and John G. Nicolay. *Abraham Lincoln: A History*. 10 vols. New York: Century, 1890.

Haymond, John A. *The Infamous Dakota War Trials of 1862*. Jefferson: McFarland, 2016.

Heagle, David. *The Great Anti-slavery Agitator*. Princeton: Streeter, 1886.

Herndon, William. *Herndon's Life of Lincoln*. 1942; reprint. New York: Da Capo, 1983.

Hoig, Stan. *The Peace Chiefs of the Cheyennes*. Norman: University of Oklahoma Press, 1980.

Holzer, Harold. *Lincoln at Cooper Union*. New York: Simon & Schuster, 2004.

———. *Lincoln President-Elect*. New York: Simon & Schuster, 2008.

Julian, George W. *The Life of Joshua R. Giddings*. Chicago: A. C. McClurg, 1892.

Kahan, Paul. *Amiable Scoundrel: Simon Cameron, Lincoln's Scandalous Secretary of War*. Lincoln: University of Nebraska Press, 2016.

Lamon, Ward Hill. *The Life of Abraham Lincoln*. Boston: James R. Osgood, 1872.

Lee, John Hancock. *The Origin and Progress of the American Party in Politics*. Philadelphia: Elliott and Gihon, 1855.

Levine, Bruce. *Thaddeus Stevens*. New York: Simon & Schuster, 2021.

Mach, Thomas S. *"Gentleman George" Hunt Pendleton*. Kent, OH: Kent State University Press, 2007.

Magdol, Edward. *Owen Lovejoy: Abolitionist in Congress*. New Brunswick: Rutgers University Press, 1967.

Marvel, William. *Lincoln's Autocrat: The Life of Edwin Stanton*. Chapel Hill: UNC Press, 2015.

Milton, George Fort. *The Eve of Conflict*. Boston: Houghton Mifflin, 1934.

Moore, Jane Ann, and William F. Moore. *Owen Lovejoy and the Coalition for Equality*. Urbana: University of Illinois Press, 2020.

Moore, William F., and Jane Ann Moore. *Collaborators for Emancipation*. Urbana: University of Illinois Press, 2014.

Morris, Roy, Jr. *The Long Pursuit*. New York: HarperCollins, 2008.

Nevins, Allan. *Frémont: Pathmarker of the West*. New York: Appleton, 1939.

Niebuhr, Gustav. *Lincoln's Bishop*. New York: Harper One, 2014.

Onstot, T. G. *Pioneers of Menard and Mason Counties*. Peoria: J. W. Franks, 1902.

Ossman, Laurie. *Great House of the South*. New York: Rizzoli, 2010.

Owen, Thomas McAdory, ed. *Transactions of the Alabama Historical Society, 1904*. Vol. 5. Montgomery: Alabama Historical Society, 1906.

Paul, Bonnie, and Richard Hart. *Lincoln's Springfield Neighborhood*. Charleston: The History Press, 2015.

Poore, Benjamin Perley. *The Life and Public Services of General Ambrose Burnside.* Providence: J. A. and R. A. Reid, 1882.

Prince, Ezra M., ed. *Transactions of the McLean County Historical Society.* Vol. 3. Bloomington: Pantagraph, 1900.

Pryor, Elizabeth Brown. *Six Encounters with Lincoln.* New York: Penguin, 2015.

Quarles, Benjamin. *Frederick Douglass.* Washington, DC: Associated Publishers, 1948.

Quatman, G. William. *A Young General and the Fall of Richmond.* Athens: Ohio University Press, 2015.

Raymond, Henry. *Lincoln, His Life and Time.* 2 vols. Chicago: Thompson and Thomas, 1891.

Reavis, L. U. *Life and Public Services of Richard Yates.* Saint Louis: J. H. Chambers, 1881.

Reep, Thomas. *Lincoln at New Salem.* Petersburg: Old Salem Lincoln League, 1927.

Rehnquist, William H. *All the Laws but One: Civil Liberties in Wartime.* New York: Knopf, 2001.

Reynolds, David. *Abe: Abraham Lincoln in His Times.* New York: Penguin Press, 2020.

Sandburg, Carl. *Lincoln: The Prairie Years and the War Years.* 1926 and 1939; reprint. Pleasantville: Reader's Digest, 1970.

Saunders, Robert. *John Archibald Campbell.* Tuscaloosa: University of Alabama Press, 1997.

Sears, Stephen W. *George B. McClellan: The Young Napoleon.* New York: Ticknor & Fields, 1988.

Seaton, Josephine. *William Winston Seaton of the* National Intelligencer*: A Biographical Sketch.* Boston: Osgood, 1871.

Shenk, Joshua. *Lincoln's Melancholy.* Boston: Mariner, 2005.

Simon, Paul. *Freedom's Champion: Elijah Lovejoy.* Carbondale: Southern Illinois University Press, 1994.

———. *Lincoln's Preparation for Greatness: The Illinois Legislative Years.* Urbana: University of Illinois Press, 1971.

Swanberg, W. A. *Sickles the Incredible.* Gettysburg: Stan Clark, 1956.

Tarbell, Ida M. *Life of Abraham Lincoln.* 4 vols. New York: Lincoln History Society, 1895.

Thomas, Benjamin. *Lincoln's New Salem.* Springfield, IL: Abraham Lincoln Association, 1934.

Thomas, Benjamin, and Harold Hyman. *Stanton: The Life and Times of Lincoln's Secretary of War.* New York: Knopf, 1962.

Vallandigham, James L. *Life of Clement L. Vallandigham.* Baltimore: Turnbull, 1872.

Van Deusen, Glyndon G. *Thurlow Weed: Wizard of the Lobby.* Boston: Little, Brown, 1947.

———. *William Henry Seward.* New York: Oxford, 1967.

Washington, John E. *They Knew Lincoln.* 1942; reprint. New York: Oxford University Press, 2018.

Weeks, Philip. *Farewell, My Nation.* Wheeling: Harlan Davidson, 1990.

Wert, Jeffry D. *General James Longstreet.* New York: Simon & Schuster, 1993.

White, Barbara. *Visits with Lincoln: Abolitionists Meet the President at the White House.* New York: Lexington, 2011.

White, Ronald C., Jr. *A. Lincoln.* New York: Random House, 2009.

Williams, T. Harry. *Lincoln and the Radicals.* Madison: University of Wisconsin Press, 1941.

Wilson, Douglas. *Honor's Voice: The Transformation of Abraham Lincoln.* New York: Random House, 1998.

Winkler, H. Donald. *Lincoln's Ladies: The Women in the Life of the Sixteenth President.* Nashville: Cumberland, 2004.

Yacovone, Donald, ed. *A Voice of Thunder: A Black Soldier's Civil War.* Urbana: University of Illinois, 1998.

COLLECTIONS OF ESSAYS AND ANALYSES

Pargas, Damian, ed. *Fugitive Slaves and Spaces of Freedom in North America.* Tallahassee: University Press of Florida, 2018.

Wert, Jeffery. *General James Longstreet.* New York: Simon & Schuster, 1994.

Wilentz, Sean, ed. *The Best American History Essays on Lincoln.* New York: Palgrave Macmillan, 2009.

JOURNALS AND ARTICLES

Adams, Carl. "Lincoln's First Freed Slave: A Review of *Bailey v. Cromwell*, 1841." *Journal of the Illinois State Historical Society* (Fall-Winter 2008), 235–59.

Adams, James Rowe. "A Confederate Spy in the White House?" *Intelligencer* (Winter/Spring 2010), 29–37.

Ames, William. "The *National Intelligencer*: Washington's Leading Political Newspaper," *Records of the Columbia Historical Society* (1966/68), 71–83.

Blight, David. "The Meaning of the Fight: Frederick Douglass and the Memory of the Fifty Fourth Massachusetts." *Massachusetts Review* 36 (Spring 1995), 141–53.

Chandler, Josephine Craven. "New Salem: Early Chapter in Lincoln's Life." *Journal of the Illinois State Historical Society* 22 (January 1930), 501–58.

Clark, Allen C. "Colonel William Winston Seaton and His Mayoralty." *Records of the Columbia Historical Society* 29–30 (1928), 1–102.

Clark, T. D. "The Slave Trade between Kentucky and the Cotton Kingdom." *Mississippi Valley Historical Review* 21 (December 1934), 331–42.

Collins, Bruce. "The Lincoln-Douglas Contest of 1858 and Illinois' Electorate." *Journal of American Studies* 20, no. 3 (December 1986), 391–420.

Corrigan, Mary Beth. "1848: The Pearl." *Washington History* 32, no. 1/2 (Fall 2020), 24–27.

Dirck, Brian. "Lincoln's Kentucky Childhood and Race." *Register of the Kentucky Historical Society* 106, no. 3/4 (Summer/Autumn 2008), 307–32.

Duncan, George W. "John Archibald Campbell." In Thomas McAdory Owen, ed. *Transactions of the Alabama Historical Society, 1904*. Vol. 5, 107–50.

Dyer, Brainerd. "The Treatment of Colored Union Troops by the Confederates, 1861–1865." *Journal of Negro History* 20 (July 1935), 273–86.

Etcheson, Nicole. "Manliness and the Political Culture of the Old Northwest, 1790–1860." *Journal of the Early Republic* 15, no. 1 (Spring 1995), 59–77.

Gertz, Elmer. "The Black Laws of Illinois." *Journal of the Illinois State Historical Society* 56 (Autumn 1963), 454–73.

Green, Fletcher M. "Duff Green, Militant Journalist of the Old School." *American Historical Review* 52 (January 1947), 247–64.

Grover, Frank. "Indian Treaties Affecting Lands in the Present State of Illinois." *Journal of the Illinois State Historical Society* 8, no. 3 (October 1915), 379–419.

Guelzo, Allen C. "Abraham Lincoln and the Doctrine of Necessity." *Journal of the Abraham Lincoln Association* 18, no. 1 (Winter 1997), 57–81.

Hart, Richard E. "Springfield's African Americans as a Part of the Lincoln Community." *Journal of the Abraham Lincoln Association* 20, no. 1 (Winter 1999), 35–54.

Hickey, James T., George W. Spotswood, C. G. Saunders, and Sarah Beck. "The Lincolns' Globe Tavern." *Journal of the Illinois State Historical Society* (Winter 1963), 629–53.

Hudson, Gossie Harold. "William Florville: Lincoln's Barber and Friend." *Negro History Bulletin* 37 (September 1974), 279–81.

Inskeep, Steve. "John Boehner on the 'Noisemakers' of the Republican Party." NPR, April 12, 2021. https://www.npr.org/2021/04/12/985722549/john-boehner-on-the-noisemakers-of-the-republican-party.

Jackson, W. Sherman. "Emancipation, Negrophobia, and Civil War Politics in Ohio, 1863–1865." *Journal of Negro History* (Summer 1980), 250–60.

Jordan, Caine, Guy Emerson Mount, and Kai Perry Parker. "A Case for Reparations at the University of Chicago." Unpublished paper, Reparations at UChicago Working Group.

Luthin, Reinhard H. "Abraham Lincoln Becomes a Republican." *Political Science Quarterly* 69 (September 1944), 420–38.

Mallam, William D. "Lincoln and the Conservatives." *The Journal of Southern History* 28, no. 1 (February 1962), 31–45.

Masur, Kate. "The African-American Delegation to Abraham Lincoln: A Reappraisal." *Civil War History* 56, no. 2 (June 2010), 117–44.

Neely, Mark. "The Political Life of New Salem, Illinois." *Lincoln Lore* (January 1981).

Noll, Mark. "Lincoln's God." *Journal of Presbyterian History* 82, no. 2 (Summer 2004), 77–88.

Prickett, Josephine G. "Joseph Gillespie." In *Transactions of the Illinois State Historical Society*, 1912. Vol. 17, 93–114.

Schwartz, Thomas F., and Anne V. Shaughnessy. "Unpublished Mary Lincoln Letters." *Journal of the Abraham Lincoln Association* 11, no. 1 (1990), 34–40.

Siegel, Peggy. "Charles Case: A Radical Republican in the Irrepressible Conflict." *Indiana Magazine of History* 107, no. 4 (December 2011), 327–60.

Smith, Charles R. "The Meaning of Lincoln's 'Such a *Sucker* as Me.'" *Journal of the Abraham Lincoln Association* 40, no. 2 (Summer 2019), 1–17.

Snay, Mitchell. "Abraham Lincoln, Owen Lovejoy, and the Emergence of the Republican Party in Illinois." *Journal of the Abraham Lincoln Association* 22, no. 1 (Winter 2001), 82–99.

Stevens, Frank E. "Life of Stephen Arnold Douglas." *Journal of the Illinois State Historical Society* 16, no. 3/4 (October 1923–January 1924), 274–673.

Taylor, Grace N. "The Blair Family in the Civil War." *Register of the Kentucky Historical Society* 39, no. 126 (January 1941), 47–57.

Wilson, Douglas L. "William H. Herndon on Lincoln's Fatalism." *Journal of the Abraham Lincoln Association* 35, no. 2 (Summer 2014), 1–17.

Wilson, Major L. "The Repressible Conflict: Seward's Concept of Progress and the Free-Soil Movement." *Journal of Southern History* 37, no. 4 (November 1971), 533–56.

Woodward, Isaiah A. "Lincoln and the Crittenden Compromise." *Negro History Bulletin* 22 (April 1959), 153–55.

Image Credits

Page xii: [Portrait of President Abraham Lincoln, half-length, seated], by Lewis E. Walker, ca. 1863. Library of Congress, Prints and Photographs Division, LC-USZ62-61374.

Page xx: [Johnson portrait of Abraham Lincoln as a youth reading in front of the fire.], by Eastman Johnson, published by W. Harring. & L. Prang & Co., Boston, Massachusetts, 1868. Library of Congress, The Alfred Whital Stern Collection of Lincolniana.

Page 13: [Abraham Lincoln, head-and-shoulders portrait, facing right. Copy of the print by Thomas Doney], by Thomas Doney and Alexander Hesler, 1860. Library of Congress, Prints and Photographs Division, LC-USZ62-23072.

Page 14: Hon. Joshua R. Giddings of Ohio, created between 1855 and 1865. Library of Congress, Prints and Photographs Division, LC-DIG-cwpbh-02821.

Page 26: [Illustrated Civil War "Union Envelopes"]: [Portr. of Stephen Douglas labeled "Patriot"], Library of Congress, Prints and Photographs Division, LC-USZ62-53591.

Page 40: Courtesy of the collection of the Massachusetts Historical Society. Owen Lovejoy, from Portraits of American Abolitionists (a collection of images of individuals representing a broad spectrum of viewpoints in the slavery debate), Mass. Historical Society. Photo. 81.420.

Page 56: Illustration of Joseph Gillespie, from Recollections of Early Illinois and Her Noted Men: Read Before the Chicago Historical Society, March 16th, 1880. United States: Fergus Print. Company, 1880.

Page 76: Hon. Thurlow Weed, created between 1855 and 1865. Library of Congress, Prints and Photographs Division, LC-DIG-cwpbh-01231.

Page 91: [Abraham Lincoln: President-elect], by Samuel G. Alschuler, 1860. Library of Congress, Prints and Photographs Division, LC-USZ62-15984.

Page 92: Gen. Duff Green, created between 1860 and 1875. Library of Congress, Prints and Photographs Division, LC-DIG-cwpbh-00011.

Page 108: William Florville, date of original unknown. From the Lincoln Financial Foundation Collection, LN-1138.

Page 118: [Print of Lincoln's cabinet based on Carpenter painting.], n.d. Library of Congress, Rare Book and Special Collections Division.

Page 133: [Abraham Lincoln, President of the United States, three-quarter length portrait, seated, facing right], by Anthony Berger, 1864. Library of Congress, Prints and Photographs Division, LC-DIG-ppmsca-19470.

Page 134: Mrs. [Jesse Benton] Fremont, Black Point, San Francisco, 1867, by C.E. Watkins., Early San Francisco views, BANC PIC 1905.07692--PIC, The Bancroft Library, University of California, Berkeley.

Page 152: [Antietam, Md. President Lincoln and Gen. George B. McClellan in the general's tent], by Alexander Gardner, 1862. Library of Congress, Prints and Photographs Division, LC-B817-7948.

Page 172: [Indian delegation in the White House Conservatory during the Civil War, with J.G. Nicolay, President Abraham Lincoln's secretary, standing in center back row and interpreter John Simpson Smith at back left] / Brady, New York, by Mathew B. Brady, 1863. Library of Congress, Prints and Photographs Division, LC-DIG-ppmsca-19914.

Page 186: Carte d' visite: Pendleton, George H. (George Hunt), 1825-1889, by Brady National Photographic Art Gallery (Washington, DC). Library of Congress, Manuscript Division.

Page 198: Illustration of Frederick Douglass, from Narrative of the life of Frederick Douglass, an American slave by Frederick Douglass, Dublin: Webb and Chapman, Gt. Brunswick-street, 1846.

Page 214: Frances L. Clalin, 4 mo. heavy artillery, Co. I 13 mo., Cavalry Co. A. 22 months / S. Masury, photographic artist, 289 Washington St., Boston., by Samuel Masury, ca. 1865. Library of Congress, Prints and Photographs Division, LC-DIG-ppmsca-30978.

Page 228: Judge John A. Campbell, created between 1855-1865. Library of Congress, Prints and Photographs Division, LC-DIG-cwpbh-01552.

Page 246: Lincoln, Mrs. Abraham, ca. 1860-1865. Library of Congress, Prints and Photographs Division, LC-DIG-cwpbh-03451.

Index